ATMOSPHERES:
AESTHETICS OF EMOTIONAL SPACES

For Alessandra

For suggestions and encouragements that have contributed to the making of this book I am grateful to my friends and colleagues Alessandro Ferrara and (in memoriam) Massimo Rosati

Atmospheres:
Aesthetics of Emotional Spaces

TONINO GRIFFERO
University of Rome Tor Vergata, Italy

TRANSLATION BY
SARAH DE SANCTIS

ASHGATE

Copyright © 2010, Gius. Laterza & Figli, All rights reserved
Published by arrangement with Marco Vigevani Agenzia Letteraria

This is a translation into English of *Atmosferologia: Estetica degli spazi emozionali*, translated by Sarah de Sanctis. This edition © 2014.

All rights reserved. No part of this publication may be reproduced, stored in a retrieval system or transmitted in any form or by any means, electronic, mechanical, photocopying, recording or otherwise without the prior permission of the publisher.

Tonino Griffero has asserted his right under the Copyright, Designs and Patents Act, 1988, to be identified as the author of this work.

Published by
Ashgate Publishing Limited
Wey Court East
Union Road
Farnham
Surrey, GU9 7PT
England

Ashgate Publishing Company
110 Cherry Street
Suite 3-1
Burlington, VT 05401-3818
USA

www.ashgate.com

British Library Cataloguing in Publication Data
A catalogue record for this book is available from the British Library.

The Library of Congress has cataloged the printed edition as follows:
Griffero, Tonino.
  Atmospheres : aesthetics of emotional spaces / by Tonino Griffero.
    pages cm
  Includes bibliographical references and index.
  ISBN 978-1-4724-2172-2 (hardback) -- ISBN 978-1-4724-2173-9 (ebook) -- ISBN 978-1-4724-2174-6 (epub) 1. Space. 2. Aesthetics, Modern. 3. Emotions (Philosophy) I. Title.
  BH301.S65G75 2014
  111'.85--dc23

2013044893

ISBN 9781472421722 (hbk)
ISBN 9781472421739 (ebk – PDF)
ISBN 9781472421746 (ebk – ePUB)

Printed in the United Kingdom by Henry Ling Limited,
at the Dorset Press, Dorchester, DT1 1HD

Contents

Introduction: Not to Leave Vagueness (but to Stay in it in the Right Way)   1

1   Atmospheric Perception   9
     1.1 Atmospheric Segmentation?   9
     1.2 Perceiving Atmospheres   11
     1.3 How One Feels Here and Now in the Felt-Body   23
     1.4 The First Impression   29
     1.5 Atmospheres as Situational Constraints   31
     1.6 Lived (Predimensional) Spaces   36
     1.7 'Affordances' and Imagine-Motor Reactions   47

2   History of the Concept of Atmosphere   55
     2.1 The Climatic Paradigm   55
     2.2 Atmosphere and Landscape   60
     2.3 Orosensory Atmosphere (and the Case of Haptics)   63
     2.4 … that 'Creates an Atmosphere'   69
     2.5 The Numinous and the 'Genius Loci'   73
     2.6 'Stimmung', 'Ambiance', Aura   75
     2.7 From 'Affordances' to Emotional Design   79
     2.8 And Art? From the Beautiful to the Atmospheric   82
     2.9 Urban Seductions   87
     2.10 The Magic of Dwelling   93
     2.11 Ecstasy of Materials   96

3   Atmospherology   101
     3.1 History of a 'Sin': Introjection and Projection   101
     3.2 Atmospheres: Not Metaphors but Quasi-things   108
     3.3 Sinaesthesias   113
     3.4 'All Out': Atmospheric Ontology   119
     3.5 Principles of a Phenomenology of Atmospheres   129

Conclusion *143*
Bibliography *151*

Index *171*

Introduction
Not to Leave Vagueness
(but to Stay in it in the Right Way)

'If no one asks me, I know; If I want to explain it to an interrogator, I do not know.' The well-known *captatio* with which Augustine introduces the enigma of time certainly holds true for atmosphere as well. That is, for a state that is hardly defined not because it is rare and unusual but, on the contrary, because it is as omnipresent – even though at times unnoticed – as the emotive situation. Just as 'fundamentally there is no state of life of man that is not already sentimentally tuned in some way' (Bollnow 1941: 54), there is probably no situation that is totally deprived of an atmospheric charge. Despite its undoubted intermittence, the atmosphere (*atmos* = exhalation or vapour, *sphaire* = sphere or globe) is therefore something we all know, even outside of the nonetheless relevant meteorological field (see *infra* 2.1). It is something in which, to paraphrase Merleau-Ponty, 'there is sense', a *logos in statu nascendi* that can even be geographically searched for – perhaps *à la* Nietzsche, in whose pathological quest for favourable climates it is hard not to recognise an improvised atmospheric diet.

In fact, not only do we speak of atmospheres continuously, we are also not surprised by being able to describe them and verify their influence on actions,[1] sometimes even on events of historical significance. We resort to them to explain certain causal interactions and to comprehend emphatic tunings that would otherwise be incomprehensible,[2] or more generally all those effects that, being out of proportion with respect to their causes, used to be attributed by pre-modern knowledge to a mysterious action *in distans*. We say that 'there is something in the air' or that 'there is something brewing', or that we feel, who knows why, like

---

1 Soentgen (1998: 72) is therefore mistaken when defining them 'anti-Faustian sentiments'.

2 'It is absolutely certain that an important element of comprehension is given by the coherence between atmospheric sensibility and atmospheric irradiation.' (Tellenbach 1968: 62 ff.)

'a fish out of water' or 'at home'. It is well-known that the atmosphere at lunch is different from that at dinner, that old furniture has more atmosphere than modern,[3] that even appetite can be stimulated by an atmosphere of warmth and trust, that sometimes a witticism is enough to change for better an initial atmosphere of diffidence, that to paint the walls means to essentially change the atmosphere of the room, that to have a coffee together creates an atmosphere of intimacy and sociality, that 'a drink seems to taste better in a dark and dimly lit bar' (Dichter 1964: 360). And also – choosing examples (almost) at random – that a small pill emanates an atmosphere of greater effectiveness, that to take off the gloves before shaking hands suggests an atmosphere of intimacy, that certain objects age well acquiring a seductive patina that makes collectors happy, that as soon as 'a shadow is thrown on our environment, our own mood changes correspondingly, as it were by reflection; we feel cold, and our own mind seems to have darkened' (Köhler 1938: 12). Furthermore, it is obvious that 'a particular piece of music can change the atmosphere in a room, […] a particular article of clothing can change the impression a person makes, […] a certain architecture can modify the expression of a city' (Seel 2005: 92), that one can tell immediately whether a film is French or American by the overall atmosphere of it. Is the aroma that, for Lévi-Strauss, assaults whoever gets to the new world truly a chemically peculiar smell or is it rather an unforgettable atmosphere symbolically condensed in a perfume? Well, in these and in countless other cases, we do indeed count on atmosphere – even though we cannot define it. Even when, feeling ill at ease or having nothing to say, we talk about the weather, we are probably discussing optical–climatic conditions that, exercising an effect on the felt body,[4] can be well defined as atmospheric.

Yet, despite this undoubted familiarity with atmosphere and with the fact that it can also be in contrast with cognitively verifiable data, the question 'what is an atmosphere?' is still – perhaps necessarily, given the reifying presupposition of the question? – not answered satisfactorily. Even knowing that the attempt at

---

    3   It has a 'moral theatricality' and a 'warmth' that renders it 'a realm of even greater privacy: they serve less as possessions than as symbolic intercessors.' (Baudrillard 2005: 16, 85)
    4   I borrow here the classical phenomenological distinction between felt-body (*Leib*) and mere, physical body (*Körper*). My use of the adjective 'corporeal' shall be understood as referring to the felt-body.

conceptualising 'floating and hardly graspable experiences' (Geiger 1911a: 156) risks 'inadvertently modelling experiences on concepts' (ibid), I will here accept the challenge, preferring overall an inevitably reductive definition of the variety of the manifestations of atmosphere[5] to the thesis according to which everything is atmospheric (and, consequently, nothing is in the proper sense). Of course, just like emotions, atmospheres too are 'curious situations that lose meaning when one tries to describe them: one has to be in them to understand them' (Galati 2002: 84). Nor does the ambiguity of the linguistic usage seem casual: 'atmosphere' can be either a neutrally descriptive expression (the atmosphere can be harmonious or suspicious), or implicitly (and positively) axiological, in the sense that by exclaiming 'what an atmosphere!' we usually express *ipso facto* a favourable condition.[6] It is obvious that this ambiguity is conditioned by the current praxis in the regional ontology in question, as emerges from the fact that when we prefer the atmosphere to the plot of a film we are probably praising its formal-authorial intensity, while when we say of a political summit that it produced a cordial atmosphere we are probably stating its failure (unless, obviously, the expectations were totally pessimistic). Atmosphere can therefore, paradoxically, be everything and nothing, a bit like 'air': it is everything or almost so when it increases the quality of life, when some enterprise succeeds thanks to the atmosphere of trust[7] or resilience (resistance, elasticity, vitality and good mood) as an efficacious barrier against negative situations,[8] yet it is almost nothing when it only indicates the superficial occultation of conflicts.

One cannot exclude that it is for this very semantic plasticity that the concept of atmosphere, although counting on a metaphorical use of the term ever since the Eighteenth century, has recently boomed,[9] especially in the psychological, aesthetological and (neo)phenomenological area.[10] First of all, that is, in all the research areas that, paying more attention to the 'veil' or the 'cloud' occulting the

---

5   Especially if we consider atmospheres as irreducible to concepts just as much as Kantian 'aesthetic ideas' (Franzini 2006).

6   In fact, a famous advertising slogan of the past ('the brandy that creates an atmosphere') felt no need to further specify the nature of that atmosphere.

7   That often 'is mistaken for a man' (Daudet 1928: 198).

8   Graf (2006).

9   Soentgen (1998: 72–73) even speaks of an *atmospheric turn*.

10 For a first approach to this, see Tellenbach (1968); Schmitz (1964 on., 1969, 1998), Böhme (1985, 1995, 1998, 2001, 2006a, 2006b), on which Battisti (2006), Hauskeller (1995, 1998, 1999, 2002), Hasse (2002a, 2002b, 2005, 2006, 2008a, 2008b).

'edge' of the thing itself (Schapp 1976: 13 ff.) than to strictly functional parameters, rejoice in the meticulous and occasionally exhausting description of phenomenical *nuances*. And obviously it flourished also in the 'aesthetic work',[11] meaning by this not only the production of atmospheres, but also their pertinent reception within the so-called widespread aesthetisation. Finally, the concept of atmosphere prospered also in those areas where demonstration gives way to persuasion and cognitively irreducible *qualia*, such as economic choices, decisional processes and even inferential psychology. In fact, even the greater 'felt' persuasiveness of some logically invalid syllogisms – like the one that from two particular and affirmative premises (some A are B, some B are C), atmospherically draws an erroneous particular and affirmative conclusion (some A are C)[12] – could be attributed to an 'atmosphere effect'.

Being philosophically interesting not *despite* but *precisely because of* this vagueness, atmosphere does not yet coincide with an exclusively subjective *nuance*. Whoever proclaims (with Conrad's Kurtz) 'the horror, the horror!', or discusses the even corporeal atmosphere (for instance, of irritability[13]) of an entire age, is obviously intending to refer to extra-subjective atmospheres. It is true that we say 'I am sad' and not 'I feel sadness around me', but only because the extreme proximity of that atmosphere and the introjectionist prejudice privileging the possessive sense of the personal pronoun,[14] both impede the external location of sadness.

> Subjects exist only through subjective facts, while subjectivity-for-someone does not already presuppose this someone as a subject. Rather, at its root, in my being affectively involved, subjectivity-for-me is such that the word 'me' is to

---

11   Which, according to Böhme (1995: 24–25; 2001: 22; 2006b: 8), includes not only art, but also design, cosmetics, advertising, scenography, urban design, etc.

12   'The premises create a mood, a sort of humoral vein, which in turn creates the atmosphere of reasoning. The positive and universal vein satisfies us the most and invites us to persuasion the most […] Instead, a syllogism based on negations and partial systems […] creates an atmosphere that is less persuasive for us' (Piattelli Palmarini 1995: 76–77). On the controversial 'atmosphere effect' see Woodsworth-Sells (1935), Sells (1936), Chapman-Chapman (1959), Begg-Denny (1969), Evans *et al.* (1993: 235–241).

13   See Lethen (2005) on the atmosphere of 'irritability' of the third decade of the twentieth century.

14   'My sadness', in fact, implies 'not that I possess it, hold it or perform it', but only that 'it hits me, regards me, touches me in the flesh.' (Schmitz 2003: 181)

be understood not so much as a pronoun but rather an adverb (like 'here' and 'now'), which does not nominate an object but characterises a milieu – just as with the word 'here' we do not refer to an object ('the here') but to what is here, in the milieu of maximum proximity. (Schmitz 1994: 15)

At the centre of our (aesthetic and phenomenological) interest there is, therefore, atmosphere – and here is a first, approximate, definition – as a qualitative-sentimental *prius*, spatially poured out, of our sensible encounter with the world. Something that is 'chronologically at the start and objectively at the peak of the hierarchy', as emerges from the fact that 'the sensibility to the differences in way-of-being or "atmosphere" existing between two colours is normally greater than the sensibility for the corresponding differences between pure chromatic qualities' (Metzger 1941: 86). Perceiving an atmosphere, therefore, means grasping a feeling in the surrounding space, definitively the most important thing for men,[15] implied by any subsequent clarification, both sensible and cognitive.[16] It means being gripped by a *something-more*, and it is precisely 'this something-more, exceeding real factuality and which nonetheless we feel with and in it, that we can call "atmospheric"' (Tellenbach 1968: 47), seeing in it an excess with respect to the place[17] and, if you like, a great part of what 'resists a "representational" attitude' (Franzini 2006: 72). In short, a

---

15 'Feelings are the most important thing in life, because only they bring power and delicacy, brightness and opacity into the world; the only thing that, generally, makes something important to men.' (Schmitz 1969: xii)

16 'We must recognize the indeterminate as a positive phenomenon. It is in this atmosphere that quality arises'. 'But in reality all things are concretions of a setting, and any explicit perception of a thing survives in a virtue of a previous communication with a certain atmosphere', like a chromatic one, for instance. And if they are objects, every one of them 'is moulded to the human action which it serves. Each one spreads round in an atmosphere of humanity', that is more or less determined. (Merleau-Ponty 2005: 7, 374, 405)

17 'An occupied space creates an atmosphere. Atmosphere is always what the individual objects that occupy places are not, the other side of their form, what perishes along with them. This explains the "invulnerability" of atmosphere, along with its dependency on a given occupied space. Atmosphere is a kind of excess effect caused by the difference between places. It cannot be analyzed by describing places, nor is it reducible to places. It comes into being each time an object occupies a place and creates an ambiance that is neither identical to the object nor able to resist without it. Atmosphere makes visible both the unity of the difference that constitutes space and the invisibility of space as a medium for the creation of forms. But it is not the same as space, which, as a medium, can never become visible.'(Luhmann 2000: 112)

'difference',[18] a 'resonance' of the felt space, filled by atmosphere not as 'a material object which fills another by espousing the form that the other imposes' (Minkowski 1936: 86) but rather as a vibration (not necessarily auditory) in which the perceived and the perceiver meet and even merge isomorphically and predualistically. It is a something-more, a *je-ne-sais-quoi* perceived by the felt-body in a given space, but never fully attributable to the objectual set of that space – hence the resort to very precise, although oxymoric, formulations, like in the case of the 'misty transparency' attributed by Goethe to the Mediterranean landscape.[19] A spatialised feeling,[20] a something-more in an affective and corporeal sense, rather than in an abstractly semantic sense: 'in all the areas of sense, atmosphere, in the perceived object, is what is *not* object but meaning. The way in which the world is for us, namely what kind of relation we have with the world in every single moment and how we feel in it, is something we experience not objectively but atmospherically' (Hauskeller 1995: 101). A something-more that, finally, escapes 'analytical' and therefore 'immobilising' perception, because 'science reduces all it touches to immobility, it transforms it into still life. While around us the world resonates with a thousand melodies, exhales a thousand perfumes, is animated by a thousand movements, that make our being vibrate and palpitate. And we take part in this life, so intense, impalpable and indefinite' (Minkowski 1936: 150).

If this vagueness cannot but irritate traditional ontology, it is welcomed instead by a renewed ontological approach. An inflationary one, founding itself both upon a phenomenology that 'in fact, at least initially, knows no negation' (ibid: 116) and upon the heuristic power of everyday language, which is therefore willing to enrol into the ordinary ontological catalogue also dimensions like atmospheres, considering them the more positively active the more they are evanescent:[21] 'when I enjoy a given thing, I linger on it, but at the same time the object becomes less of an

---

18 'The atmosphere of a thing extends itself precisely wherever the presence of this thing entails a difference.' (Hauskeller 1995: 33)

19 A transparency devoid of distinctness because of the bright intensity, according to Lehmann (1986: 155–156, 159, 190 and *passim*).

20 Atmosphere would not benefit, for instance, from an excessive formal vividness: 'no one would like to live in an infinitely vivid place, where everything is patently connected to everything else [...] We don't wish to live in a goldfish bowl; we would be overwhelmed by a multiplicity of evocative signs.' (Lynch 1981: 143)

21 Speaking of 'emotionally tuned space' (Stroker 1977) might in fact make one mistakenly suppose the previous existence of a pre-emotional space (Böhme 2006a:122).

"object" to me, and the sensorial pleasure it gives to me becomes less "sensorial". The "contours" of the object and the way in which it invests me lose something of their precision, while upon everything an atmosphere of discrete fascination is cast, which indeed I enjoy' (ibid: 187). One might wonder (see *infra* especially 3.4 and 3.5) what the criteria of identity and identifiability of atmospheres are, whether they exist independently from the subject or at least from his awareness; if and to what extent they supervene on given features and materials; whether they constitute a semantic or *de dicto* vagueness (the atmospheric description designates a given situation in a vague way) or instead, as we like to think, a metaphysical or *de re* vagueness (the atmospheric description designates a vague entity in a precise way), analogous to that attributable to many other quasi-things, such as colours, shadows, etc. In any case, one thing must be restated: clarity is not 'an absolute value [...] It only represents a form of life, one of the many. For nothing in the world, in the name of clarity, would we renounce obscurity, night, mystery and the intense life palpitating in these phenomena, offering itself to us' (ibid: 137–138).

In short, we would never renounce vagueness (in this case, the atmospheric one), from which one must therefore never exit. If anything, it is a matter of learning to stay in it in the right way, especially preferring, to naïve sentimentalism, 'a reflective and emancipated relation with one's perception' (Hasse 2005: 362; see also 2000:163), namely one in which the affective experience is integrated by a reflection not devoid of critical potentialities. If 'learning how to relate to atmospheres makes the single man into a member, and critical interpreter, of the world we live in today' (Böhme 2006a: 53), it is because only an adequate atmospheric competence (both productive and receptive) could immunise us from the media-emotional manipulation which the aesthetisation of politics and social life in the late-capitalistic 'scenic' economy results in. Providing that, of course, we admit that the unintentionality which phenomenology returns to 'is not that which is prior to philosophy or prior to reflection [but] the unreflected which is understood and conquered by the reflective' (Merleau-Ponty 1964: 19; see 1945: 18): that is, an immediacy grasped by a philosophy that for its aesthetic,[22] or rather aesthesiological, nature, aspires to present itself as the first philosophy.

---

22 In the sense in which 'aesthetic' is 'what engages our senses, arouses in us sensations and feelings and thus imprints on our consciousness.' (Zur Lippe 1987: 17)

Chapter 1
Atmospheric Perception

1.1 Atmospheric Segmentation?

The atmospheric – while uniting and allowing for a productive tuning – divides at the same time, given that 'through the entire world of human life, under the sign of the atmospheric, just as in the animal reign under the sign of the olfactory, there are numerous invisible, yet selective and efficacious, frontiers' (Tellenbach 1968: 56). That is, segmentations that are natural as much as socio-cultural, like that (more violent than one would imagine) between the 'happy few' self-elected priests of good taste and all 'the others'. With their facilitating factors of unification, objects undoubtedly guarantee representational, and therefore ontological, advantages on the basis of dualisms (*in primis* that between mind and body) that would even count as the evolutionary answer of the species.[1] And yet, as soon as the cognitive distance (required by representation and judgment so as to overcome the roughness of lived experience) is reduced, as soon as one leaves behind the thingness typical of naïve physicalism as well as the obsessive epistemic causalism, things change and it is not so much dualisms that impose themselves on us for their undisputable aesthetic primal character, but rather emotional situations that involve us on the affective-corporeal level. And their ontological primal character, on the contrary, suggests the hypothesis – opposed to that of evolutionary psychology – that the separation between things and meanings is only a late phenomenon in biophysical evolution (being, moreover, exclusively human) with respect to the more primal symbioticity.

In this sense, the basic ontological elements would not be things but (atmospheric) meanings, namely 'that kind of living system of meanings which makes the concrete essence of the object immediately recognizable, and allows its "sensible properties" to appear only through that essence. [...] In the normal subject

---

[1] It is *Descartes' Baby* (Bloom 2004: 177 ff.).

the object "speaks" and is significant, the arrangement of colours straight away "means" something' (Merleau-Ponty 2005: 151) – notwithstanding that, following Aristotle, what is prior in experience can turn out to be cognitively successive (and more enigmatic). Why on earth, in fact, should solid and contoured bodies be more real than vague entities, which we experience without referring them to solidity,[2] such as fluids, gas processes or even quasi-things like atmospheres? So much so that atmospheres, far from being abstractions or mere possibilities, preserving their identity in our (especially involuntary) memory, seem to guarantee even 'the immutable preserved in what is past' (Tellenbach 1968: 31). Be it the innumerable and elegant examples of atmospheric memories of the *Recherche* (from the *Madeleine* onwards) or Léon Daudet's more prosaic pea soup,[3] what every good novel exemplifies extensively is that our lived experience – especially if untied from generally reifying senses like sight and touch – is not segmented first of all into discrete objects, but in feelings poured out in the surrounding space, felt by the felt-body before any analytical distinction.

Due to their priority and (relative) objectivity, atmospheres must certainly then be registered in the ontological repertory originated by our ordinary, intuitive and pragmatically efficacious segmentation of reality (which is firstly aesthesiological, then socio-cultural and so on). In short, it is a matter of affective and corporeal conditions aroused in the subject by external situations;[4] they are pre-dualistic and, in principle, opaque to the so-called expert knowledge and yet, as invariants obtained from a flux, still classifiable into a familiar and sufficiently systematic repertory (atmospheric topics) of affective-emotional kinds:[5] a phenomenologically

---

2 'If the inelastic fluid is already almost entirely devoid of its own specific shape, only the gas is utterly devoid of it, *despite the fact that it can still be experienced*, for instance in the resistance of moving air' (Klages 1929–32: 963–964; my emphasis). 'We find no normative reason for the fact that it is daylight and a step distance that present the world to us as it is. Why could it not be twilight and a thousand step distance that present the world in a more correct way?' (Schapp 2004: 95)

3 Attracted to the nurse that, at the La Charité hospital, distributed it to the patients, Léon Daudet (1928: 127) remembers 'how delicious it was and how the sight and the perfume [...] of that pea soup suited her blonde hair [...] Ever since, every pea soup has stayed alive and clear in my memory'.

4 As the sociologist also admits: 'by perception I mean a process of contemporaneous irradiation of the social goods or men and the perceptive activity of corporeal feeling.' (Löw 2001: 195–196)

5 See the catalogue of it proposed by Tellenbach (1968: 63) on the basis of the criteria of temperature, tension and consistency (dirty-filthy vs. pure; fresh-icy vs warm-hot;

'true' repertory, as it is passively perceived,[6] almost as if it were the point of view of things.[7]

1.2 Perceiving Atmospheres

Philosophers, one could say, have so far only interpreted the world, in various ways: now the point is to perceive it. Also atmospherically. Then it might be convenient to begin by precisely defining, though with no pretentions of exhaustiveness and systematicity, what kind of perception the atmospheric one is, starting also from what it is not.

a. First of all, like ordinary perception, it is never only the belief of perceiving. While counting on the same reality index (owing to the identity of the real and the perceived), atmospheric perception is, nonetheless, never the unaffective and anaesthetic perception tackled by psychology handbooks, thus fatally confusing experience and experiment. It is only because of a logistic-epistemic strabismus, in fact, that perception is thought-of as 'if the external world were behind a door and we were in front of it, full of curiosity. Instead, opening an eye is not at all similar to looking through a door lock' (Piana 1979: 19): it is rather living significant impressions possibly without ascetic and/or reductionistic shortcuts.[8] That is, to have an experience and not the distancing-constative process that specialised psychology limits itself to, namely not the mere passive-reflective registration of a portion of the visual field by an immobile eye thought of along the model of the camera obscura or the 'open window'. If it is untrue that 'we stop seeing when we close our eyes' (Minkowski 1936: 132), it is precisely because the optical

---

perturbing-hostile-foreign vs. familiar-friendly-intimate, etc.).

6 'I cannot perceive [an object] without attributing to it at the same time the possibility of impressing me in this or that way. The relation is always mutual, so that perceiving something always also means exposing oneself to its influence area or immerging oneself into its atmosphere, which is the same' (Hauskeller 1995: 155). For a convincing critique of oculocentrism see Pallasmaa (2005).

7 Griffero (2005a).

8 'Visual habits have blurred the attention for things; hurriedly studied and apprehended words and concepts have surpassed sensations, thereby narcotising them.' (Rumpf 1994: 8)

reduction of the perceptive – despite being probably the evolutionary outcome of the weakening of animal olfaction – is probably much rarer than the affectively and synaesthetically engaging perception that interests us here.

b.   Atmospheric perception, as we have anticipated, does not concern cohesive, solid, continuous objects mobile only through contact, nor discrete forms and movements, but rather chaotic-multiple situations (see *infra* 1.6) endowed with their own internal significance[9] and whose phenomenical efficiency must be radically disjointed from the physical stimulus. Borrowing a term established in aesthetics, philosophical anthropology and hermeneutics, we could therefore identify atmospheric percepts with the 'significances',[10] in particular with emotional saliences at least partly cognitively penetrable, in that they derive more from a 'noticing' than a purely optical seeing,[11] and they are in any case so immediate that they need no deciphering.[12]

> The eye comes always ancient to its work, obsessed by its own past and by old and new insinuations of the ear, nose, tongue, fingers, heart, and brain. It functions not as an instrument self-powered and alone, but as a dutiful member of a complex and capricious organism. Not only how but what it sees is regulated by need and prejudice. It selects, rejects, organizes, discriminates, associates, classifies, analyzes, constructs. It does not so much mirror as take and make; and what it takes and makes it sees not bare, as items without attributes, but

---

9   'Every perception of something unique, for instance a colour, a thing or a quasi-thing, is therefore from the beginning also the perception *that* something is in a certain way, the perception of states of things that do not manifest themselves necessarily in an explicit way, while they can instead be profoundly immersed in the chaotic-multiple significance of the situation.' (Schmitz 2002b: 18)

10 'No perception without a lived significance [...] no objectification (perception, concept, knowledge) realised by the "I" and to be incorporated by the person in the absence of a significance lived by the "Es" and by the emotional stratum.' (Rothacker 1948: 172). See Scholtz 1992.

11 In fact, our senses are always 'to a large degree informed senses' (Seel 2005: 50). See the objections to Danto (2001).

12 'What is felt is not a visual quality but a face of the world, a certain *atmosphere* expressing itself, and not giving itself for reading or deciphering but for feeling in an immediate way, like in the moment when one feels the storm in the air or when one feels joy or sadness.' (Dufrenne 1991: 32, my emphasis)

as things, as food, as people, as enemies, as stars, as weapons. Nothing is seen nakedly or naked. (Goodman 1968: 7–8)

According to the organic species-specific constitution and the psychic-existential situation, in perceiving the senses select, in fact, as significant (and *ipso facto* as real), within an ampler repertory of possibilities, something one is motivated by independently from the psycho-physical conditioning.[13]

> The physiological processes in the sense organs, in the nerve cells and in the ganglia, do not motivate me even if they condition, in my consciousness, psychophysically, the appearances of sense data, apprehensions, and psychic lived experiences. What I do not 'know', what does not stand over against me in my lived experiences, in my representing, thinking and acting, as the represented, perceived, remembered, thought, etc., does not 'determine' me as a mind. And what is not intentionally included in my experiences, even if unattended or implicit, does not motivate me, not even unconsciously. (Husserl 1990: 243)

c.   The situation, it is true, is intensely perceived on the atmospheric level mostly when it escapes the ordinary pragmatic relationship; like when an unexpected climatic event, impeding our activities, unexpectedly attracts attention over its own autonomous emotional value. Yet, far from being an exceptional event, cause of ineffable losses or unheard-of discoveries, atmospheric perception is largely nothing but one of the variants of ordinary perception, in which 'the state of *perceiving* consciousness as *directly* conditioned by something absolutely *foreign* to the soul'[14] (Klages 1921: 212–213) is sensed.

---

13   'From the biological field to the maximally spiritual one we recognise as the engine of the entrance in the world, of the exploration and opening of the world, of the amplifying and annihilation of the world, a vital, emotional and existential participation in the absence of which there is generally no knowledge, no content of experience or knowing.' (Rothacker 1934: 98)

14   'The man who, walking, trips over a stone of the pavement that sticks out, and after this somehow or other has to notice it, feels that his perception has been […] extorted from him.' (Klages 1927: 130)

> We see colours, hear sounds, smell perfumes, taste the sweet, the sour, the bitter, the salted; with touch we sense pressure, the hot, the cold, the wet, the rough, the smooth, the dry; but we do not see our own seeing, hear our own hearing, smell our own smelling, taste our own tasting, touch our own touching. […] Finally, we feel sadness, joy, hope, love, expectation, veneration, hatred, and therefore something that *moves* the soul, but we do not feel our own feeling […] To live experiences with sentiment means living the attractive force of images […] Our soul mirrors the world, but not…the mirror! (ibid: 290–292)

Such variant is certainly, at times, subversive enough, with respect to the lethal familiarity, to allow for a renewed look on things and places that has something of a rapture, breaking 'the surface of visual habits' until 'from the cracks the forgotten daemonic character of things erupts' (Böhme 1988: 230), and in which the phenomenological 'that' reveals to be irreducible to the cognitive 'what'.

> An inhibition of familiar sensa is very apt to leave us a prey to vague terrors respecting a circumambient world of causal operations. In the dark there are vague presences, doubtfully feared; in the silence, the irresistible causal efficacy of nature presses itself upon us; in the vagueness of the low hum of insects in an August woodland, the inflow into ourselves of feelings from enveloping nature overwhelms us; in the dim consciousness of half-sleep, the presentations of sense fade away, and we are left with the *vague feeling of influences from vague things around us*. (Whitehead 2010: 176, my emphasis)

Yet, it is not necessary here to identify perception with impulse,[15] given that, after all, it already falls within that common experience that gives us the world, phenomenologically, as it is, and which aetiology follows only afterwards. If, in fact, 'the phenomenon itself is a bearer of meaning' (Klages 1921: 254), it is erroneous to 'intend the thing as if I had here the thing and there the idea, because I instead perceive the thing in its idea. In front of me I do not see two things, but I have in front of my eyes the thing in its idea. Which is why I cannot at all imagine what else the thing could be without its idea' (Schapp 2004: 141).

---

15 Barbaras (2004).

d. Perceiving atmospherically is not grasping (presumed) elementary sense-data and, only afterwards or *per accidens*, states of things,[16] but it is instead being involved by things or, even better, situations. After all, 'much closer to us than all sensations are the things themselves [...] In order to hear a bare sound we have to listen away from things, divert our ear from them, i.e listen abstractly' (Heidegger 1977a: 156). Not only do we always 'hear the storm whistling in the chimney, [...] the three-motored plane, [...] the Mercedes in immediate distinction from the Volkswagen [Adler in the original, AN]' (ibid), but, even when the meaning remains obscure, we do not regress at all to presumed (unaffective) sense-data, because we still refer, physiognomically, to a unit of meaning within a situational background. In fact, 'to be aware of a fire as merely a set of hues and shapes in motion instead of experiencing the exciting violence of the flames presupposes a very specific, rare and artificial attitude' (Arnheim 1966: 63); the same goes for perceiving a face as an object instead of 'its look and its expression', or Paris as a collection of perceptions instead of the 'style' of the perceptions suggested by the city (Merleau-Ponty 2005: 327–328). Atmospheric perception is therefore a holistic and emotional being-in.the-world. 'Only because one moves between things and has to do with them, only if one is in the world and does not have it before oneself, one can feel [...] One is never in a vacuum, but always "with" things' (Lipps 1977: 77–78), with 'the desk at which I am now writing [...], likewise [with] the flavor of the tobacco I am now inhaling from my pipe, or the noise of the traffic in the street below my window' (Koffka 1922: 532): in short, with what is now here-for-me, both affectively and corporeally. Atmospheric perception is not explicated, in the final analysis, through a 'separatistic sensualism' (Schmitz 1978: 9), nor, following Kant, through the synthesis of an otherwise confused sensorial multiplicity, but always having to do, vice versa, with a 'matter [...] "pregnant" with its form' (Merleau-Ponty 1964: 12), with situations that cannot be partitioned into those numerical singularities[17] upon whose constellations only one can build

---

16 'As of Cleon's son we perceive not that he is Cleon's son, but that he is a white object, as the fact of his being Cleon's son is accessory to the whiteness.' (Aristotle 1907: 111)

17 According to Schmitz (2002a: 134), Plato mistakes for pure thought the more archaic notion of *noein* ('perception of situations'), thus creating the conditions for the consequent dichotomy between abstract thought and passive and acephalous perception.

abstractive constructions of prognostic value.[18] In atmospheric perception one is rather affectively and corporeally involved in a situation, for instance in 'an atmosphere propagating into the glance, the voice and innumerable other signs' (Schmitz 1978: 42), and whose petulant focalisation would even represent a pathology. Perceived silence and darkness, in fact, are not simple *qualia* (or will we have to posit the existence of waves and particles of darkness?), but complex atmospheric *qualia*, filled with motor and synaesthetic suggestions and possibly – only under particular conditions of epiphanic (mystical) or almost hypnotic (habitual acts) disembodiment – also absolute *qualia*, untied from situations that semanticise them[19] and only afterwards translatable into *qualia* predicatively tied to material supports.

e. Although there certainly are atmospheres, mainly of a social kind, whose corporeal effect is scarce and anyway not easy to observe (the economic, political situation etc.), perceiving atmospheres mostly means being touched by them in the felt-body. Which sets a limit to the spread view that notices in the contemporary world (electronic proceedings, iconic surrogates, scientification of the therapeutic practice and psychotherapy[20]) enormous processes of anaesthetisation and de-localisation of the sensible presence, following both the kinetic routine imposed by the new media and, paradoxically, the aesthetisation of reality: in fact, 'where everything is beautiful, nothing is beautiful any more. Continued excitement leads to indifference' (Welsch 1997: 121). The fact that the perceiver's visual world does not coincide with his visual field and with what there is in the stimulus – namely, the fact that it might be something more, less or even distorted[21] – does not only mean that atmospheric perception is direct and deambulatory, kinaesthetic[22] and

---

18 What else is a licence if not the impossibility of 'abandoning oneself' to lived experiences? (Verhoog 2003: 140–141).
19 Thus Schmitz (1978: 210 ff.) reinterprets Husserl's 'eidetic vision': as the (disembodied) perception of absolute impressions.
20 'For generations, psychoanalysts will shrink from perception like vampires from light.' (Huppertz 2003: 182; see also 181 and 186).
21 See Massironi (1998: 33–35).
22 In the sense in which for Arnheim (1966: 83, 81) 'the feeling of movement' is 'an inherent feature of visual perception itself' cognitively not producible 'unless the proper perceptual features are present'.

affectively engaging,[23] synaesthetic or at least polymodal, but most of all that it means 'to render oneself present to something through the body' (Merleau-Ponty 1964: 52), or better through the felt-body understood as the extraorganic dimension and the absolute place one can only access in the first person. Understood as:

> What he [man] can feel of himself in the surroundings of his physical body, without basing himself on the attestation of the five senses (sight, hearing, touch, olfaction, taste) and of the perceptive bodily scheme (that is, of the usual representative construct of one's own physical body derived from visual and tactile experiences). The living body is populated by bodily drives such as anguish, pain, hunger, thirst, breathing, pleasure, affective involvement on the part of feelings. It is indivisibly extended without surfaces in the form of a pre-dimensional volume (that is, without a numerable dimension, for instance not three-dimensional) which has its dynamics in contraction and expansion. (Schmitz 2007: 15–16)

Contrary to the cognitivist vulgate, perception, as we are trying to outline it, is not an inner process of elaboration of signals that, from the outside, through physical (and physicalistically definable) stimuli, reach the brain through the different sensorial channels (the metaphysical hiatus between the physical and the psychic sensation would anyway stay unanswered). It is rather, although on a psycho-physical background, a 'communication of the felt-body with meaningful impressions' (Schmitz 2002b: 38; 2005a: 147–149), its distension into situations to the point of being modified by it, in the light of a vital dynamism at times antagonistic, at times supportive. To sum up, atmospheric perception is a

> synaesthetic and sensorymotor unity of experience [that] allows one to holistically sense complex situations: the nuance, the mood, the atmosphere and the significance they possess. In this way the expert develops, in the end, a 'seventh sense', a sensibility or a presentiment, an intuitive perception of situations. (Fuchs 2003: 77)

---

23 Perhaps even visceral-affective, if we wish to distinguish (Spitz 1965) between perception founded on the autonomic nervous system (kinaesthetic organisation) and that which replaces it throughout the formation of the 'I' (diacritical organisation), based on the peripheral sense organs.

f.   We must add, though, that the holistic perception of atmospheric feelings in the pre-dimensional space has much in common with the vital involuntary experiences that (always) lead to adequate semi-automatic reactions. Like a driver avoiding a danger by corporeally using the optic channel (the look forwards, sideways and backwards, thanks to rearview mirrors) and the tactile-vibratory channel (hands, feet and torso), a person who lives an atmospheric feeling knows immediately how to behave: 'he who is content can jump around; he who is sad can moan and sit dull or as if he was shattered; he who is ashamed can lower his head, shrug his shoulders; he who is irremediably desperate can burst into a clamorous laughter, etc.: no one that is thus involved has to awkwardly wonder how it is done' (Schmitz 1990: 305).

g.   If 'each thing tells us with one look how it is to the touch or how it should be handled' (Fuchs 2003: 76), if 'our eyes and ears also react to haptic moments' (Rothacker 1966: 339), perhaps grasping 'the resonance of things in the drama of the human life world' (Rumpf 2003: 252), then we can undoubtedly think of atmospheric perception also as the (extraintellectual, of course) comprehension of the expression of our 'surroundings', including the directed tensions that are inherent to the perceived and *Gestaltically* extended also to 'inanimate objects, such as mountains, clouds, sirens, machines' (Arnheim 1966: 52). But just as in 'it is hot' the heat is not the attribute of a substance, so the atmospheric quality is not so much the property of a thing as instead (see *infra* 3.4) a quasi-thing, not less autonomous with respect to things than a melody is with respect to simple noise.[24] In other words, it is a lived quality (in a transitive sense), not conjectured or analogically deduced but encountered[25] in its ante-predicative Gestaltic organisation, and at least initially foreign to the interiority of the subject.

Yet, a clarification is due: whether we compare them to expressive qualities or ways-of-being, to physiognomic characters or tertiary qualities, atmospheres are not at all an extrinsic integration of anterior qualities – for instance 'tectonic'

---

24   For the expert sommelier, the aroma of wine, for instance, 'is made autonomous […] on a kind of minimal level like a melody or a motive, or like an catchy chord when one enjoys listening to music' (Schmitz 1978: 217), becoming the 'occasion' for the irradiation of that specific aroma.

25   Namely that kind of 'perceptive performance that is different both from the directly perceived and from the merely imagined.' (Massironi 1998: 108)

qualities (round, angular, discontinuous, etc.) and 'global qualities' of the material (rough, hard, strident, etc.).[26] The cheerful and the friendly, the proud and the obscure, the feminine, the masculine and the childlike, to refer to Metzger's list, are rather the proper *prius* of our encounter with the world, and not simply a practical-emotional tonality gregarious with respect to the preliminary (and in any case non-projective) perceptive constitution of objective formations.[27] Precisely because they are non-subjective 'neither with regard to their localisation nor with regard to their cause' (Metzger 1941: 78) and because they can be assimilated to a fluid or 'an "essence" that can be distilled from its "bearer" and of which another can be impregnated' (ibid: 83), it seems that ways-of-being can be compared with atmospheres, which, though, should be thought of as a synthesis of the three, only relatively different, Gestaltic qualities mentioned above. Let us limit ourselves to the decisive point: there is no perceptively anterior scene to the 'Gestaltic qualities of "global consciousness"',[28] i.e. those atmospheric tonalisations that 'permeate and color all the objects and events that are involved in an experience', thus qualifying (also in an aesthetic sense) 'all the constituents to which it applies in a thoroughgoing fashion' (Dewey 1989: 75) – be it the so called Caravaggio-like quality or the threatening look of clouds in the mountains.

h.   Affectively involving the felt-body in its quality of embodied perception, atmospheric perception is perfected not so much through knowledge but rather by way of an exercise, also mimetic, that is not semiotically founded upon sign reference – 'at the first sight of an enraged person, we do not notice those lines on the face in which rage manifests itself but, relying on the effect produced in ourselves, we believe to see rage itself' (Klages 1923: 40). This exercise rather constitutes (by testing a sentimental resistance, in this case) a sort of non-theoretical but aesthesiological demonstration of the external world.

---

26   Metzger (1941: 77).
27   Precisely for this reason 'much less rich in sense than it might seem at first sight.' (Piana 1979: 49–50)
28   'In the sense that today is given to this term, that is including also the way in which the external world is lived; but it is better to call these qualities, following the current use, not feelings but 'moods', or also 'atmosphere', 'climate' and the like.' (Metzger 1941: 88)

> The impulse to development and vital expansion runs up against something external in which life finds its confines, a resistance that thwarts and limits it. And on this original experience of resistance then lies every further certainty of a reality external to us. Only through the experience of this resistance is the initial and yet undistinguished unity of man with his world divided into the opposed poles of the self and the objectual world. (Bollnow 1956: 113)

Moreover, it is unnecessary to dramatise (existentially and/or psychopathologically) such resistance, given that, in partial contrast with the existential analytic of the first Heidegger, it can surely happen that 'reality presents itself as something that gives joy, expands my being there and increases my strength' (ibid: 114), like 'the security towards one's own specific being [that] provides [man] also with the possibility of conceding to other things and men their own specific being' (ibid: 127).

Like any other perception, though, atmospheric perception also has, inevitably, its own blind spot:[29] it therefore necessarily implies also a non-perception.[30] We are not referring here so much to the inexhaustible phenomenological transcendence of the object, but rather to the obliteration of what, although present on the retina, is foreign, unwanted and tabooed.[31] It is an obliteration that is mostly unaware – as in the classical biological example of the perceived image being concealed by the previous search image (or at least the usual search tone)[32] – but that is sometimes perfected in a sort of art of non-perception,[33] which is obviously necessary to avoid the paralysis entailed by the strong emotional involvement, but that is already in act, more simply, whenever there is an intra-atmospheric conflict between

---

29 'To see something is constantly to oversee something else. There is no vision without a blind spot.' (Welsch 1997: 25)

30 'Hence the "milieu" is only what I experience as "effective" on me', that is to say, 'a "milieu thing" belongs to an "*intermediate sphere*", lying between our perceptual content and its objects on the one hand and those objectively thought objects on the other', given that we 'frequently experience the *effectiveness* of *something* that we do *not* perceive', of 'everything with *whose existence or absence*, with whose being so or other than so, I practically "reckon".' (Scheler 1973: 139, 140)

31 See Böhme (2001: 32 ff.).

32 Uexküll (2010: 113–118).

33 See Hauskeller (2003a: 169): a block of visual field that – we say this as an incidental comment–, in principle, invalids the ideological 'pretension of sense' of Modernity (Marquard 1986: 41).

the emotionally valorised detail (even elevated to the symbol of an age) and the culturally underestimatable rest.

i. We have thus enrolled also atmospheric perception into the catalogue of passivities: namely of what, to put it with Merleau-Ponty, is more a being-perceived than a perceiving. And yet, while being wary of the relativistic thesis according to which, for instance, 'in nature we generally see only what we have learned to see, and we see as is required by the style of the time' (Lehmann 1986: 141), it frankly seems impossible to entirely de-historicise atmospheric perception. Suffice it to think of the growing positivity (in the Western world) of every atmospheric power tied to sun exposure – from the health-related enthusiasm for sun baths to the thinning out of woods, from open air trips to (even artificial) tan – 'after long periods of a real mania for shadow' (Hellpach 1960a: 82) in which enclosed premises, North-facing houses, hats, gloves and parasols were preferred. But think mostly – we linger here on one of the many possible examples – of what is perceived in travel: a sensorially reduced perception (no smells, sounds or touch) devoid of spatial profundity, where the greater the speed the more it is downgraded to a mutable theatrical scene, implying on one side a space degraded to non-place,[34] on the other a standardised time antithetic to the lived one. Well, would we dare to claim that such perception is *a priori* incapable of arousing specific and authentic atmospheres?

The answer can only be negative. In fact, the perception in movement that we get from the window (of the car, the train, the plane, etc.), framing its objects in an almost pictorial way, generates atmospheres. Atmospheres that are usually occasional, but sometimes also so recurring (both a blessing and a curse of commuting!) that one grows fond of them like to a sort of everyday punctuation – like when the glimpse of the first known blocks signals with certainty, as metric as affective, that one is home. And is it not a particular (melancholic) atmosphere that offered by the indiscreet gaze from the train on the back of things? On the aesthetic and construction-related misery of unknown peripheries and meagre vegetable

---

34 Who transits in non-places 'becomes no more than what he does or experiences in the role of passenger, customer, or driver. […] Subjected to a gentle form of possession, to which he surrenders himself with more or less talent or conviction, he tastes for a while – like anyone who is possessed – the passive joys of identity-loss, and the more active pleasure of role-playing.' (Augé 1995: 103)

plots growing despite the rails; on more or less symbolic thresholds between the country and the city; on urban filaments extended enough to annihilate every trace of countryside; and on the more humble back of pretentious monumental buildings and, mostly, of common houses (neglected balconies and yards, clothes hanging and sad 'brownish pantries', to put it with Paolo Conte),[35] whose intimacy one is almost ashamed of looking at? Even if it undergoes an enormous 'modal reduction' (Hauskeller 1995: 185) and even spatial, chromatic distortions, etc. (glasses, windows, mirrors), perception in travel has in its protective cabin a sort of 'wandering "bubble", able to cut out parallel territories' (Tarpino 2008: 109). In the dynamic contrast between an almost unperceivable close-up, a relatively mutable medium shot and a background that almost coincides with the line of the horizon, one could then atmospherically grasp a historical and cultural depth;[36] in the glimpsed landscape, for example from the motorway, one could perceive a picturesque atmosphere; or even, in the touristic sign of a place of historical interest exempting us from visiting it, we could sense an atmosphere of joy 'from the mere knowledge of its proximity' (Augé 1995: 97), in its quality of a *memento* of something that goes irremediably lost in blurred and derealised experiences. The (Kantianly?) detached and casual character of these eradicated perceptions[37] arouses, in fact, a *sui generis* atmosphere that is impossible in direct contact, being formed by the unpredictable combination between external reality and internal reality (to which can also contribute, in the case of the train, what one is very likely reading), as well as between the non-places of the supermodernity in travel and the places of tradition that the first ones run along. The large scale neutralisation both of the historical-natural density of the crossed places and of the travellers' nature, produced by rest areas, is maybe contrasted or compensated by the touristic signs that, signalling detours of aesthetic-historical-commercial interest, performatively

---

35 'The railway, which often passes behind the houses making up the town, catches provincials off guard in the privacy of their daily lives, behind the facade, on the garden side, the kitchen or bedroom side' (Augé 1995: 99) 'But at night between us there is almost no dialogue', adds, not by chance, Paolo Conte (the Italian original is 'Ma la sera tra noi non c'è quasi dialogo', from the song *La ricostruzione del Mocambo*).

36 See Osborne (2000: 171) and Andrews (2005: 96–97).

37 'For the driver, the landscape becomes a mere image, inviting him to the play of cognitive faculties but without touching him more directly. In this sense the long-range driver of our times is the perfect aesthete.' (Hauskeller 1995: 182)

and constitutively[38] solicit an imaginative translation, not devoid of regrets, of the only topological indications of something one will perhaps never see again.[39] We thus find out, in the final analysis, that also the derealising and sensorially deprived perception is not devoid of its own atmospheric charge, possibly lived not outside but inside the very cabin, like in the gigantic American cars characterised by 'great size, davenport seats, soft springs, and insulation [...] soft cushions, soft tires, power steering and monotonously smooth pavements.' (Hall 1966: 60, 177)

Now that we have demonstrated, with the travel example, how the historicity of perceptive conditions does not at all exclude their (perhaps even mutable) atmospheric power, the time has come to interrogate ourselves on the phenomenological presuppositions of atmospheric perception.

1.3 How One Feels Here and Now in the Felt-Body

Sartre rightly sets the philosophy of transcendence implicit in Husserl's intentionality[40] against the 'alimentary' philosophy of immanence that claims to assimilate everything to consciousness. It would be necessary to take 'everything out' (even ourselves!) thus freeing ourselves from 'interior life', bringing terror and magic back into things and making supposedly subjective reactions like hatred, love, fear and fondness into properties of things and forms of discovery of the world. What matters to us here – as is certainly clear by now – is to take out atmospheric feelings, namely to see them as self-manifested phenomena irreducible to mere correlates of consciousness, beyond whose phenomenic surface it is meaningless to proceed[41] – especially so towards the view of essences or of

---

38 Explicitly inviting the traveller to a certain action, perhaps depicted on the sign, and, at the same time, giving a different overall image of the city, region or country one is crossing (Andrews 2005: 98–99).

39 As the poster in the office domesticates the wild landscape it reproduces, so 'the Autoroute becomes a kind of room, a corridor. The Autoroute's framed pictures, liminally perched between motorway and landscape, adorn the invisible walls of our long, monotonous, "non places"' (Andrews 2005: 100). See Augé (1995: 97).

40 Sartre (2002). We prescind here from the fact that Husserl would later fall back into the dogma of immanence with the reduction of the object to noematic correlate of the noetic act (see Schmitz 1996: 88–93).

41 It is the 'principle of all principles', that is, 'that every originary presentive intuition is a legitimizing source of cognition, that everything originarily (so to speak, in

being's Being, given that 'from a phenomenological perspective, preliminarily renouncing any value judgement, the surface is in fact something as alive and as important as depth is' (Minkowski 1936: 219). If, on the reflective level, the identified atmosphere is also what resists the variation of assumptions and the overcoming of introspective prejudices – that is, a 'phenomenological revision' (Schmitz 2002b: 36–37) – as well as something that can be asked to condensate itself into a judgement (on the atmospheric quality), on the subjective affective level there is only the perception of the quality of the apparition.

Yet this approach is influenced not by classical phenomenology, but rather by the heterodox science of the phenomenon sketched by Ludwig Klages – a true stone guest in every discourse on atmosphere – namely a science 'of elementary souls' (Klages 1929–32: 1138) 'appearing phenomenically' (Klages 1921: 262) as (originary) real images and being the daemonic *nimbus* of things. This holds true provided that this science's primacy of the optical over the felt-body,[42] as well as its heuristically excessive role of language (be it even the language pregnant with mythic-daemonic *Erlebnisse*), is limited, enhancing instead – following the universalisation of the Goethian principle of the immanence of theory in the phenomena themselves – its ability to stay 'in contact with reality' (Klages 1929–32: 617), escaping the materialistic and/or logistic reification.[43] Klages' phenomenology is undoubtedly precious to our approach, precisely as it addresses not things but 'significant contents, whether they give joy or are menacing' (Klages 1979: 523), that is, phenomenic characters on whose basis unheard-of kinds of knowledge can be built – a 'science of "autumn sensorial contents"', for instance, or of 'daily' or 'nightly sensorial contents'. Characters (or essences) like night and day, nearness and farness, Orient and Occident, right and left, light and darkness, sound and silence etc. are, in fact, just like atmospheres, 'situations, quasi-things, orientations of the felt-body' (Grossheim 1994: 237), perceivable by the soul only by prescinding from the scientist reductionism that made the world disenchanted

---

its "personal" actuality) offered to us in "intuition" is to be accepted simply as what it is presented as being, but also only within the limits in which it is presented there.' (Husserl 1982: 43)

42   Unfortunately asserted as a merely topologic paradigm (Klages 1929–32: 972–973).

43   'Among the representatives of the science of phenomena or, as it is said, of "phenomenology", there are unfortunately many false prophets', formalist enough to refer to 'appearances without what appears in them.' (Klages 1964: 440, 441)

and that, erasing its '*content of distance*' (Klages 1922: 163)[44] and proceeding to a pragmatically oriented reification, tore away its *nimbus*, preserved instead by the eros of distance. In other words, this can be achieved only by reacting to the systematic theft of the expressive or atmospheric value of things[45] and their images by reductionist physicalism, and not necessarily, in Klages' terms, by the spirit as the adversary of life.[46]

Distance itself (contemplative but also emotional)[47] can then be a privileged condition for atmospheric irradiation, especially under the visual profile. It is well-known, in fact, that 'how much more easily the leave-taker is loved! For the flame burns more purely for those vanishing in the distance, fueled by the fleeting scrap of material waving from the ship or railway window. Separation penetrates the disappearing person like a pigment and steeps him in gentle radiance' (Benjamin 1996: 450). Klages then teaches us also how (atmospherically) precise and non-figurative it is to say, with the language of common sense, that 'twilight comes, falls, lights up, withdraws; the day rises and disappears; the distance opens up; clouds push, wander, hurry, sweep away, sail, vanish, gather; the moon hides and so forth' (Klages 1929–32: 187). Finally, he teaches us how the experience of the atmospheric can at times be, following a sort of Eraclitean metamorphism, unique and unrepeatable. In fact,

> if the reality of sensorial impressions is a reality of happening, then it is also something unique and unrepeatable. Within the lived yellow of a rose fall not only its perfume, the summer heat, the blue of the sky, but also that period of life

---

44 'The call of the tawny owl at the beginning of February coming from the ancient city parks; the cry of the quail in full night or full midday, when the sun weighs on mature wheat fields; a song that fades into the streets: these [...] events [...] can be wrapped in the brightness of distance, exercising over us an inexpressible fascination.' (Kunz 1946: 288 ff.)

45 'We would laugh if the housewife wished to define water as cuisine liquid because it is particularly apt at cooking food; yet we are fundamentally doing the same thing when, *a posteriori*, we make reality into a toolbox for man's work because we have only tested it from this point of view.' (Klages 1974:712)

46 'The doctrine of facts, and even more the one of causes, are the peculiar form of conceptual violence over reality needed by the spirit in us so as to operatively dominate reality.' (ibid: 331)

47 'Contemplation does not consist in accurately getting rid of feelings with the aim of participating in a presumed pure knowledge, but in receiving the impulses to the evaluation of the feelings' depth.' (Klages 1964: 622)

that will not come back twice and that was occupied by the impression we are talking about: within the lived yellow of a withered plant falls not only autumn as a whole, but also the uniqueness of the place and time that no autumn to come will ever present again to me. (ibid: 174–175)

Within certain limits, we can compare atmospheres precisely with this yellow as a transmodal *Gestalt*, lived in a situational mutability both subjective[48] and objective – about which one might perhaps speak of 'momentary science' (Minssen 2004: 20) – with images, preconceptual impressions[49] or with 'meaning units such as sky, earth, night, brightness, darkness, tree, animal, stone etc., or such as running, standing still, lying, being awake, sleeping and so forth' (Klages 1929–32: 426). It is therefore not surprising that, in restating how images assail us from outside, 'expanding or contracting' (ibid: 1103), Klages can assimilate them to 'atmospheric pressure' (Klages 1964: 426).

But this thematisation of the atmospheric presupposes a (neo)phenomenological redefinition of philosophy in the terms of a 'self-reflection of man regarding the way in which he orientates within his environment' (Schmitz 1990: 5). It therefore claims the right to express, indeed, 'how one feels' (Schmitz 1994: 11), namely to examine experience so as to discern (without physicalistic[50] and epistemic guarantees) its atmospheric charge in the light of an aesthesiologic sensibility. Such sensibility is also hermeneutic, in a twofold sense: in fact, on the one hand, the comprehension could be nothing but the correspondence between atmospheric intuition and atmospheric irradiation (Tellenbach 1968: 62–63),[51] on the other hand through atmosphere itself – borrowing here what is said about mood – 'the world is already "interpreted" in an entirely specific way, and from this originary interpretation of life and world […] all understanding is governed to begin with'

---

48 'My seeing, hearing, tasting etc. are as little someone else's seeing, hearing and tasting as my dreaming is someone else's dreaming.' (ibid: 377)

49 'There is not *the* light, *the* heat, *the* sound, but there really is – even for us – the *character* of light, heat, sound. The world made of coagulated "ideas" offers, in a way, the silhouette of a reality once made of living gods.' (Klages 1929–32: 202)

50 And after all 'a physicalist laughing at a joke never believed to be laughing at oscillations of air, light and atoms.' (Rothacker 1934: 43)

51 'The intuition of the atmospheric is an organ that allows us to grasp what characterises, in an entirely immediate and unitary way, the world of our neighbour and our own environment.' (Tellenbach 1968: 49)

(Bollnow 1956: 57). What interests us here is *how* and not *why* we feel (in the felt-body) the way we feel; that is to say, we are interested in what it means, for a subjectivity whose self-conscience is not attributive *ipso facto*,[52] to be touched and involved by forms that are pathically and axiologically qualified, and thanks to which it is still at one with the world – for instance how we can be sad or happy (atmospherically) before any linguistic-reflective self-attribution.

Subject to an inevitable marginalisation as philosophy of art, aesthetics might therefore find here a new life. It could happen if, while not neglecting the aesthetic work and the ubiquity of design (which we all are at least co-responsible for),[53] it thematised the emotional (atmospheric) and perhaps even persuasive effect[54] exercised over the felt-body by environments and works, landscapes and advertisements, things and quasi-things (natural or artificial), possibly also in order to learn how to live more intensely what is present. At the centre of *this* (neo)phenomenological aesthetics, oriented to the phenomenic characters and the impressions stemming out of them, we find (as we know) the felt-body with its extradualistic motions. Unlike the physical body, which is stable, extended, endowed with a surface, divisible into parts occupying a relative local space, and which therefore is a legitimate object of natural sciences (anatomy *in primis*), the felt-body[55] is vice versa devoid of surface and occupies an 'absolute' and non-geometrical space; it is capable of self-auscultation without organic mediations and, because it exceeds the skin contour, it only occasionally coincides with the physical body. Manifest in the affective sphere and, in a completely different

---

52 It is therefore exempt from the infinite regress implied by the self-attribution of properties. In order to be able to identify a given property with myself, I should already be able to count on self-consciousness, and so forth: a rethinking of subjectivity, based on oscillation rather than stratification (Schmitz 2002b: 25; 1969: 52 and mostly 1992, 1995) that, though, falls outside our topic.

53 'We are all designers. We manipulate the environment, the better to serve our needs. We select what items to own, which to have around us. We build, buy, arrange, and restructure: all this is a form of design. [...] Through these personal acts of design, we transform the otherwise anonymous, commonplace things and spaces of everyday life into our own things and places.' (Norman 2005: 224)

54 Images, for instance, 'do not only take atmosphere into account, they create it. Images themselves are this atmosphere and not only its representation; so their effectiveness usually proves persuasive.' (Mersch 2002: 36)

55 We freely borrow here the 'economy of corporeality' elaborated by Schmitz (1965: 169 ff.; 1966; 1990: 115–205, 275–320).

way from the physical body,[56] appearing in accordance with a polarised rhythm (contraction or narrowness/ expansion or vastness) whose extremes, both unaware, are paralysing terror (embodiment) and total relaxation (disembodiment), it is articulated not into discrete parts but into 'corporeal isles'. These isles should be understood as extradimensional spaces of variable duration and configuration,[57] of a merely accessory functional value.[58] They are the perceptive and non-anatomical zones (head, chest, sole of the foot, etc.)[59] in which the felt-body identifies itself each time[60] and that do not confuse themselves with the 'bodily schema' (hence, otherwise, the famous illusion of the phantom limb) – which is necessarily more stable[61] for its necessary function reactive towards the world,[62] but emerges only at a certain point in a person's development. It is then corporeal communication with all the perceived (immobile or in movement) that, while adequately explaining the already mentioned excess of the perceived with respect to the seen[63] as well as the extrareflective-situational intelligence of external motor suggestions, also explains

---

56 Hence a new topography of lived corporeality as 'anatomy of half-light, requiring first of all the practice of a new vision' (Schmitz 1965: 283), no less hard than psychological introspection.

57 Corporeal isles can, in fact, change, disappear or be generated *ex novo* (ibid: 151).

58 Think of the indeterminate zone concerned by pleasure during a massage, of the cold felt by a feverish person whatever the environmental temperature, of the thirst extended to the oral cavity but indivisible, of the tiredness accompanying awakening that is not dividable into the different parts of the physical body, etc.

59 'The physical felt-body gives itself to each person in a discrete form with immediate feeling – it gives itself as divided into isles with no continued link between them – and we are normally unaware of the unusual character of this fact simply because these isles of the felt-body can be easily inserted, with the help of bodily schema, into the physical body we own, of whose continuous extension we are persuaded by our eyes and hands.' (ibid: 35–36)

60 'A corporeal isle that we feel – like for instance the hand – is not describable through the sentence *I feel my hand*, because, if anything, what is felt (namely the hand) is nothing but the feeling itself and it is not the feeling of an I that has the hand as its object, either: it is, instead, nothing but a conscious being-hand.' (Böhme 2003: 38)

61 'What normal man would ever think of having an image of himself made by floating confused isles? And, in any case, the task of painting a portrait according not to the bodily schema but to the material felt-body is yet to be achieved by surrealist painters.' (Schmitz 1965: 27–28)

62 'For man it is usually a point of honour that his material body has an extensive continuity, a precise confine and a constant articulation, in conformity with the bodily schema; only thus can he "face" the world surrounding him.' (ibid: 32)

63 'The felt-body communication of incorporating kind constructs with the gaze, as with an antenna, a spatial field unitarily and integrally organised, inclusive not only of the seen object, but also of our felt-body that we sense is being touched and which, with

the fact that one can perceive the atmospherically oppressive or elating character of a given environment.

1.4 The First Impression

A phenomenological aesthetics of atmosphere must rehabilitate the so-called first impression.[64] That is to say, the involuntary life experiences that, 'almost' as servomechanisms beyond both doubt and selective or conceptual discretion, function as a global response (emotive, motivational and value-related). We might even speak of *insight*, but only if we do not explain it, like Köhler does, in projectivistic[65] terms that, after all, do not exclude deceit.[66] The first impression is an affective corporeal involvement that, interrupting the habitual observational and pragmatic flux, can, for this very immediacy,[67] represent for the subject an identity certificate much better than the *cogito* – and, even more so, better than objective facts, which as such are ours as much as others', in principle. The first impression, which is certainly amendable (even though only because initially assumed in its unanalysable certainty), is always atmospheric, even if it had a merely contextual value. This is why 'the sensible working-class woman [...] sees at a glance a slight anger in her returning husband and a mute irritation in her son' (Klages 1964: 379), without being able to analytically explain the link between physiognomic traits and the impressions she draws from them. This is also why general Augereau cannot explain himself why, in the presence of Napoleon, 'he has felt himself

---

its specific dynamics, guides the movement of our visible and touchable physical body.' (Schmitz 2002b: 45)

64 Griffero (2009a).

65 'For when we are in an irritable mood, and now discover something that more or less fits this inner situation, the object in question will at once appear as an entirely adequate cause of intense anger.' (Köhler 1992: 335, see also 1938: 23–27)

66 'If, finding myself in a mood of relief after a brilliant exam, I find that everyone around me has a happier appearance than usual, this certainly means that I projected my joy in them, but at the same time I have also deceived myself about their real disposition.' (Klages 1921: 248)

67 'Someone having a consciousness exists only through the facts, subjective to him, of his being affectively touched'. In other words, 'the commander of the ship of life must always have fallen outside his cabin, in the waves of affective involvement, in order to assume the role of commander in the cabin.' (Schmitz 2005a: 77, 89)

overwhelmed from the very first' (Le Bon 2009: 123). For the same reason a figure, and sometimes even the sound of a voice, immediately arouse fondness or antipathy. More generally, this is why we feel something when visiting a certain apartment for the first time, when we witness a natural phenomenon or when we meet a stranger. In all these cases we live an affective and corporeal perception that undergoes an immediate evaluation and has expressive consequences (excitement, paralysing terror, jumping from joy, blushing, goose bumps),[68] whose explanation, though – especially if in a culturalist fashion, as much as it could be partially correct – almost always sounds like a flat rationalisation *ex post*.[69]

Against the attempts (physicalistically understandable but phenomenologically useless) at quantifying this first impression[70] we shall set the (willingly naïve) thesis according to which the first impression ceases 'when in he who receives the impression there is nothing left that could co-resound during the act in which something is recorded and understood' (Eckstein 1937: 102). There is an equally predictable objection according to which we never analyse the first impression, but only the first memory we have of it, which is largely influenced by the specific (also interpretative) personality of the perceiver.[71] To this objection we shall reply that the necessarily reflective character of the analysis of the unreflected is far from excluding that the first impression might 'seem' immediate[72] and might prescind from logical comparison, the observation of genetic-causal links and the evaluation of its truth or falsity (in a strictly epistemic sense). As for the possible uncertainty of the first impression, it will suffice not to confuse formal certainty with content certainty, given that an atmosphere of uncertainty is not necessary a

---

68 See Hasse (2005: 112–113).

69 'The occasion and cause of our inclinations is not the evaluating comprehension of certain character traits of the other, but rather a modification that immediately happens in ourselves.' (Klages 1976: 17)

70 A century ago experimental studies spoke of three minutes, contemporary studies established instead that it takes thirty thousandths of a second (seemingly, the time necessary to the extracortical area to like or dislike a face and even to judge its reliability). See Willis-Todorov (2006).

71 Eckstein (1937: 50, 70, 89).

72 Here is a high-coloured description of this immediacy: 'it is the personal and hereditary spirit in its totality that initially commands vision and hearing: the organising, coordinating, creating spirit. It ensures its global gripping on a minimal part of the vast universe', generating an image that is 'something springing immediately out of an act of moral and mental synthesis, preceding the sensations of aspect, relief and colour, maybe purely material and physical.' (Daudet 1928: 98, 91)

less certain atmosphere than an atmosphere whose content is certain (happy, sad, etc.). Despite being supported by quasi-things that are not clear and distinct,[73] the first and indemonstrable impression influences and directs with its atmospheric charge every subsequent reflection and perception (hence the instructiveness of the studies on the so-called 'mere-exposure effect' and imprinting). It is therefore not surprising that, in life as in literature, the first time is charged with an enormous yet fragile atmospheric potentiality.

> The thing that makes the very first sight of a village or town in the landscape so incomparable and so irretrievable is that in it remoteness reverberates in its closest association with proximity. Habit has not yet done its work. As we start to find our bearings, all of a sudden the landscape vanishes like the façade of a house as we cross the threshold. The façade has yet to achieve dominance as a result of repeated, ultimately habitual exploration. Once we have begun to feel right in a place, the original image can never be reconstituted. (Benjamin 2009: 84)

1.5 Atmospheres as Situational Constraints

If we do not want to risk totally identifying atmospheres and feelings (or emotions), we must restate that atmospheres are indeed feelings, but mostly external ones, effused into a (not yet clarified) spatial dimension and tied to situations.

But then, what is a situation, exactly? In our sense, a multiple and chaotic state of things that can be distinguished from others precisely thanks to its peculiar atmospheric tone. Then, an atmospheric phenomenology will be nothing but a special declination of a more general philosophy of situations.[74] In a nutshell: if to each constructive and functional level of the animal organism corresponds an equally specific level of the *Umwelt*, could we not hypothesise that atmosphere

---

73 Thus Scheler thinks of the *milieu* as an intermediate layer between perceived content and its objects, but also as the immediate manifestation of value as the object's messenger: just like 'a man can be distressing and repugnant, agreeable, or sympathetic to us without our being able to indicate *how* this comes about', so 'in any comprehension of our *milieu*, for example, we immediately grasp the unanalysed totality and its value; but again, in the value of the totality we grasp partial values in which individual represented objects [*Bildgegenstände*] are "situated".' (Scheler 1973: 17, 18)

74 See Griffero (2009b).

also belongs to the latter? Moreover, just like man is the only animal that can, to an extent, reflect on his own *Umwelt* and compare it to others – thereby transcending, at least from a theoretical-hypothetical perspective, the constraints of his own 'perceptual world' and 'effector world' – could he not also be the only animal able to thematise the atmospheric tones he finds himself situated in, as well as potentially imagine other ones? Consider the well-known example of the same oak tree, having different meanings in different *Umwelten*:[75] it is, for instance, a potential few cords of wood for the forester; a threatening daemon for the little girl, to whom the knobby bark resembles the deformed face of a man; a solid roof for the fox resting between its roots; a nest for the owl on the branch, and so forth. The same object, in a strictly physicalist sense, therefore presents different tones in different species-typical *Umwelten* (utility tone, threat tone, recovery and support tone, etc.), to the point that 'each environment cuts out of the oak a certain piece, the characteristics of which are suited to form the perception mark carriers as well as the effect-mark carriers of their functional cycles' (Uexküll 2010: 130–131). Now, why should we not add to these strictly biological tones (the medium, nourishment, the enemy, sex), i.e. to these significances,[76] also the atmospheric ones, thereby reducing the objection according to which the practical-emotive tone of perception is too vague to undermine the grasping of objective formations?[77]

The hypothesis is therefore that atmospheric impression enjoys the same priority that is normally (besides, maybe precisely by the virtue of an intrinsically positive atmosphere)[78] attributed to the general figural moment with respect to its components: that is, to the wood, for instance, as perceived before the single trees. The hypothesis is, therefore, that some atmospheric value is perceived in the whole environment in which one finds oneself, much before the potential atmosphere of its single elements is perceived, and so much before one is able describe them analytically. Colours, for instance, before being perceived as properties of the objects, are perceived in their interaction with the colour of the contiguous objects

---

75 Uexküll (2010: 126 ff.).

76 For an interesting list of equivalent terms (lived space, invite characters, stimulating forms, emotional characters, etc.) see Rothacker (1948: 161).

77 Piana (1979: 49–50).

78 According to Norman (2005: 26) positive affection always induces to preferring the big picture and not to concentrate upon details.

and even with the air interposed between our eye and the perceived, to the point that they 'are no longer condensed into surface colours, but are diffused round about objects and become atmospheric colours': it is 'as if the thing is thrust outside itself' (Merleau-Ponty 2005: 310, 372) – and it is not exaggerated to define such ecstasy as coexistence or communion.

> Sensation is intentional because I find that in the sensible a certain rhythm of existence is put forward [...] If the qualities radiate around them a certain mode of existence, if they have the power to cast a spell [...] this is because the sentient subject does not posit them as objects, but enters into a sympathetic relation with them, makes them his own and finds in them his momentary law [...] I say that fountain-pen is black, and I see it as black under the sun's rays. But this blackness is less the sensible quality of blackness than a sombre power which radiates from the object, even when it is overlaid with reflected light, and it is visible only in the sense in which moral blackness is visible [...] Every thing appears to us through a medium to which it lends its own fundamental quality; this piece of wood is neither a collection of colours and tactile data, not even their total *Gestalt*, but something from which there emanates a woody essence; these 'sensory givens' modulate a certain theme or illustrate a certain style which is the wood itself, and which creates, round this piece of wood and the perception I have of it, a horizon of significance. (ibid: 248, 355–356, 523)

If philosophy is, from this perspective (as we already mentioned), a reflection on how one feels here and now in the felt-body, a philosophy of atmospheres will then be nothing but a reflection on the atmospheric power of situations, on how 'the rise of a new atmosphere gives existence a different dye, another tone, a new mood disposition, before one can speak, in a positive or negative sense, of new saliences or even new meanings' (Tellenbach 1968: 73). Moving away from a phenomenological and existentialistic tradition by now consolidated, situations should be here redefined starting from their atmospheric irradiations. Without being substances or accidents, relations or single things, but being rather a significance anterior to identification[79] (which is necessary only to the pragmatic

---

79 'Single relations (as states of things) emerge only out of the diffused significance and single things, which are not relations, only thus become possible.' (Schmitz 2005a: 49)

forma mentis), situations are multiplicities (absolutely or relatively) chaotic: that is, in them the identity or diversity of elements stays undetermined. They are instances of this 'pre-personal lived experience' (Schmitz 2005a: 22) to which, as we have seen, we adequately react – in an fleeting and pre-analytic way – precisely because we have atmospherically perceived its poured out significance.[80] But the definition of a situation in terms of atmosphere – i.e. of pervasive quality (Dewey) that is irreducible to discrete elements – presupposes first of all that we silence the psychological-reductionist prejudice. That is to say, the prejudice that – starting from the physiologistic elementarism of the *Theaetetus* and passing by the Aristotelian thesis for which, unlike the sensibles of each sense and the common sensibles,[81] situations are perceivable only by accident and through an intellectual synthesis (*De anima* 425a 20 ff.; 430 26b; *Metaph.* 1027b) – reaches the Kantian idea of the necessity of a synthesis.[82]

This is not the place to proceed, with Schmitz, to a detailed classification of situations (relatively or absolutely chaotic, in act or persisting, founding or inclusive, sudden or segmented, etc.) and the examination of their possible intertwine in second order atmospheres. It is enough to restate that the situational constraint is always also an atmospheric constraint, reading in this light also Heidegger's 'they'. If we speak in front of an audience, for instance

> the Other's presence remains undifferentiated [...] But neither do we apprehend a plural look [...] If on the other hand, I want to verify that my thought has been well understood and if in turn I look at the audience, then I shall suddenly see heads and eyes appear. When objectivised the prenumerical reality of the Other is decomposed and pluralised [...] It is for this prenumerical concrete reality

---

80 That is, for Schmitz, 'facts, programmes and problems'. Situations would therefore be 'the dwellings, springs and primary partners of the entire human and animal behaviour; all thinking and feeling, willing, representing and doing draws from situations, falls back in them and lingers on them in an analytical and combining way only through provisional steps about single themes obtained from situations and their constellations.' (Schmitz 2003: 91)

81 'According to accident it is said sensible, for instance if the pale thing would be son of Diares: for according to accident this is perceived, because the pale thing has happened this which is perceived.' (*De anima*, 418a 20–23)

82 'Kantian rationalism is, in this case, a late abortion of physiologism.' (Schmitz 1978: 194)

that we ought to reserve the term 'they' rather than for human reality's state of unauthenticity. (Sartre 1969: 281–282)

Finally, a clarification. The desubjectification of atmospheres attempted here must not lead us to forget that a situation, probably never devoid of some atmospheric charge,[83] is still relative to a subject (we shall go back to this: see *infra* Conclusion),[84] who feels touched by something partially undecipherable. And it is thanks to these corporeal suggestions pushing him to this or that reaction,[85] and possibly to a sort of cooperative or supportive incorporation,[86] that he gains his own identity. Yet his identity is still constrained, given that the subject bumps into in the 'quality of the situation' (Thibaud 2003a: 288) unexpectedly, nor can he change anything in a projective sense[87] – especially when a certain tiredness[88] or an almost pathological uncertainty[89] in him, weakening the pre-existing bodily

---

83 *Contra* Schmitz (1998: 178).
84 'An urgent work, a headache, three phone calls, an antiaircraft drill, three guests at the same time, one of whom falls off the stairs, the lack of cigarettes, etc.: all these things together or in a few minutes' time make most people "lose their mind". They have "chaotic" impressions.' (Rothacker 1966: 141)
85 Situations 'dynamically embrace and hold both subject and object under control even in a corporeal sense, as is demonstrated by the motor reactions traced or suggested by the situation itself.' (Schmitz 1990: 67)
86 Think of a cobra and a mongoose fighting: 'the movements of the two animals are not separated by latent periods and reaction times: they form an organic unit, compact like the movements of a single body.' (Buytendijk 1956: 153)
87 Heidegger himself, while opting for a compromising solution (the mood is partly objective, partly subjective) (Heidegger 1995: 89), observes that any transference onto things of the emotional effect over us 'does not happen by chance or arbitrarily, but evidently because we find something *about things* which demands of its own accord, as it were, that we address and name them in this way and not otherwise [...] In that case, we are no longer transferring something, but in some way *apprehending* it *from the things themselves*. (ibid: p. 85).
88 'Especially when we meet other people for the first time [...] *before* any consideration, judgement, comparison, reasoning etc. on these men, we often have a feeling that a certain atmosphere penetrates and formally wraps us, like a psychic cloud. It is what often happens, of course, especially when we are internally "tired" or fatigued, when we are not permeated by a vigorous autonomous experience or we do not address another object in a particularly focused way.' (Walther 1955: 77)
89 It is 'atmospherisation' that torments Ivan Karamazov. 'When self-confidence is threatened by the upsetting of moral consciousness, on whose indisputable validity trust must mostly be built, the existence experiencing the scission might be dissolved into an

economy, seems indeed to be favouring the bursting out of the atmospheric.[90] If the variable intensity of the atmospheric impression therefore also depends on the subject, its phenomenic apparition must be framed in the sphere of Husserl's passive synthesis,[91] which can be here summed up in the fact that 'we can do nothing at all' about perceived atmospheres, since 'no "synthetising" subject could give rise to bonds where there are none' (Piana 1979: 31, 40).

1.6 Lived (Predimensional) Spaces

We have often said that atmospheres are spatialised feelings: that is to say, they are the specific emotional quality of a given 'lived space'. By this concept (that had a massive philosophical success in the first half of the twentieth century and that was now brought back to the fore in social sciences, where they even speak of a *spatial turn*) we here mean, on first approximation, the space we experience in the lifeworld and to which plane geometry turns out to be completely blind. For instance, geometry is incapable of justifying the (not only metaphorical) volume of a Sunday silence or the narrowness of a living room (perhaps metrically identical to another which is yet perceived as more spacious); the enormous difference between the space filled with directional saliences where the dancer moves and the anodyne one of someone crossing the same ball room for no reason; the different length of a journey for someone who strolls casually and someone with a precise destination in mind, but also, banally, for those who leave and those who return. This very extradimensional and non-epistemic sense of space brings a fundamental contraposition to light. While physical space, made of places and measurable distances, enjoys an abstract uniformity (isotropy and Euclidean three-dimensionality), 'lived' space claims to have an absoluteness and an irreversibility tied to the felt-body (above/below, right/left,

---

atmospherisation. A new pathological existential figure can be born out of this dissolution, one that obtains by force what it was previously denied.' (Tellenbach 1968: 95; see also 91)

90   'At those times when we allow ourselves simply to be in the world without actively assuming it, or in cases of illness favouring this passive attitude.' (Merleau-Ponty 2005: 310)

91   See Husserl (1977: 177).

up/down) and to our actions[92] – as revealed, although with all due differences, in a phenomenological-psychopathological sphere and also in an anthropological-existentialistic one (Heidegger, Binswanger, Minkowski, Straus, Dürckheim, Merleau-Ponty, Bachelard, Bollnow) following the more remote discovery of the (geographically and historically different) experiences of spatiality[93] in the area of both *Kunstwissenschaft* and *Kulturmorphologie*.

It is only because man has a lived space that it makes sense to say that there is not enough space; that we want our own space; that we need it; that there is too much of it, so we find shelter in narrowness; that we can or cannot have it; that we can make it (thus creating a void that was not there before). In fact, both its genesis and its effects are psychosocial and relatively independent from physical ontology.[94] Man, in fact, is not first of all 'in' space like in a big container (i.e. in an invariable and pragmatically useful system of reference of things and places, mutually defined by position and distance) but 'in' predimensional lived spaces,[95] including the atmospheric ones: 'besides the physical and geometrical distance which stands between myself and all things, a "lived" distance binds me to things which count and exist for me, and links them to each other. This distance measures the "scope" of my life at every moment' (Merleau-Ponty 2005: 333). Hence not only a relatively different perception of space by different generations, ethnic groups, genders and cultures, but also a sort of iconic polydaemonism of spaces.

> For the spirit clinging to life, there are first of all as many spaces and times as the images it is possible to have a lived experience of, in a space-time sense: therefore not only a nightly space next to a daily one, a domestic one next to a celestial one, the space of a wood next to the space of a temple, an East, a

---

92 'A room that can be traversed in one or two steps gives an entirely different experience from a room requiring fifteen or twenty steps. A room with a ceiling you can touch is quite different from one with a ceiling eleven feet high.' (Hall 1966: 54)

93 See Pinotti (2005).

94 'Man does not end with the limits of his body or the area comprising his immediate activity. Rather is the range of the person constituted by the sum of effects emanating from him temporally and spatially. In the same way, a city consists of its total effects which extend beyond its immediate confines.' (Simmel 1950: 415)

95 For instance 'the space of sound, the space of wind blowing against us and sweeps us away with it, the space of gestures, the space of water for the swimmer and the diver with his eyes closed.' (Schmitz 2005b: 109)

South, a West, a North; but possibly also as many house spaces as the houses, and finally as many house spaces as the moments of interiorisation of the spatial manifestation through which the house takes shape. (Klages 2005: 24)

Far from sketching the (philosophical) history of lived space,[96] it is sufficient here to highlight the turning points that anticipate and prepare the theory of atmospheric space. We can start with Martin Heidegger (1927), for whom the vulgar (quantitative) conception of spatiality consists of the neutralisation of a more originary 'circumspection' [*Umsicht*], at the centre of which lies the emotive attunement. He made 'true' dwelling and building, as well as the 'place' as a non-isotropic spatial determination, into a sort of poetical correspondence to the appeal of Being or, in his terms, to the essential fourfold (earth, sky, divinities, mortals).[97] Immediately afterwards, we must remember Eugène Minkowski, with his subtle analysis (1933) of the non-metric but qualitative value of 'distance' and its possible pathological deformations, as well as that of clear space and dark space on the basis of the conviction that, far from moving in space, it is the I that creates space with a sort of 'spatial dynamism *a priori*' (Minkowski 1936: 58). But maybe Erwin Straus' distinction[98] – focused on the felt-body,[99] between a gnosic perception, relative to 'the *what* of the given in its object character', and a pathic feeling, relative to 'the *how* of its being' (Straus 1980: 12), exemplified by the contrast both between geography and landscape and between walking and dancing – is even more significant. Precisely in the space of dancing, where subject and partner are at one, one could allegedly experience the originary lived space, which is, for Straus (differently from the practical-orientative meaning it assumes in other authors) a presential-homogeneous-ecstatic-unaware space, even pathological in its irreducibility to a historical and localistic determinateness. It must therefore be said from the start that, if the spatiality of atmospherically paradigmatic conditions (twilight, darkness, fog) was only the pathic-landscape spatiality typified by

---

96 See Griffero (2010).
97 'Accordingly, spaces receive their being from locations and not from "space".' (Heidegger 1977b: 332)
98 L. Binswanger immediately referred to this (1933).
99 'A concrete transcendental of the experience of spatiality, an apriorism for everyday orientating practices, which found even objective judgements of a geographical, astronomical and cosmological nature.' (Pinotti 2005: 9)

Straus, then it could be entirely assimilated to the incommunicable one of the autistic subject:[100] an exceptionality and marginality that we must avoid here, by carefully avoiding the identification of atmospheric power and a-directionality.

Karlfried von Dürckheim's inquiry into lived space starting from the 'surrounding reality of the felt-body' (1932: 36) is particularly relevant. We shall prescind here from his many and slightly nitpicking distinctions, but an anticipation of atmosphere can be found in what he calls 'functional space': it exists in the operative variant, based on non-objective but felt distance and closeness; then in the self-related variant where the space exceeds the self like the felt-body (from the skin or dress to the chair one is sat on and the car one is travelling in, even up to the home, the homeland and the space of movement; in the vital-personal variant it also involves the community);[101] but also and mostly in the variant of the essence space, with its physiognomic-qualitative characters,[102] to which the delicate dialogue between visible forms, light and air would also contribute. In fact, it is by virtue of the 'affordances' (ibid: 16), which for us are *tout court* atmospheric, that one 'feels "solemn" in a church, "objective" in a laboratory, etc. […] One unwillingly moves differently in a church or in a workplace, in a wood or a street, in a Northern landscape or a Southern one, at home or at someone else's place' (ibid: 34, 49). And this is certainly not due to projectivistic reasons.

> Every natural space is also felt like the space of a specific life. Here there is not a transference of vitality starting from the sphere of the human so that, so to speak, particular natural beings living their life in that space are empathised. It is rather a matter of a life expressing itself starting from nature itself: a life whose day, form and history give sense and meaning to the being-so of the space. (ibid: 45)

---

100 Straus (2005b: 84–85).
101 'Church means also "Sunday". The different spaces of a house have the quality of their hour […] Every space in its overall quality is co-determined by the quality of the hour in which it is present and by the quality of the functions and life that are realised there.' (Dürckheim 1932: 107)
102 In particular, character features (a space can be heroic, harsh, pleasant, etc.), emotional qualities (a room, for instance, can be 'serene') and position qualities (the space addresses us in a free or oppressive way, etc.).

> The specific existence of the vital qualities of different spaces becomes evident and tangible mostly in the moments of passage from a space to another. It is therefore clear how the overall vital behaviour changes when one leaves the house to go out; when one leaves the street to enter the fields, then penetrates into a wood or, once surpassed the last houses, gets to the countryside; or when a very congested city road turns into a quiet corner. (ibid: 40)

Of course, one can love a vast space while another can love a narrow one.[103] But this is precisely because 'all men overall feel these position-qualities, even though one feels good and another does not' (ibid: 79). And here one can note[104] at least a sketched distinction between an essence (in our sense, atmosphere) and a mood that does not necessarily correspond to it. The atmospheric is favoured by an afinalistic relation to space,[105] by a 'certain passivity and a vast availability' (ibid: 71), if not even by a not excessively outlined personality. In Dürckheim, the atmospheric seems like a compromise solution – unfortunately largely relegated to the infantile and artistic sphere – between the lived sense immanent in the present space and the more or less contingent vital directions of the subject.

Dürckheim might be the first European who broke the two-millennia long illusion that man is an a-spatial innerness and that space is only a reservoir for external objects.[106] Still, he was certainly less influential than Merleau-Ponty, to whom we owe the divulgation of the (by now consolidated) critique of the physical-geometrical space in the name of perception, which counts as a primordial, anonymous and ante-predicative pact with the world. According to him, all fundamental spatial determinations are therefore lived: from depth – reinterpreted as 'a possibility of a subject involved in the world' (Merleau-Ponty 2005: 311) with his felt-body – to movement, ascribable to a 'variation of the subject's hold on his world' (ibid: 312), to the high and low as meaning directions (both physical and desiring) of the 'essential structure of our being' (ibid: 331). All these dimensions, as 'great affective entities' (ibid: 332) as well

---

103   The child, for instance, prefers closed spaces (like nests or caves) and absolutely private ones.
104   See Hasse (2005: 142).
105   'It suffices to utter the word "finalistic space" and a world – indeed, the world of essence – collapses.' (Dürckheim 1932: 82)
106   As emphatically stated by Schmitz (2005b: 111).

as synaesthetic ones, constitute a (mythical or anthropological) lived space whose symbolical pre-theoretical and pre-thetic pregnancy should be reawakened by the phenomenologist. Without being petrified by it, he should recognise that it is the anonymous operative intentionality of primordial perception that legitimises the relatively (if not entirely) objective nature of the emotionally connoted space we have defined as atmospheric.

This line of research must then be integrated with Otto Friedrich Bollnow's analysis of spatiality as 'existential' (in a Heideggerian sense), totally other than metric space, and of its bonds with moods. Being anisotropic[107] and, due to this, being the principle of any axiology, the lived and emotionally tuned space that Bollnow considers – be it the archetypal space of the house or the non-linear hodologic one – is truly really close to our atmospheric space, although his entire discourse is a little bit penalised both by the statement that there can be a 'space of action devoid of emotional mood' (Bollnow 2004: 256) and, once again, by a weak solution to the problem of the subjective or objective character of atmosphere.

> Even in the same man, his need of space varies according to his psychic condition and his various necessities [...] On the other hand, the character of the space surrounding man also retroacts on his mood. We therefore have a twofold influence: the man's psychic condition determines the character of the surrounding space, and vice versa the space then retroacts on his psychic state. Every concrete space in which the man finds himself, be it internal or external, has as such a determined mood character (*Stimmung*); it has, so to speak, human qualities which, in turn, influence – in the form of the most elementary determinations – the experience of narrowness and vastness of a certain space [...] Space has its determined mood, both as inner space and as landscape. It can be serene, light, dark, dull, solemn, etc., and this mood character is transferred to the man who lingers in it. In particular, it is atmospheric conditions that act, as serene, radiant, oppressive, etc., on man. And so even man himself is

---

107 'Space is far from homogeneous, because particular meanings are immanent to each of its places. In it, one can distinguish favoured regions and regions to avoid [...] Just like, for us, the sun rises every morning in the East on the solid earth even though we have known "better" for ages thanks to the Copernican system, so for us, notwithstanding all knowledge of the infinity of cosmic space, the space concretely lived by us still remains, in its essence, something finite.' (Bollnow 2004: 69, 302)

permeated from the inside by a certain mood, and is incline to transfer it also to the surrounding space – and here the concept of transferring can be used only in a provisional sense to clarify, for now, this immediate co-belonging and accordance. There is a mood in both human soul and a landscape or an enclosed internal space, and the two things are in principle only two aspects of one unitary being-tuned [...] The mood itself is nothing subjective "in" man and nothing objective – as something that could be found "outside" in his environment – but it regards man in its yet undivided unity with his *Umwelt*. (ibid: 230–231)

This is an isomorphic irenicism, as we know, that is far from isolated[108] and that reoccurs also in the suggestive 'philosophy of detail' by Gaston Bachelard (1994: 222), to whom we owe a careful phenomenological thematisation of the resonances aroused by a corpus of (irreducible) poetic images of space. That is to say, pre-reflective, allusive and dreamlike images in which space, taken away from 'utilitarian geometrical notions.' (ibid: 55) as well as psychoanalytical and metaphorising deferrals, functions as an archetypal shelter for the reverie, and also as the presupposition for any subsequent axiology. In fact, everyone would allegedly coincide with the spaces they lived-imagined![109] And especially when this topophilia is condensed into the house, which is examined by Bachelard in all the aspects capable of atmospheric irradiation (roof, ceiling, basement, stairs, rooms, the angular and the round, wardrobes, chests, drawers, doors, shells, inkpots, etc.). In fact, he speaks of avolumetric spatialities (mainly intimacies)[110]

---

108 'In this essential relation between the mood of the I [...] and the spatiality of the world there is nothing genetically primary or genetically secondary, nothing that is the cause or the effect, condition or conditioned, inducer or induced, not even reason or consequence. Even what we call, indeed, trepidation of the soul rather consists of a restriction of the world and the sky, and vice versa the restriction of the world and the sky consists of the trepidation of our soul.' (Binswanger 1933: 200)
109 'Each one of us, then, should speak of his roads, his crossroads, his roadside benches; each one of us should make a surveyor's map of his lost fields and meadows. [...] Thus we cover the universe with drawings we have lived. These drawings need not be exact. They need only to be tonalized on the mode of our inner space.' (Bachelard 1994: 11–12)
110 Drawers, chests and wardrobes, for instance, turn out to be 'hybrid objects, subject-objects [that] like us, through us and for us, [...] have a quality of intimacy.' (ibid: 78)

charged with corporeal suggestions,[111] of a specific atmosphere of the act of polishing,[112] of spaces objectively charged with determined impressions – the forest, for instance, as real 'psychological transcendent' (ibid: 188)[113] – and of immanent[114] and transmodal emotional qualities: 'for the sense of taste or smell, the problem might be even more interesting than for the sense of vision [...] But a whiff of perfume, or even the slightest odor can create an entire environment in the world of the imagination' (ibid: 174). The abovementioned irenicism is here founded upon a psychic-imaginative consonance between subject and object whose poetic expression would curiously function as a relief.

> The two kinds of space, intimate space and exterior space, keep encouraging each other, as it were, in their growth. To designate space that has been experienced as affective space, which psychologists do very rightly, does not, however, go to the root of space dreams. The poet goes deeper when he uncovers a poetic space that does not enclose us in affectivity. Indeed, whatever the affectivity that colors a given space, whether sad or ponderous, once it is poetically expressed, the sadness is diminished, the ponderousness lightened. [...] When a poet tells me that he "knows a type of sadness that smells of pineapple," I myself feel less sad, I feel gently sad. (ibid: 201–202)

One can remedy the uncertainty about the subjective (projective) or objective (quasi-thing) nature of atmospheres, though, only by means of more radical positions. For example, one could resort to the neophenomenological position

---

111 In nest-objects, for instance, 'physically, the creature endowed with a sense of refuge, huddles up to itself, takes to cover, hides away, lies snug, concealed', whereas 'the round being propagates its roundness, together with the calm of all roundness.' (ibid: 91, 239)

112 'The minute we [...] practice phenomenology while polishing a piece of old furniture, we sense new impressions come into being beneath this familiar domestic duty.' (ibid: 67)

113 'We do not have to be long in the woods to experience the always rather anxious impression of "going deeper and deeper" into a limitless world', in a world that is *always* ancestral, given that 'in the reign of the imagination, there are no young forests.' (ibid: 185, 188)

114 'A gloomy life, or a gloomy person, marks an entire universe with more than just a pervading coloration. Even things become crystallizations of sadness, regret or nostalgia.' (ibid: 143)

held by Hermann Schmitz, to whom we owe not so much yet another reflection on the lived space (maybe on the subversive character of walking the city, counting on proper names[115] of places capable of evoking absences[116] like in De Certeau, or of surrogating a richer sensibility like in Benjamin[117] and of historicising even non-places[118]) but rather an ambitious and systematic correction of the prevailing spatial conception. No matter if it is the *topos* or place as an area circumscribed by bodies (Aristotle), the metrical *spatium* (Descartes) or the space as the sensible transcendent of man (Kant). Schmitz, in fact, looks at the space experienced through our 'corporeal presence',[119] that is, how one feels within the sphere of oscillation of the anisotropic narrowness/vastness polarity in us. In short, he also looks at the atmosphere that, although largely unconscious,[120] permeates our entire life and not only its exceptional moments.

For Schmitz, there are three levels of experience of space.[121] First of all a) *local space* (*Ortsraum*), founded on relative dimensions devoid of their own features (straight line, divisibility into parts, surfaces, reversibility, distance, place, etc.), which can be explained – so as not to end up in an infinite regress – only by starting from a corporeal space, such as b) *directional space* (*Richtungsraum*), pregeometrical dominion of a motility that is not (yet) reduced to local translation (expiration, gestural expressiveness, dance, sport, glance, etc.) and that is rather

---

115   'In the spaces brutally lit by an alien reason, proper names carve out pockets of hidden and familiar meanings. [...] These names create a nowhere in places; they change them into passages.' (De Certeau 1984: 104) With their magical power they inspire the walker and, ceasing to be proper, they constitute 'local authorities.' (ibid: 106)

116   '"*Here*, there used to be a bakery." "*That's* where old lady Dupuis used to live." It is striking here that the places people live in are like the presences of diverse absences. What can be seen designates what is no longer there [...] Demonstratives indicate the invisible identities of the visible [...] Places are fragmentary and inward-turning histories [...] symbolizations encysted in the pain or pleasure of the body.' (ibid: 108)

117   'The sensuality in street names – certainly the only sort which citizens of the town, if need be, can still perceive. For what do we know of streetcorners, curbstones, the architecture of the pavement – we who have never felt heat, filth, and the edges of stones beneath our naked soles, and have never scrutinized the uneven placement of the paving stones with an eye toward bedding down on them.' (Benjamin 1999: 517)

118   Thus Augè (1995: 69–70; see also 2008: 63 ff.).

119   See Schmitz (1967), Böhme (2006a: 88–89, 122).

120   Petzold (1991) sees in it an intertwine between subliminal and supraliminal information, as well as the mnestic resonance of these impressions.

121   For a summary of what follows see Schmitz (1967: 134; 1990: 181; 2002b: 66–69 and mostly 2005a: 186–204).

founded upon the narrowness/vastness dynamic, as well as being the starting point of a corporeal communication with the surrounding environment: a communication whose prelocal directionality depends on motor suggestions.

> Optical objects exercise not only a function of orientation, but also a function of attraction. That is, [...] not only do they attract the observer's attention, they also induce him to come close [...] The very sight of an open door, a piece of furniture of surprising shape and colour, a glance at a distance, a source of light are often enough to make a man engage in a finalised movement. (Révész 1938: 91)

Directional space, in turn, is rooted into an even more originary spatiality, devoid both of surfaces and of dimensions: it is c) the *space of vastness* (*Weiteraum*), the place of the 'primitive presence'[122] as the extradimentional *a priori* of our corporeal feeling. This is the climatic space (the one that, for instance, makes us say that 'there is tension in the air') and the sound space; the olfactive space irreducible to a figure[123] and the space of silence; the space of the swimmer (surrounded by volumes without width, height or depth) and the space of corporeal isles; the space of feeling and the space enlightened in its peculiar atmospheric voluminousness.[124] And again, the empty space, the distressing space of twilight, the space of ecstasy, even the (fundamental and yet unnoticed) unarticulated background that accompanies each of our optical-kinetic motions forwards. Finally, the ability to walk with others without clashing thanks to the somatic control of the glance, the instinctive and undetermined tendency to run away in case of panic, the open air we breathe when we leave a sultry space, the thermal-optical field to which we expose ourselves when we doze in the sun. These, then, are the three levels of experience of the space. While being, luckily,

---

122 Given, for Schmitz (1990: 280), by the series 'here-now-being-this-I'.

123 Because of its 'naïve' spatiality, 'what smells and tastes cannot be measured, numbered, divided and, for these reasons, it cannot even be communicated in an objective way [...] It is indissolubly tied to the whole of a mood' (Tellenbach 1968: 28–29), without any scission between gnostic and perceptive components.

124 Hasse (2005: 61).

melted together in adult life (and particularly in the atmospheric power immanent to dwelling),[125] they still remain, at times, relatively distinct.

> When a burning sensation, an itch and so forth seem to indicate an undesired visit, the prevailing hand gets there swiftly, with no need to look for it in a relative place (defined by position and distance); we locate just as rapidly the place of the sting, although such place is usually not yet recorded into the bodily perceptive schema: that is, it is identified in a place that is no less absolute than that of the hand heading for it. (Schmitz 2006: 30)

The first localisation, to which we get 'guided only by the absolute place of the corporeal isle now manifest and by the habitual trajectories of the motor-bodily schema' (Schmitz 1990: 291), is evidently the absolute one. The second one, which is instead possible only by means of subsequent focalisations of our finger, is relative.

What interests us here is that, in the space of feeling (*Gefühlsraum*),[126] there are three different levels of atmospheric charge corresponding to local space, directional space and the absolute space of vastness. In fact, the atmospheres corresponding to the space of vastness are a) atmospheres centred on the felt-body, devoid of borders like pure moods, and from which full extensions (satisfaction) or empty ones (desperation) derive. The atmospheres corresponding to the directional space are instead b) vector atmospheres: emotions whose objectual terminations lead to (mistakenly) talk of intentional feelings. They can be unilateral, like those that exalt or depress, but also omnilateral, centrifugal, centripetal or undecided like what is rightly defined 'presentiment'. Finally, the corresponding atmospheres of local space are c) the atmospheres that, in this or that object, find their point of condensation and/or anchoring. There are therefore

---

125 Which is 'culture of feelings in a closed space'. 'The spatiality of feelings becomes here so efficacious that men always need again these places of dwelling – instead of a simple sheltered accommodations – in order to capture feelings, in a way, administrate them and model them on these places'. In a nutshell, 'to dwell is to dispose of the atmospheric.' (Schmitz 1990: 318–320)

126 Obviously, the thesis according to which 'feelings are spatially extended [...] would be inconceivable or even comical if it were referred to local space' given that, in that case, 'a feeling would be perhaps a sort of sphere or a triangle in the stomach or in the proximity of the head.' (Schmitz 1990: 292)

as many kinds of atmosphere as there are forms of spatiality, and even the banal local space (surfaces-points-distances), rationalistic and pragmatically functional to man's ex-centricity,[127] is far from devoid of atmospheric power (although a derived one). As is also admitted in sociology, it is spaces themselves that develop 'their own potentiality, that can influence feelings. This potentiality of the spaces [can] be called "atmosphere"' (Löw 2001: 204). By enhancing the role of this atmosphere as lived space, especially in an age of break with the traditional bond between communities and their places (virtual world and globalisation), we also commit to a sort of critical countermovement.

1.7 'Affordances' and Imagine-Motor Reactions

Imagine that while sleeping, we feel cold.[128] We could a) cover ourselves more, without waking up, b) wake up a little bit and think 'I am cold', c) wake up completely, objectively-causalistically perceive the fact that the cold comes from the window, and maybe solve the problem. Now, one could compare atmospheric experience with the first of these situations. That is, with a primitive, involuntary perception that is anterior to distancing, founded upon mimetic-kinaesthetic and semi-automatic reactions[129] – which are the more perfect the less one thinks about them, and through which the felt-body senses tensions and expressive orientations in the surrounding world. It is the case, for instance, of the tactile involvement not only of the arm but of the whole of the perceiver's body; the same happens with the almost perfect fusion of optical and motor in the driver,[130] or in a person walking without clashing against the others. In short, it is a 'sensory vigilance' required by 'selective and very close reactions, that have to swiftly decide for a determined possibility within an enormous number of possibilities' (Hellpach

---

127 'Man learns to draw, project, trace and inscribe his fantasies onto a surface' and thus also 'as object, to spatially insert himself between objects and, as subject, to break free from this order by assuming the role of who contemplates and plans.' (Schmitz 2005a: 213)

128 For this example, see Székely (1932: 227 ff.).

129 In a different context, Becking (1928) identifies a music style, for instance, starting from the hand movement that accompanies the listening of it.

130 'The optical and the motor sphere are capable from the start – and not only through learning processes – of elastically adapting to each other.' (Schmitz 1966: 299)

1960a: 61). Atmospheric perceptions can also be ascribed to this kind of 'cognitive unconscious'.[131]

As for the often mentioned motor suggestions, we can first of all think of the 'internal reproduction of movements' (Klages 1964: 447); of directional tensions[132] that are immediately and physiognomically[133] perceivable in even static[134] lines and forms (Wölfflin *docet*), and where 'the felt-body, which we feel immediately, and the perceived form perfectly coincide' (Schmitz 1966: 42). Prescinding here from a general formal physiognomy,[135] we simply refer to the *Gestaltic* principle of isomorphism, if not even to adverbial rather than adjectival properties.[136] So, 'a weeping willow does not look sad because it looks like a sad person. It is more adequate to state that since the shape, direction, and flexibility of willow branches covey the expression of passive hanging, a comparison with the structurally similar psychophysical pattern of sadness in humans may impose itself secondarily' (Arnheim 1966: 64). In this case, we have 'not anthropomorphic metaphors of action, but an adequate reproduction of the motor suggestions coming from the forms and *immanent to them*' (Schmitz 1966: 38; my emphasis), i.e. what we might call transmodal characters.[137] Atmospheres then seem to be

---

131 Lakoff-Johnson (1999).

132 See Arnheim (1966: 64), for whom the perceived is the outcome of a conflict between the perceptive forces inherent to the stimulating situation and the forces of the perceiving organism.

133 Koffka (1999: 359–364) speaks of 'physiognomic characters', that is, expressive qualities effective on our behaviour.

134 That is, also when 'in the form of the line, the element of movement now seems spatially almost petrified', given that 'at the basis of every comprehension of the line there is a lived experience of movement, as some linguistic expressions can testify even now: the road "proceeds", "turns", "goes up", "goes down", "winds"; the spiral "turns", the vine "twists", the edge of the rock "plummets", two lines "meet" or "run parallel" etc.' (Klages 1929–32: 51–52). 'That the road "goes" or "leads" from here to there, that it "runs" through a field, "winds" along a brook, that the rigid spiral "twirls", the still branch "twists", the slope of the mountain "goes up" to the top, the side of the rock "plummets" down steeply' (Klages 1923: 56 and see 1929–32: 179–180), all this demonstrates the rhythmic character of life as a whole, and its resistance to the barriers imposed (according to Klages) by its own antagonist (the spirit).

135 Schmitz (1966: 55, 109 ff.) verifies, for instance, the corporeal and even sexual effect of various elements (the straight line, the angular, the curved, the spiralling).

136 That is, properties applying to the behaviour and dynamics of things rather than things in themselves (Arnheim 1966: 208).

137 'The human body has the property of heat, an ice cube has the property of cold; but the colours in a painting are also "warm" and those of another are "cold". The bark of a

bridge-qualities, founded on a corporeal communication whose prototype is the fusion with the instrument that the musician or the athlete can achieve, and due to which 'knowledge manifests itself only in doing and, also from a subjective point of view, one knows that he knows it exclusively while doing it' (Buytendijk 1956: 203). That is, atmospheres are suggestions that are as 'immediately and frankly perceivable as sounds or smells are' (Schmitz 1978: 41).[138] They also are virtual movements[139] – as admitted both by the nineteenth-century 'Carpenter law' (according to which every perceived or imagined movement unconsciously excites in us the stimulus to make the same movement) and by the contemporary and all too known theory of mirror neurons. A person is much more recognisable from his motor or gestural behaviour, the tone of his voice and the (seductive, ironic, etc.) quality of his look – that is, evidently, from shadowy and impalpable tertiary qualities – rather than from his eye colour, weight and height. In the same way, in artistic styles, we recognise corporeal dispositions[140] that are certainly not reducible to an intentional *Kunstwollen*. Also, in the same way, about a given space we perceive, first of all, an atmospheric quality, according to modalities that are irreducible to the hydraulic model of psychic filling of the extra-psychic world[141] – to which the aesthetics of empathy always slightly refers to. Just like the motor suggestions that permeate them, in fact, atmospheres can be prototypically (see *infra* 3.5) antagonistic (and then we resist them or surrender to them) or supportive (and then we welcome them).

---

tree is rough but so is the clamour of a bull mooing or the climate of the Pamir plateau; the knife is sharp, but the whistle of the locomotive and the smell of vinegar are no less sharp. The thing-properties of sound and those of colour have absolutely nothing in common, and yet we speak with no hesitation of "auditory dyes" and "chromatic tonalities". Height characterises the mount, depth characterises the well; but sounds are also distinguished from one another for the same characters.' (Klages 1921: 250)

138   'The eye also feels oppressed, for instance, in narrow valleys and going through rock walls that lie at a very short distance [...] that is, it has also tactile needs'. This is due to the fact that 'spaces also tangibly refer to lived experiences and rhythmical needs.' (Rothacker 1966: 297)

139   Like in the inadvertent virtual movement, induced by the fact that the expected movement is not made (Palàgyi 1925: 106 ff.).

140   'Corporeal dispositions, thanks to the artistic creation, turn into works of art by means of the motor suggestions both of the felt-body and of formal developments.' (Schmitz 1966: 83)

141   So that 'the sense passes, like in a game of communicating vessels, from a subject that is full of it to an object that lacks it.' (Pinotti 1997a: 28)

Keep in mind, though, that atmospheres also imply reactions that we could call image-motor, that is, reflective-motor responses, preconscious or semiconscious, aroused not so much by physical stimuli but rather by images (even just thought of). The organism reacts, for instance, to (external or internal) erotic images or images that break some taboo not only through physiological processes and muscle effects (excitements and shivers, heart pulsation and salivation, etc.), but also through 'mood variations and objective inversions lived in the subjectivity of the whole behaviour' (Rothacker 1966: 337). For instance, the fact that we obey certain words even without understanding their meaning is due to the atmosphere suggested even just by their sound image. It is almost obvious, at this point, to link the theme of motor and image-motor reactions to the Heideggerian topic of 'handiness' as significance and, above all, with Gibson's affordances (although, for us, they are not restricted to the visual): namely, the 'affordances of objects, which convey messages about their possible uses, actions and functions' (Norman 2002: 82). The several reflections on empathy (although here interpreted differently) are also instructive.

> The tree, which we see standing erect and resisting the powerful attack of the wind, arouses in us the representation of strength. The massive rock, steep and sheer, inflexibly resisting the influence of gravity and storms, awakens in us the representation of obstinacy. (Hilger 1928: 24)

> An armchair, for instance, manifestly invites one to take a seat, the handle and spout of the jug invite a handy grasping and pouring; the architectonic space invites to occupy the space and freely walk around. (Lipps 1908: 207)

> When I say that this rock is unclimbable, it is certain that this attribute, like that of being big or little, straight and oblique, and indeed *like all attributes in general*, can be conferred upon it only by the project of climbing it, and by a human presence. (Merleau-Ponty 2005: 510; my emphasis)

With the discovery of situational atmospheric power it was ascertained that man is not surrounded by things that are devoid of meaning – as can be inferred from animal comprehension, prototypical of infantile thought (apparently up to the age of two) and of symbolical thought at every latitude[142] – but by things and quasi-things always already affectively connoted. The animal

> comprehends expressions only in the momentaneity of its action and orientation [...] It does not grasp the other objectively in its being-in-itself – that would be a form of knowledge; instead, as it experiences the world, it experiences it in general in the form of a world that manifests itself, contrasts and cooperates. For the animal, everything is expression: colour as well as sound and smell, the forms as well as the way of moving. It lives only on manifestations. (Straus 1956: 201)

After all, also in man's lifeworld there is nothing rarer than the perception of an inexpressive object: on the contrary, it is perhaps atmospheric power itself[143] that makes it possible for mere sensation to become a real perception.[144]

The idea – very briefly – is that not only pragmatic-behavioural[145] but also atmospheric *qualia* function as (transmodal) affordances, i.e. as ecological invites or meanings that are ontologically rooted in things and quasi-things. One reacts to them – and we should make this clear – not necessarily with a behaviour,[146] but at times also with a distancing (which is, to an extent, always aesthetic). 'The perceiving of an affordance is not a process of perceiving a value-free physical object to which meaning is somehow added in a way that no one has been able to agree upon; it is a process of perceiving a value-rich ecological object' (Gibson 1986: 140). Therefore, the perceiving of an atmospheric affordance seems to

---

142 'The further back one goes, the less one can separate the qualities of the object from sentimental values.' (Hauskeller 1995: 37)

143 'Only atmospheric perception makes this world into [man's] world, a place in which and with which he can live, and which can regard him in a friendly or unfriendly way. Such perception therefore lies at the principle of both collective and individual development.' (ibid: 144)

144 'The psychotic anaffective perceives, but the perceived does not regard him nor does it touch him [...] The apathetic, in seeing, hearing and touching, etc., perceives nothing. It is therefore a person's affective participation that turns a sensation into a perception.' (Katz 1960: 209 ff.)

145 As is posited instead by Gibson (1986: 225).

146 'When a child falls into water, it does not matter whether one finds a bath pleasurable or not: it requires immediate rescue independently from the present mood.' (Bollnow 1956: 135)

'demand' a special objectivity, just like the Kantian judgement of taste: for instance, it is legitimate to expect that the unease and the feeling of being spied on aroused in us by a dark wood – not allowing free locomotion or observation (darkness, fog, badly outlined things like foliage, bushes etc.), as well as being filled with undecipherable sounds of unknown origin – is affectively and corporeally felt by anyone who shares such an experience.

> In the dark, where it is not possible to cast a glance, 'it' spies on us from behind the trees, although we do not wonder what it is that spies on us from that place. It is something totally undetermined, it is the act of spying itself. *The spaces lying between what is seen and what lies behind,* [...] namely the very background against which perceivable things stand out, has lost its neutrality. What makes us shudder is not the tree or the bush we see, the rustle of the tree tops or the cry of the owl we hear, but rather everything that is hidden, all the surrounding space from which the tree and the bush, the rustle and the cry stick out: what makes us shudder is the very *darkness and what is hidden as such.* (Conrad 1958: 43)

Everyone 'gets easily lost in the wood. Which can have something frankly disquieting about it. Man never reaches the secure field of open view. Behind every bush there could be an enemy hiding. Twilight, that is, semi-darkness, is part of the wood's essence. Single things lose their precise outlines and melt into an omni-pervasive medium' (Bollnow 2004: 218–219). The disquietude can certainly be greater for the city person than for the lumberjack, but certainly the wood has, for everyone, characters that impede a projection of joy or light-heartedness. In opposition to the associationist temptation or, even worse, the conventionalist one, we must restate that the atmosphere of disquietude aroused by the wood does not derive from the thought of fear, but is rather the immediate irradiation of a quasi-thing feeling that is spatially poured out. Association, if anything, comes after and it is certainly not arbitrary,[147] given that 'phenomenically, it is not the reference

---

147 'Thus someone, for instance, reminds me of someone else. But not as if the latter came to my mind for his resemblance to the first; it is rather the fact that the one reminds me of the other that constitutes this resemblance. In fact, this resemblance does not consist in a coincidence of details that have already been known, defined and clarified in each of the two physiognomies as such. It is not identifiable in the *a posteriori* comparison. A physiognomy reminds me of another by the virtue of the fact that it enters a direction which is constrained

that produces the atmosphere, but it is the atmosphere that makes the reference possible' (Hauskeller 1995: 139).[148]

Since we support here the antiseparatist thesis on the relation between perception and value, it seems legitimate that we explicitly speak of atmospheric affordances. Forms, whether they are static or in motion, do not merely express apparent causal relations[149] and pragmatic affordances – 'each thing says what it is [...] a fruit says, "Eat me"; water says, "Drink me"; thunder says, "Fear me"; and woman says "Love me"' (Koffka 1999: 7) – but also tertiary qualities or sentimental (and therefore atmospheric) ones that permeate the space in which they are perceived. This can be said in many ways. Either in a pathetic way: 'it is not true that I feel my sadness in the willow, my pride in the cliff, my joy in the cloud; rather, the willow, the cliff and the cloud are (when they do not give themselves as objects of my knowledge) animated in themselves: daemons and souls identical to myself' (Lessing 1926: 27). Or in the manner of anthropology of childhood: 'what rolls and is round invites one to make it roll; what is high up invites one to lift it up higher and throw it down; what is empty invites one to fill it and what is full to empty it; what is open invites one to fumble in it, crawl in it, cross it; someone crying invites one to cry with them and someone laughing to laugh with them' (Langeveld 1968: 89). Yet, anyway you put it, it is clear that, just as expressive qualities are for *Gestalt* psychology, atmospheres are also 'perceptive ingredients inside facts themselves', 'shivers of meaning present in [quasi] things' (Bozzi 1998: 88 ff.),[150] that are relatively inter-observable and no less repeatable than perspective properties.[151] They are pathic affordances responsible for our spontaneous-intuitive evaluations and aroused by accumulation centres that – in both a causal-topologic and an axiologic and motivational sense (salience,

---

thanks to the parallel with the second physiognomy: without reciprocity, neither would be what we only now know. The memory founds relations.' (Lipps 1977: 91–92)

148   Even for a projectivist theory of empathy, in fact, 'the object must be made so and so, in order for me to be able to project this or that feeling on it.' (Pinotti 1997: 29)

149   Massironi (1998: 230–232).

150   'Even in an emotionally connoted space, therefore, the distinction between primary and secondary qualities disappears. The form of things speaks here in expressive characters in the same way colours do. Forms and colours have an equivalent emotive salience and, in their physiognomic content, they can support and help each other but also neutralise each other and arouse discordant experiences.' (Ströker 1977: 26)

151   Putnam (1999: 159).

preferability, etc.) – fill the multidimensional sensory continuum which, properly, the world of experience consists of.[152] In short, following Wertheimer, 'black is lugubrious yet before being black', because the lugubrious, far from being the product of occasional subjective vibrations, is a general atmosphere irradiated by the black before any analytical examination (at least in certain cultures). In *Gestaltic* terms, it is a polymodal emotional completion that integrates, perhaps not only culturally,[153] the merely sensorial asset,[154] arousing an 'emerging superstructure' (ibid: 111) felt as objective by a community.

---

152 For an account of the affinity between our phenomenological approach (Griffero 2005c) and experimental phenomenology of perception, see Bianchi (2005).
153 As Hauskeller posits instead (1995: 132): 'one same colour can then conciliate, in itself, semi-objective phenomenic characters of opposed quality on the basis of their heterogeneous origins, where once a characteristic trait prevails, then another characteristic trait, then again a fusion, according to the interpretation of the present characters of the environment and of the specific situation of the perceiving subject involved (with his personal structure, his individual experiences and his momentary moods).'
154 See Massironi (1998: 119; 2000: 111 ff.).

Chapter 2
History of the Concept of Atmosphere

2.1 The Climatic Paradigm

> Today has been at least the fifth day of sirocco, the most horrible wind there is; we must thank God if we do not permanently feel stupid; normal people do not demand that one should work in these conditions and one must be very impertinent indeed to be brave enough to write something that will have to be read by reasonable people. Sonnets originate from the bridal between Italian brain and the sirocco. (quoted in Hellpach 1960b: 315)

If one considers climatic atmosphere as paradigmatic,[1] not even rather banal observations like this one, sent by the historian Niebuhr from Rome at Christmas 1819, must be underestimated. By saying 'what suffocating weather!' (on a very hot summer day) or 'what oppressive weather!' (on a foggy autumn day), we are expressing the fact that the sticky drowsiness and the vaguely bad mood we got in can be referred not so much to objects or specific events but rather to a certain atmosphere. Namely, to a sort of nomad feeling that is, so to speak, in the air; one of those 'things that happen' (Landweer 2004: 485) and that we feel *in* our felt-body. Climatic impressions or atmospheres, in fact, imply a feeling (depressing or electrifying, exciting or unnerving, etc.) poured out into a space:[2] a space that, as we have seen, (see *supra* 1.6) is not local but extradimensional, holistically and synaesthetically perceived, endowed with voluminousness and vectoriality (one could say, for instance, that hatred is centripetal and esteem is centrifugal). 'The grey, humid November weather, the sultriness before a storm, the dim evening atmosphere, the seducing spring atmosphere, the soft air during a drizzle in the

---

[1] Like in Japanese culture. See Watsuji (1961), on which Soentgen (1998: 70 ff.)
[2] 'It is hard for us to specify the characteristic of a feeling without descriptive concepts of a spatial nature.' (Hippius 1936: 315).

countryside on a summer night, the harsh and dry coldness of a new and sunny winter morning' (Schmitz 1978: 14): these are the examples of the climatic atmospheres that, perceived as external powers by more archaic cultures, were subsequently internalised to the point that 'nothing [in] man's affective feeling is external to climate' (Schmitz 1967: 51). Think of the emblematic case of wind, whose enigmatic dynamicity – one 'cannot see it, nor does one know where it comes from and where it goes' (Volz 1910: 59)[3] and it exists only if, and only when, one perceives its effect – significantly influenced even the theological notion of spirit. Think also of the contemplation of clouds (*cloudspotting*) that, transcending the cliché that sees in it a prophetic or strictly meteorological interpretation, regards the formal specificities of the clouds (cumulus, stratus, nimbostratus, cirrocumulus, etc.) as the expression of 'the atmosphere's moods' (Pretor-Pinney 2006: 11) and therefore – if you will excuse the wordplay – precisely the variable atmospheric values of atmosphere.

The phenomenic-perceptive whole that we mistakenly believe to domesticate, theoretically and emotionally, by calling it 'climate' seems therefore an excellent example of atmosphere as an unwilling feeling present in the space. It is not by chance that someone who examines 'our psyche, as it reacts to weather and climate' – that is, as a 'geopsyche' (Hellpach 1960b: 101) responsible for phenotypical variations – attributes to psychosomatic agents of the natural environment (such as weather and climate, ground and landscape) not only perceivable influxes (impressions), but also non-perceivable ones (tonic, and especially vasotonic) about which we can speak of atmospheric 'tone' or 'accent'. 'For instance, we perceive air as being "cumbersome", "unnerving", "feeble", "heavy", "rigid", "harsh", "biting", "stingy", "suffocating", "sneaky" and by these words we attribute to its mildness, warmth, heat, coldness, windiness or freshness a particular "note", which cannot be simply identified with the heat, cold, calmness and the like' (ibid: 105). An example of a specific climatic atmosphere is the oppressive heat of a summer afternoon, influencing everything and almost casting a monochromatic aura over all things. Analogously, the atmosphere of oppression (heaviness and inertia) of a gloomy autumn day, and the debilitating atmosphere of electricity (excitement and

---

3   'A phenomenon fully invisible itself that escapes the steadily dominant sense of sight, showing itself uniquely in its mediated effects on water and clouds, on branches and boats, on balloons, in noises and sounds.' (thus wrote Minssen 2003: 92 when describing the marine experience of the wind)

psychophysical tension) – which is due to sultriness, the air excited by the storm, unstable weather (in March or April) but also to the climate of a heated debate – all these are climatic as well as sentimental atmospheres, and not only for neuropaths or metereopathics.

a. We might start from *fog*, which is far from metaphorical even when it affects a melancholic person, given that he would first of all consult an optician. The only exception is the solitary person, who sees in it some comfort that 'fills the abyss surrounding him' (Benjamin 1999: 337). In fact, fog is an unlocalised feeling of oppression that, still, is spatially extended like a veil which, dissolving the contours of all things and depriving them of their salience,[4] endows them with a 'new balefulness' (Bollnow 2004: 219) analogous to the 'total dematerialisation of the surrounding world' (ibid: 221) produced by snowfall. To have a 'foggy mind' is therefore the literal expression of the atmospheric perception of a wizened world, in which every pre-view becomes impossible, in whose grey indifference we feel depressed and lonely and in which (given that under such circumstances we only hear sounds) there is 'a feeling of unreality, of a fluctuation in the empty space' (ibid) – which is often accompanied by the typical and impalpable humidity, melting within itself both sensible impressions and occult tonic influxes.

b. The different *parts of the day* are also atmospheric: from the unbearable inaugural vividness of *the dawn* (Nietzsche *docet*!) to the midday daemonicity that takes away *ab extra*, and almost freezes the flow of our life. But we must mention, above all, the primitive and poetic charm of the *night*: its obscurity, today threatened by artificial light and by a rhythm that knows no lights and shades, leads to the disappearance of distances, the perturbing autonomy of the sound from things, a certain lack of motor freedom and a paralysing isolation from things, and finally a regression to the animistic and prelogical extra-objectual spatiality.[5]

---

4 Hence the traditional representation of *acedia* as a cloud (*caligo*) hanging over the subject.

5 See Schmitz (1969: 389 f.); Bollnow (2004: 225–226, 229). 'We are also able to enjoy the charm of the night, to be inspired by its poetry and to listen carefully to what all this poetry tells us about life […] The night, in reality, surpasses by far the limits of the day and reveals to us secrets that the day and the light will ignore forever.' Therefore, 'the not-seeing of biology becomes the life of obscurity, the life of the night.' (Minkowski 1936: 138, 139)

That is, to a 'pure depth without foreground or background, without surfaces and without any distance separating it from me', whose unity is, though, for some, 'the mystical unity of the *mana*' (Merleau-Ponty 2005: 330); for others, it is 'the cradle of the I, the *principium individuationis.*' (Hauskeller 1995: 127).

Perhaps, *twilight* is even more atmospheric than the night, as it is a peculiar 'medium of indeterminacy' (Böhme 1998: 31). That is, the moment when, perhaps once the fog has descended and the contours of things have been progressively dissolved,[6] semi-darkness favours at times a certain levity,[7] at times sadness,[8] if not even a real disquietude;[9] at times the sense of the futility of things,[10] and often, once spatial directionality has faded, extreme and antithetical moods such as full satisfaction or absolute desperation. And obviously – it is not by chance that it

---

6 Modelled on the daily space, where 'one also perceives the interval between things, namely this apparent nothing.' (Bollnow 2004: 216)

7 'Sometimes [...] I happen to let myself be embraced by semi-darkness. I put down the pen and watch the night slowly fall upon the earth, spread all around, wrap itself around me. The profile of objects gets more and more blurred and is progressively dissolved into the shade of the evening until it disappears into the darkness of the night. But, at the same time, objects seem to exit their immobility, acquiring strange, mobile shapes full of charm and poetry, animated with a new life, animated with a nightly life. The world around me is filled with spectres, with imprecise, living, mysterious images. And I mingle myself with this new world; I adhere to its form and, penetrating it, I drink from the spring of the mystery it hides. I become almost lighter, less material, I detach myself from the ground – one could say – so as to become akin to the images surrounding me. I abhor, at that point, the immobility of the objects of precise contours, be them objects or my thought that moulds to them. [...] Should I renounce [...] this form of life? Not for anything in the world.' (Minkowski 1936: 155)

8 'The sun has long since gone down [...] the meadow is damp, and a coolness comes from the forests. Something unknown is about me and is looking thoughtfully. What! Are you still living, Zarathustra? Why? What for? Whereby? Where to? Where? How? Is it not folly to go on living? — Ah, my friends; it is the evening that questions thus from within me. Forgive me my sadness! Evening has come.' (Nietzsche 2005: 95)

9 'Where the dividing lines between perception and sensorial deceit disappear, there is born a threatening spectral world, which one can never grasp and which changes continuously. Every bush blurring into semi-darkness turns into a menacing figure.' (Bollnow 2004: 222)

10 'The least friendly of all the parts of the day, for me, has always been late afternoon. The hours around five and six o' clock have no proper character, they oscillate between the brightness of the early afternoon and the grey colour of the evening, and have as such something bright-greyish and turbid about them [...] In spring things go particularly bad with this time of the day; given that there is not even space for it before evening arrives, it limits itself to a crepuscular existence, and it easily infects us with the feeling of a certain futility of things.' (Ratzel 1905: 174)

seems to come from above – it can even favour mystical inspiration: 'the semi-darkness that glimmers in vaulted halls, or beneath the branches of a lofty forest glade, strangely quickened and stirred by the mysterious play of half-lights, has always spoken eloquently to the soul, and the builders of temples, mosques and churches have made full use of it' (Otto 1936: 71). What favours the atmospheric irradiation of twilight – understandably little noticeable at the latitudes where the transition from day to night is almost immediate – is, in short, precisely the indeterminacy that can be found both in the object (loss of differences) and in the subject, whose perception 'is reduced to its first and ultimate element: a premonitory feeling' (Böhme 1998: 32).

> There is especially an evening or moonlight mood, perhaps even a morning mood. The full clarity of the day is instead less favourable to moods. The objective and precise way in which the objectual world can be known and embraceable with our gaze leaves no space for the emergence of moods, which rather presuppose a certain crepuscular state, in which contours disappear and every single thing starts dissolving into an imprecise general impression […] The receptivity of the mood presupposes in man himself a state in which every determined will is slackened and he regresses to an undetermined sentimental state. (Bollnow 1956: 144–145)

Obviously, our list of examples might continue. We could remember, for instance, the specific atmospheric power of the different latitudes,[11] of urban life in comparison with rural life and also that of the different days of the week, given that there is, for instance, 'a Sunday mood; its quietness, in which what usually fills up the streets stops, is something that can weigh on someone, petrifying them' (Lipps 1977: 97). Notwithstanding this indisputable intertwine between human atmospheres and climatic atmospheres, the latter might still appear less coercive

---

11   In the Southern air 'sweet doing nothing' allegedly imposes itself, because 'everything becomes "more pleasant", one becomes nonchalant, one lets oneself go more easily, one is more unkempt, tension decreases, just like exactness and productivity. At first one is outraged, but after a while one feels that in such an "air" one cannot do otherwise. Therefore the impulsive, intuitive, sentimental aspects of the I come to the fore; one becomes more at ease, but "more of a man".' (Hellpach 1960b: 146–147)

that the first ones,[12] due to the fact that in some cases one can at least mitigate them with a different clothing or by moving elsewhere. Only, by doing so, one does nothing but pass to other atmospheres: the no less specific one of the bed[13] or that of clothing. In fact, 'our body is surrounded by a whole system of "atmospheres" through its apparel, which is rarely one-layered and, rather, mostly multi-layered: these atmospheres could be called – and more rightly than many atmospheric thickenings of the air, considering their net separation – "atmospheric bodies of the apparel"' (Hellpach 1960b: 235).

2.2 Atmosphere and Landscape

It is well-known. The 'first image we have of places and landscapes [...] has surprise (sometimes shock) and a certain atmosphere in it' (Daudet 1928: 62): that is, atmospherically speaking, often something unique and unrepeatable. Nevertheless, it would be obvious to re-read the classical theories of landscape,[14] and maybe also those of garden art, in generically atmospheric terms, and be contented with the link – first identified by Simmel, although unfortunately in a still too projectivistic key – between mood, landscape and atmosphere. It is not sufficient to refer the relative objectivity of the landscape as 'spiritual form' to the *Stimmung*, namely to the 'unifying powers of the soul' (Simmel 2007: 24). It is, rather, a matter of understanding whether it is possible to reinterpret the aesthetic-environmental segmentation we call landscape in atmospheric terms, thus identifying what – cutting across 'the dichotomy of subjective-objective' (Gibson 1986: 129) – ascribes an aesthetic identity to places[15] precisely in the global impression aroused by a given sentimental-atmospheric affordance.

---

12   Croome (2003: 196).

13   'Especially in the city, the atmospheric element of the bed is no longer the overheated, ventilation-free and suffocating atmosphere there once was in alcoves and in deep and obscure corners; devoid of light and aeration and with a mass of heavy layers of feathers.' (Hellpach 1960a: 102)

14   For an overview of some of them, see Griffero (2005b).

15   Namely that 'character that is inherent to the place and identifies it as that particular place and, in this sense, it is as "objective" as other determinations we use in order to identify a specific part of the territory.' (D'Angelo 2001: 127)

A re-thinking of landscape in atmospheric terms, though, presupposes a few conditions that must be met. a) First of all, we must admit that both landscape and atmosphere do not exist in the same way as cats and tables – that is, detached, three-dimensional objects that are usually convex and movable independently from other objects, and that are relatively durable and identical even in motion – but rather as clouds and shades. At a closer look, they also exist in the same way as entities that are certainly more solid than the latter, but whose (inferior) borders are undetermined and incomplete, such as mountains.[16] That is, they exist in the same way as many other entities that, while being fundamental under the anthropic and mesoscopic perceptive profile, turn out to be superfluous under the predictive-scientific one (Mark-Smith n.d.: 4, 17). b) We must then hypothesize that it is possible to refer the characters of a landscape to ecological affordances, especially to those devoid of pragmatic indications that – while being determined by physical reasons[17] – present themselves as formal and qualitative niches inviting the perceiver to linger on them contemplatively, thus exposing himself to the irradiation of their atmosphere. c) Finally, we cannot deny the fact that such landscape-atmospheric affordances constrain the emotional disposition of their perceiver from the outside. Even if we reduced a landscape to a certain qualified 'hierarchy of nested units' (Gibson 1986: 22), it would still irradiate an atmosphere for non-projective reasons, given that 'when we are transported into a given impression, we do not look *towards* it, but rather *starting from* it' (Smuda 1986: 57).[18]

---

16   Mark-Smith (2003).
17   In fact, it can be the case that 'a change in affordance is thus signified by natural chemical changes of greening, ripening, flowering, and fading.' (Gibson 1986: 97)
18   'The landscape does not express the mood (*Stimmung*), but it possess it; the mood hovers there, filling it and permeating it, just like the light shining on it and just like the aroma coming from it; the mood does not co-belong to the overall impression of the landscape, nor does it let itself be detached from it by means of abstraction as if it were a particular component of it' (Baensch 1924: 2). 'When we attribute a mood to a landscape, especially in certain atmospheric conditions, or to a room […], it is not at all an *a posteriori* and merely analogical transfer, it is rather a direct and originarily precise description […] In such a way we do not ascribe, for instance, a soul to the landscape, but we mean that man and world are jointly included in (and permeated by) a given mood. Therefore, the mood does not pertain to an isolated "inner life" of man, but it is man that is inserted into the whole of the landscape.' (Bollnow 1956: 39–40)

These are some of the reasons why a renewed aesthetics of nature, paying attention to the link between expressive environmental qualities and emotive states, could thematise landscapes in atmospheric terms,[19] recognising in them forms (broadly speaking) whose ecstasies[20] make the subject 'feel' affectively and corporeally the place he is in. This is an atmospheric realism admitted even by Caspar David Friedrich: 'you know my house and the splendid view one can enjoy from it. This place, usually beautiful, that always announced to me joy and life, today, for the first time, talks to me about caducity and death. The sky is grim and stormy and today, for the first time, it coats the splendid mounts and multicoloured fields with its uniform winter cover. Nature lays out pale before me' (Friedrich 1989: 94). What animates his grim presentiments is still, in fact, an objective change in the sky and the light in the environmental asset: in other words, a feeling so immanent to the material characters of the landscape that it is cognitively impenetrable to a great extent. The aesthetic identity of a landscape could therefore be precisely the atmosphere we sense in it, mainly in a semi-conscious way:[21] that is, in a sort of psychophysical condition that accompanies and influences our life, like a continuous base. So,

> for the adult who grew up in the mountains, the first sight of a lowland is [...] a true, oppressive desolation [but] on the other hand there is also a reverse malaise provoked by the landscape, that is, a genuine landscape nostalgia of the plain-dweller who goes to the mountains; these are oppressive states provoked by emerging high grounds, the walls of the valleys, the 'narrowness' of the horizon – states that can occasionally reach the point of angst. (Hellpach 1960b: 163)

Finally, it might be worth recalling that the atmospheric nature of the landscape, given the plastic nature of such a concept, does no longer fully justify claims like the following.

---

19 See D'Angelo (2009: 31–32).

20 Which perhaps, externalising themselves up to re-modulating the surrounding *medium*, play a co-evolutionary role like other organs (as in the case of symbiosis between insects and flower plants).

21 'A number of visual semi-conscious and obscure lived experiences have their origin in the narrowness or vastness, brightness or darkness, variety or uniformity of nature, even in all those moments when it is not consciously lived and therefore does not come to be a landscape.' (Hellpach 1960b: 256–257)

> The majority of today's people, being crammed in big cities and used from their youth to smoking chimney stacks, to the din of street noise and to a night as bright as day, have no longer any criterion to evaluate the beauty of a landscape: they believe they are already glimpsing nature at the sight of a potato field, and are greatly satisfied if some starlings and sparrows tweet on the few trees on the main road. (Klages 1998: 33–34)

Industrial chimney stacks, car traffic, perennial lightning: these are all states of affairs that undoubtedly constitute the occasion for the bursting out of (new) atmospheres, which simply add up to those we perceive as more natural, like 'the sublime sadness of the desert, the graveness of high peaks, the melancholic appeal of faraway moors, the mysterious texture of a tall tree wood, the palpitation of the coast with the glimmer of the sea' (ibid: 39–40). Even if 'the face of the continents turned, little by little, into one big Chicago surrounded by fields' (ibid: 41), it would still irradiate its peculiar (possibly negative) atmosphere. It is all a matter of attributing to the term 'atmospheric' not an exclusively positive value (the soul *à la* Klages) but only the characteristic – purely formal, in this sense – of acting affectively over the perceiver's felt-body.

2.3 Orosensory Atmosphere (and the Case of Haptics)

If it is generally superfluous to wonder what is the most atmospheric sense, it is less so for a philosophy that questions the hegemony of sight and touch: 'so far there has never been a philosophy whose conceptual elaboration was guided by what one can hear, smell and taste' (Klages 1929–32: 296).[22] Only in this sense does the atmospheric primacy often attributed to smell seem sharable. In fact, not having 'precise and defined edges, angles, faces and colours' but 'mutable and imprecise limits, as they are made up of gas substances' (Gusman 2004: 24) and involving the olfactive system, which is strictly connected to the cerebral zone (hypothalamus) destined to the elaboration of emotions and to immediate

---

22 'The world of sounds, smells, tastes and temperatures as well as the world of intracorporeal impressions were never able to determine the path of the most elevated reflection.' (Klages 1964: 462)

response, smells are the most evocative thing there is. Even as the outcome of variable factors (flora and fauna, food, clothing, construction material, religious cults, etc.), they identify with extreme precision, as 'fields' and 'olfactive landscapes' (natural and cultural), our birthplace, the social group (whose identity is somehow guaranteed precisely by a hegemonic olfactive field), the individual as such (even pathologically, remember the ancient medical practice of olfactive diagnosis) and, by the virtue of a perceptive ethnocentrism, his other, or rather the Other in general – who is, in fact, almost always also olfactively emarginated. It is not by chance that 'to smell' means both, transitively, to breath in the smells of the external world and, intransitively, to let our own smell perspire, which, elevated to a *principium individuationis*, has (unfortunately) often suggested a regarding of social difference as a prejudicial matter of odour. Good smell has always made one desirable, as well as being an index of moral value – as is shown by the *topos* of the smell of holiness, the almost universal tendency by religious cults to use perfumes in order to favour the atmosphere of spiritual gathering, but also the Arab custom of smelling the mood of the bride.[23] Bad smell, instead, isolates.[24] In fact racism, in its intolerable circularity (people smell like the place and the place smells like people), inevitably refers to stink – no matter if it condemns the supposed reek of niggers, the disgusting smell of butter that apparently Japanese people smell in Europeans or the infamous *foetor judaicus*.

It seems, therefore, that one mostly smells an atmosphere, breathes it in, and that therefore 'in smell is preserved what is eternal of the past: the atmospheric' (Tellenbach 1968: 31). It seems that 'smells are atmospheric more than any other sense phenomenon' (Böhme 1998: 50) and that they suggest the first and undeletable impression of the environment, giving a rhythm – the morning coffee, freshly baked bread, flowers in bloom etc. – to everyday and seasonal life. This is emblematically confirmed by the daydreaming by Léon Daudet, who, while having a certain auditory and 'ocular avidity'– blatantly under the influence of

---

23 'Arabs recognize that smell and disposition may be linked. [...] The olfactory boundary constitutes for the Arabs an informal distance-setting mechanism in contrast to the visual mechanisms of the Westerner.' (Hall 1966: 160)

24 Especially if *agathos* meant 'devoid of bad smell.' (Hauskeller 1995: 97)

poets of aura such as Baudelaire[25] and mostly Proust[26] – believes he can breathe in from women (as if perfume summarized their entire world) a specific atmospheric fragrance, 'different according to the flora of the province in which they were born, loved and lived' (Daudet 1928: 113). The same goes for Ivan Illich's ethical-ecological reflections.

> Both living and dead bodies have an aura. This aura takes up space and gives the body a presence beyond the confines of its skin. [...] Odor is a trace that dwelling leaves on the environment. As fleeting as each person's aura might be, the atmosphere of a given space has its own kind of permanence, comparable to the building style characteristic of a neighbourhood. This aura, when sensed by the nose, reveals the non-dimensional properties of a given space; just as the eyes perceive height and depth and the feet measure distance, the nose perceives the quality of an interior. (Illich 1987: 52)

It follows that 'for the nose, a city without an aura is literally a "nowhere," a *u-topia*' (ibid), and that even peace – referable to hospitality and, even before that, to the liturgy of the *ecclesia* – (used to) take place in the psychologically non-replaceable atmosphere of the *conspiratio*, understood precisely as sharing of air, of the smell of the others and therefore also of the spirit.[27]

For some, the smell is the symptom of the other, the foreigner or the woman, the tramp or the poor, the race but even misery,[28] given that 'prescinding from extreme cases, no observation of the proletarian's misery – and all the less the most realistic account of such misery – will be, for us, as sensuously and immediately upsetting as the atmosphere we find while entering a basement or a dive' (Simmel 1907: 548). For others, 'smell is […] atmosphere itself', something that, impregnating the lived space, 'involves us or makes us communicate with the atmosphere'; something we 'breathe in' and that allows us to penetrate it 'through all the pores

---

25   'One comes, perhaps, upon a flask of memories / in whose escaping scent a soul returns to life' (Baudelaire 2008: 97). See Carnevali (2006: 137–139).

26   'For the past to be able to come back to life in all its might, charged with the immense happiness it promises, its *ambiance* must let itself be smelled: the lure of a perfume must fluctuate in the air, an *aura* must manifest itself.' (Carnevali 2006: 129)

27   See Illich (2002).

28   As Daudet (1928: 120) rightly says: 'pension: the term alone is already a nasal overview of it'.

of [our] being' and that 'can become unbreathable as much on the physical level as on the moral one' (Minkowski 1936: 116, 118, 117). Nor can we forget the usual figurative (metonymical) value of 'smell' – 'the smell of a past age', 'the smell of a distant land' but also 'the sweet smell of money' or 'of power', etc. – nor its evocative and, jointly, achronistically comforting power.

> The scent is the inaccessible refuge of the *mémoire involontaire*. It is unlikely that it will associate itself with a visual image; of all sensual impressions it will ally itself only with the same scent. If the recognition of a scent is more privileged to provide consolation than any other recollection, this may be so because it deeply drugs the sense of time. A scent may drown years in the odor it recalls. (Benjamin 2011: 180)

After all, it is precisely olfactive atmosphere that 'democratic' sensorial anthropology[29] could profitably insist on. In fact, it stigmatizes the progressive atrophy of olfaction, seeing in the triumphant march of personal hygiene and deodorisation[30] a seriously odor-phobic tendency which is only partially compensated by the understandably defensive development of the main distance receptors (sight and hearing): 'if humans had noses like rats, they would be forever tied to the full array of emotional shifts occurring in persons around them' (Hall 1966: 39).

But what are the reasons for this atmospheric centrality of olfaction, or better of the 'oral sensorium (olfaction and taste)[31] as 'sense of proximity' (Tellenbach 1968: 27)? a) The first reason is certainly its essentiality, given that the oral sensorium is the only one that is always and even involuntarily active (due to survival),[32] both in breathing and in nutrition. This invasiveness is what induced

---

    29 See Le Breton (2006) and Gusman (2004).
    30 See, obviously, Corbin (1988).
    31 Unity of olfaction, taste and epidermic sensibility of the oral mucosa (thus Edinger 1911).
    32 Bizzozzero (1997: 19–20); Hauskeller (1995: 16 and n. 3).

Kant to judge olfaction, a little unilaterally,[33] as an illiberal sense[34] – and in fact it can be escaped by the schizophrenic patient only by 'rejecting food and defending himself from air by means of the "asthma crisis"' to the point of turning his situation into the 'atmospheric persistence of the delirious mood' (ibid: 160–161). b) The second reason is that, due to its close bond with knowledge (hence the almost mystic reference of knowledge to taste: *sapientia* from *sapor*), the oral sensorium does not separate the gnostic from the perceptive, at least until it passes from aesthetic orientation to the analytical and culturally modifiable one (the gourmet and the chemist). c) The third and particularly relevant reason is that in olfaction and taste, more than in the other senses, any distinction between sign and meaning collapses: 'we do not understand *what* is expressed in it, although it can show through, but rather what this sensible datum is expressed in *as such*. Of course, the scent (of a flower) can be somehow a sign referring to something it (the flower) designates, but in such a way that the two elements form a unity of experience' (ibid: 31–32). Instead of allegorically[35] referring to a social group, a region or a city, odour melts with them, allowing (more than taste)[36] for a tuning or a fusion (positive or negative, it does not matter) of man with his environment,[37] to the point that 'there is no here and there. Odour acts over us with no limits; to put it differently: we immerge ourselves in it' (Tellenbach 1968: 27). d) The fourth reason can be retraced in the phylogenetic but also ontogenetic primacy of

---

33 Forgetting that a delicious smell can also elevate and be liberating: 'here the mode of communication is in full correspondence with the mode of freedom (as sociability).' (Tellenbach 1968: 26)

34 'Smell is taste at a distance, so to speak, and others are forced to share the pleasures of it, whether they want to or not. And thus smell is contrary to freedom and less sociable than taste' but it is also too intimate, because 'taking something in through smell (in the lungs) is even more intimate than taking something in through the absorptive vessels of the mouth or throat.' (Kant 2006: 50)

35 '*Every* intimacy with things is alien to the allegorical intention. To touch on things means, for it, to violate them. To recognize things means, for it, to see through them.' (Benjamin 1999: 336)

36 A rather isolating sense, after all, because in it the body is alone, with no relation or alternation with the others (Mattenklott 1984: 182).

37 'During World War II in France I observed that the aroma of French bread freshly removed from the oven at 4:00 A.M. could bring a speeding jeep to a screaming halt' (Hall 1966: 50). 'What can be perceived through olfaction is always homogeneous. The olfactive perceived always penetrates into the subject like a flux of the world as it presents itself in olfaction [...] In the activity of both olfaction and taste the subject melts with the world just like when it presents itself in smell and taste.' (Tellenbach 1968: 20, 27)

the oral sensorium. In fact, we entrust ourselves entirely to our first experienced orosensory atmosphere,[38] namely the maternal one, and we elevate it to territorial mark and later to condition of possibility for any subsequent atmosphere of trust necessary for a correct development of the personality.[39] From a non-physicalist perspective, therefore, sight (which is also the last sense to be completed) should give way to olfaction, whose different sense-tonic reactions[40] at times work as true identifying atmospheres: 'after all, it is with the nose that one can establish whether one is in East or West Berlin' (Böhme 1998: 49).

The oral sense (and olfaction in particular) seems then to exemplify the atmospheric perfectly.[41] Just like atmosphere, in fact, odour nullifies the separation between subject and object: 'smelling a person's body odour is the most intimate perception of them; they penetrate, so to speak, in a gaseous form into our most sensory inner being' (Simmel 1997: 119). Just like atmosphere, it is also ineffable,[42] localisable only *ex post* and, in any case, only with the help of other senses (especially sight)[43] but also structurally transitory, given the possibility that habit might neutralise even the most repellent smell. Finally, just like atmosphere, it is an absolutely phenomenic quality and it is therefore irreducible to an attribution of a substance.

There are therefore visual atmospheres (see *supra* 2.2), auditory atmospheres (see *infra* 2.8), but perhaps mostly orosensory atmospheres. Yet, touch should not

---

38   To which taste also corresponds in the form of the primitive, involuntary and constant touching of the oral cavity (external world) by the tongue (subject): see Schmitz (1965: 305 ff.).

39   See Tellenbach (1968: 50–51) and Blankenburg (1998: 144).

40   That is, sensible (pleasure, disgust, etc.) and tonic (headache, dizziness, etc.) as well as variable (the same smell at times attracts, at other times disgusts) (Hellpach 1960b: 77).

41   Unlike other sensibles, taste and smell are not easily communicable, they cannot be willingly recalled nor can they be suppressed for long and intentionally through their organs (nose and mouth), because survival itself is at stake.

42   'The smelly and the savoury cannot be measured nor calculated; they cannot be divided nor, for these reasons, objectively communicated' but they are 'of non-figural nature.' (Tellenbach 1968: 27)

43   See Henning (1916: 29, 33). Also where smells 'are optically constrained through the inclusion into a perceptive totality, they still remain "given smells" and are still only apparently localisable. They never lose more than a part of their inobjectual character; in fact, smell does not become objectual as such, but it merely has a centre in the object without ceasing to fill the entire space.' (Hauskeller 1995: 91)

be underestimated either, in its miraculous capacity to put us in contact with the other than ourselves,[44] and in its paradigmatic value with respect to subsequent experiences – even if they are directed at diminishing the importance of touch itself.[45] In fact, touch limits our expansion while realistically proving the existence of the external world[46] and its sentimental qualities (indifference, aggressiveness, etc.) – one certainly cannot pretend not to touch or not to be touched, while one can pretend not to see or hear[47] – and therefore offers intense specific atmospheres. What is soft to touch is more repellent than things seen or heard can be; the rough and the velvety, even if illusory, are such penetrating qualities that they also impregnate other sensorial fields (in fact, one can 'see' the metallic coldness of a packaging and the velvety softness of a dress) and they produce atmospheric impressions, mainly aesthetic-social ones, even after their denial. And this also happens when the noble character of marble gives way to the coarseness of marbled wood, when a solid wall turns out to be made in plasterboard or the woody warmth of a shelf reveals itself to be an illusory effect of masonite. Therefore, not only is the atmospheric not circumscribed to some senses, but what produces it is not exclusively the contemplative distance of sight and hearing, but also the proximity made possible by olfaction, taste and touch.

2.4 … that 'Creates an Atmosphere'

'Every living personality […] is somehow surrounded by a subtle cloud emanating from it and that, spreading out in the atmosphere, links it back to the latter', by a nimbus to which personality, gestures, words and actions contribute, and of which 'the halo surrounding the saints' head' is 'a symbol, and a rather rough one' (Minkowski 1936: 119). One could also speak of an 'atmospheric integral' (Tellenbach 1968: 56, 59) that, hovering around people,[48] families, peoples,

---

44   'Is it then not a miracle that we can "touch" something, establish an immediate contact with beings and things?' (Minkowski 1936: 180)
45   'It is always touch that reveals to us the sense of immediate contact, of that immediate contact we then use in order to devalue touch.' (ibid)
46   Without touch, the world 'entirely deprived of any foothold and of any cohesion […] would evaporate, so to speak, or turn to dust.' (ibid)
47   Hauskeller (1995: 158–159).
48   See Rudert (1964).

cultures and religions, is felt by their members and even more by those external to them, who perhaps see in it the tangible mark of their exclusion. The atmospheric thus also goes into politics.

Is it not easier to understand the contagious and irrational collective enthusiasm, aroused by words in which 'a startling image which fills and besets the mind' (Le Bon 2009: 63) is condensed, under the atmospheric profile rather than the political one? Is it not (politically) precise to say that 'a right-wing (or left-wing) wind is blowing' in the country, that there is 'defeat in the air' and that 'people live in the nightmare of terrorism'? Is the otherwise inexplicable success of a fashion or a charismatic leader not mainly atmospheric? Democratic systems also make use of political atmospheres, understood as the outcome of an unscrupulous 'impression technique'[49] or at least of a certain 'communicative design' (Böhme 2006a: 166), especially when the 'vote of belonging' gives way to the more aleatory 'vote of opinion'. More in general, this happens in all the institutions where consensus is also built on the *mise-en-scène* and on the aesthetisation of the real. Thus we can explain the prestige and indefinable aura of whoever 'is something and, thus, plays a role' (Plessner 1999: 55), of the distance demanded by a public persona, hiding *de facto* the originary aura – as such intolerable – of her own psychism.[50] As intense as it is ephemeral – 'from the moment prestige is called in question, it ceases to be prestige' (Le Bon 2009: 127) – the atmospheric authoritativeness of a person is, nonetheless, nothing but the reverse of the equally atmospheric *rumours* that damage (being almost a *damnatio in effigie*) her image and which, as is well known, end up being confirmed by any denial. In this sense, all of the feelings that social life rests on are somehow atmospheric.

> Right, morals, religion, esteem as respect for what is worthy of it, all lie on the authority of feelings. Every obligation, apart from the purely theoretical one of irrefutable evidence, has to do with being captivated by feelings [...] In the absence of the captivation by the authority, right would no longer have any

---

49 Schmitz (1998: 182; and especially 1999a).
50 Hinting at 'something that should exist and be effective without being "there"', this aura suggests reliability, credibility, univocity of intents etc. 'Prestige advances the plans and actions of the person within the cloud of an aura of force [*Kraftnimbus*] specific to him; it produces space and commands respect.' (Plessner 1999: 55, 60)

pathos and would degenerate into the amusement of any intention able to impose itself. (Schmitz 2005a: 242)

Atmospheric power likely also plays a role in the success of any project and strategic move, as is easily demonstrated by the sociology of everyday life and linguistic pragmatics, (phenomenological) aesthetics and proxemics, etc. It is certainly not only in order to preserve his indispensable 'flight distance'[51] that the general director places a social distance between himself and his interlocutors, so that he makes the details of his body indistinguishable (warmth, smell, details, etc.). Nor is this the only reason why he chooses an office destined, for several reasons – vastness, refined furnishing, the distance of desk from the door, the former's largeness, the apparent *nonchalance*, the pleasant view on the outside and consequent natural lightning, etc. – to inhibit the visitor, reducing his self-esteem or (if what prevails is the mimetic identification with the boss) arousing in him the pride of membership. There are too many and too easy examples that one could make of the atmospheric-ceremonial techniques by which every social institution tries to control and maintain the impressions it seeks to arouse. Social atmosphere is ultimately nothing but the outcome of the cunning exploitation of 'the attributes that are required of a performer for the work of successfully staging a character' (Goffman 1956: 132) by means of a communication that can also be non-verbal and unintentional.

Thus, more often then we think, we vote for a (political) atmosphere, just like we acritically obey charismatic or prestigious people[52] and we are more willing to buy drinks that, to put it with an old advertisement, 'create an atmosphere' (notice the automatically positive connotation of the term). That is to say that when we choose, we always adhere (also with our corporeal affectiveness) to a certain ritual *mise-en-scène* (of an idea, of the self, of a product),[53] namely to an atmosphere whose artificiality – whose dyscrasia, for instance, between the behind-the-scenes and the on-stage – is only noticed by experts and a very disenchanted audience.

---

51 See Hall (1966: 11 and ff.)
52 'Prestige in reality is a sort of domination exercised on our mind by an individual, a work, or an idea. This domination entirely paralyses our critical faculty and fills our soul with astonishment and respect.' (Le Bon 2009: 119)
53 'Consumption is a ritual process whose primary function is to make sense of the inchoate flux of events.' (Douglas-Isherwood 1996: 43)

This happens, for instance, when we pass from the living room to the (untidy) bathroom, or from the prestigious frontal façade to the melancholic back of many buildings, or from the dining room to the kitchen (or, even worse, to the back kitchen or storage room) of the most refined restaurant, and maybe from the sophisticated-looking dish to the coarse way in which it is truly prepared. The role of the pedagogic atmosphere in every educational process that avoids authoritativeness and spontaneism is just as evident. This is shown in many aspects, from the very banal choice of setting chairs and tables frontally (institutional-authoritative atmosphere) to the cunning creation of a common background for tutor and pupils, made of reciprocity, interaction but mostly trust,[54] in the general conviction that emotive moods are more educative than the methodological or content solutions adopted each time (which holds true for love as well).[55]

At the heart of every social (and socio-symbolic) relation we thus find atmosphere. That is, the whole of words, gestures, corporeal suggestions, gazes and clichés that, guaranteeing a shared emotional 'agenda' of ideas and projects, implicitly restates social and axiological hierarchies, often by means of the reactivation of previous atmospheres, perhaps idealised ones. Just like the *habitus*, the atmosphere which social relations are immersed in can also be objectified in situations unconsciously perceived by the felt-body as familiar (furniture, clothing, kitchen). Even the 'quiet caress of beige carpets or the thin clamminess of tattered, garish linoleum, the harsh smell of bleach or perfumes as imperceptible as a negative scent' (Bourdieu 1984: 77), are after all nothing but atmospheres revealing of a certain social style. Does not the huge success of gossip in turn derive precisely from the relaxing and sharing atmosphere generated so as to make up for the absence of deeper connections? And is the push for an emergency politics also in democratic countries not the consequence of today's endemic terroristic atmosphere, the more penetrating the less it is referable to identifiable enemies? Finally – but the list of examples could go on – does not the meaning of a party as such consist precisely in the peculiar 'atmospherisation' (Assmann 1989:

---

54 Thus in Bollnow's 'appellative' pedagogy (Bollnow 1964), without denying the heuristic value of discontinuity (Giammusso 2008: 140–150). See also Koubek (2000).

55 Characterised, according to Schmitz (2005a: 107), by an atmosphere of co-belonging, whose stability does not decline to being routine and whose freedom is not confused with abuse.

15) through which it renews communal bonds and enhances the sensoriality (in all its possible variations) of those who participate in it?

2.5 The Numinous and the 'Genius Loci'

A theory of the spatiality of feelings cannot but acknowledge its debt towards the theory, also aesthesiologic, of the numinous. The *mysterium tremendum* is, in fact, the atmosphere that fluctuates in the air in a given place, without a whence and a where-to, but that arouses a 'faint shiver' (Otto 1936: 132) or assaults the subject to the point of blinding him, paralysing him or, in any case, disaggregating his personal order.

> Let us follow [this feeling] up with every effort of sympathy and imaginative intuition wherever it is to be found, in the lives of those around us, in sudden, string ebullitions of personal piety and the frames of mind such ebullitions evince, in the fixed and ordered solemnities of rites and liturgies, and again in the atmosphere that *clings* to old religious monuments and buildings, to temples and to churches [...] The feeling of it may [...] pervad[e] the mind with a tranquil mood of deepest worship. It may pass over into a more set and lasting attitude of the soul, continuing, as it were, thrillingly vibrant and resonant, until at last it dies away and the soul resumes its 'profane', non-religious mood of everyday experience. (ibid: 12)

There could thus (also) be an atmospheric explanation for the lived experience of powers that 'surprise'[56] and that perhaps are nothing but the personification of climatic feelings,[57] and the same could be said even of the authoritativeness of monotheisms. Just like the numinous, in fact, every atmosphere a) is the more deeply felt and therefore 'known', the less it is linguistically circumscribable;[58]

---

56 See van der Leeuw (1938: 7 ff.).
57 See Schmitz (1977: 149; 1990: 439).
58 'Revelation does not mean a mere passing over into the intelligible and comprehensible. Something may be profoundly and intimately known in feeling for the bliss it brings or the agitation it produces, and yet the understanding may find no concept for it. To know and to understand conceptually are two different things, are often even

b) can be produced, but not communicated, in a rational way; c) involves the felt-body with consequences on the physical one, as well ('it is hair-rising', 'it makes you shiver', 'it gives you goose bumps', etc.); d) is contagious, 'like stored-up electricity, discharging itself upon anyone who comes too near' (ibid: 18); e) is attractive precisely because it is terrifying (analogously to the sublime); f) supervenes upon sensible data that are, in any case, only the *occasio* for it;[59] g) finally, is active, of course, on emotionally predisposed souls because '"impression" presupposes something able to receive impressions, and that is just what the mind is not, if in itself it is only a "tabula rasa"' (ibid: 164).[60] This is enough to consider, if not religion *tout court*, at least the holy, as 'an experience of determined atmospheres' (Soentgen 1998: 90), perhaps second in intensity only to the erotic.[61] Mystique teaches, in fact, that one falls into God in the same way in which one loses oneself in the sea or in the air; than one feels God in oneself and at the same time one feels oneself in God; and that one feels the presence of the holy beyond and before any dualism, like a 'mystery forming an atmospheric tissue' (Schmitz 1969: 133) and enmeshing whoever experiences it.

Something very similar can be also said of the *genius loci*, namely an experience today overshadowed due to the fact that 'the "pure" place turns into something aspiritual' and '"pure" spirit into something that has no place' (Kozljanič 2004 II: 264), whereas it would be both an aesthetic and an "ethical" duty to make adequate

---

mutually exclusive and contrasted. The mysterious obscurity of the numen is by no means tantamount to unknowableness.' (Otto 1936: 139)

59 Since 'it issues from the deepest foundation of cognitive apprehension that the soul possesses, and, though it of course comes into being in and amid the sensory data and empirical material of the natural world and cannot anticipate or dispense with those, yet it does not arise out of them, but only by their means. They are the incitement, the stimulus, and the occasion for the numinous experience to become astir and, in so doing, to begin at first with a naïve immediacy of reaction to be interfused and interwoven with the present world of sensuous experience.' (ibid: 112)

60 'Like all other *primal psychical elements*, it [the sacred] emerges in due course in the developing life of human mind and spirit and is thenceforward simply present. Of course it can only emerge if and when certain conditions are fulfilled, conditions involving a proper development of the bodily organs and the other powers of mental and emotional life in general, a due growth in suggestibility and spontaneity and responsiveness to external impressions and internal experiences. But such conditions *are no more than conditions; they are not its causes or constituent elements.*' (ibid: 124, my emphasis)

61 See Rappe (1995, for a summary, see pp. 312–323).

architectural projects.[62] Just like atmosphere, the *genius loci* is not 'a secondary moment or maybe even a parasitic character' (Kuhlmann 1998: 4) of physical data, nor is it only the epiphenomenon of architectonic subjectivism. Vice versa, it consists in 'making a space into a place, namely discovering the potential sense present in a given environment' (ibid: 18) in the form of an overall mood or, to put it more esoterically, in corresponding to the region so as to let the thing abide in itself.[63] The best way to put it is Goethe's ('The Four Seasons'): 'Always to me was the field, and the wood, and the rock, and the garden / only space, but thou mak'st them, my beloved, a place'.[64] When space has or acquires an atmospheric charge, it expresses a *genius loci*. Regardless of whether it concerns 'archetypes of natural places' (Norberg-Schulz 1980: 47) or it relates to the various cultural-geographical perspectives, the *genius loci* is, in any case, something more precise than the banal inhabitative specificity of Northern (romantic) places, Mediterranean (classical) ones and desert (cosmic) ones.[65] It is the local condensation of a semiclimatic atmosphere,[66] so much so that it could be said that 'in a clear prosaic city, like Berlin, for instance, [the Daemonic] would scarcely find occasion to manifest itself' (Goethe 2005: 344 ff.).

2.6 'Stimmung', 'Ambiance', Aura

It may not by a chance that 'in the period between the two wars, European culture starts feeling the increasing need for atmospheric concepts' (Carnevali 2006:121). Let us remember that of mood (*Stimmung*), which, besides, is often translated precisely as 'atmosphere'. 'The opacity of a rainy day rests on my soul. Something hits me in the form of *Stimmung* in which I feel consulted in myself and in a

---

62 'The *ethos* is the place of dwelling built by man and transformed in time through an incessant process so as to make it apt for life.' (Venturi Ferriolo 2009: 17)
63 Heidegger (1966: 77 ff.).
64 Goethe (1866: 87).
65 See Norberg-Schulz (1980: 47 ff.) and, for a summary, Kozljanič (2004 II: 315 ff.).
66 'Local divine atmospheres are part of the immense realm of supra-personal and objective feelings, which partly lie [..], like weather, without a place and simply, so to speak, "in the air", or more precisely in the space of vastness; and partly are also condensed in determined places and around certain objects, often only as fleeting evocations.' (Schmitz 1977: 133 f.)

certain direction: the world seems different, the way I "feel" changes. I am forced to retreat from the certainties of observable and definable reality like this and that in order to abandon myself to the ineffable that is present as mood' (Lipps 1977: 97). Then, there is the concept of *ambiance*, which can be understood as 'value of *mise-en-scène*' (Böhme 2006a: 157), set against the presence quality as a *valeur d'ambiance* (i.e. as a system of abstracts signs) or seen as a quasi-thing guaranteeing the correct balance between physical (external) and psychic (internal). *Ambiance*

> permeates space and time, bursts equally out of the universe and of ourselves; and it is in us, consciousnesses, persons and peoples, like an incursion of the universal [...] that is neither quantitative nor qualitative and participates in both and has in life its own life, dissimulated and yet revealable [...] *Ambiance* is not confused with thought, and yet it serves as a means for thought. It is not confused with sensation, and yet it propagates it, increases or decreases it, it commands every sensation [...] If we could grasp it, we would intervene in the organism much better than we do today, because it is an incalculable force, an extract of force, something that is for force what volatile alcohol is for wine. (Daudet 1928: 16–17)

This term – which, due to the metaphorisation of the *air ambient* and the symbolist predilection for the evocative suffix-*ance* (emblematic in Baudelaire's *correspondances*), has recently[67] come to signify 'not [...] an ambient, a world as a physical and cultural world, but rather a sort of ethereal substance that can be perceived and felt' (Carnevali 2006: 119) – is used by Daudet to indicate, indeed, a synthetic 'substance' (both pre- and extra-dualistic), that is quantitative-qualitative and can be holistically intuited, very similar to the atmospheric. It 'draws, from the outside, from the quantitative, immediately resumed by the qualitative psychic receptor' (Daudet 1928: 26), and, almost like the spiritual body (or *pneuma*) mostly theorised in Renaissance,[68] it links all things without nullifying their specificity. Being localisable in the epithelial *sensorium*, as is testified by the reactions to material and mental impressions (perspiration, shivers, goosebumps, etc.),

---

67 See Carnevali (2006: 118 ff.).
68 See Griffero (2006c).

ambiance 'ensures our contact with reality' (ibid: 21) and is therefore allegedly 'indispensable for our mental balance' (ibid: 23). But it is fundamental for organic health as well – since it is also a sort of cell emanation of the endothelial tissue (organs and glands) – and even for public and political health, because there could be no historical event, fashion, dominant idea that would not depend on the (contagious) collective aura, whether actual[69] or inherited.[70] That is, even (curious) therapeutic indications – as diverse as deliria, namely the pathological modes of absence of aura or atmosphere[71] – allegedly derive from the possibility of grasping, especially in darkness and silence,[72] this spiritual-material aura[73] and drawing from it a consciousness that is the outcome of 'the fusion of the two auras: that of he who wants to know, the subject; and that of the object to which he applies his desire to know' (ibid: 48).

It is certainly unnecessary here to embrace the physiologic-esoteric twist that, as we can see, Daudet imposes on the idea of atmosphere (aura and *ambiance*).[74] Being 'the prelude of an upsetting which the individual will neither be responsible for nor in control of, but only the passive scene of' (Carnevali 2006: 134),

---

69   'This is to say that the greater part of historical problems are, like organic problems, problems of spirit, atmosphere, influence, aura.' (Daudet 1928: 245)

70   'I rather believe in the aura, the mysterious function of the skin, in its still obscure laws (likely epithelial and epidermic) that are for organic nature what wind – from the breeze to the hurricane – is for nature itself. The blow is close to the shiver and the aura, and this is where great frenzies and common terrors, hidden and no longer only individual presentments, as well as epidemics believed to be mental but truly cutaneous are explained.' (ibid: 244)

71   'We are constantly immerged in aura', but 'every emotion that comes from the spirit or from the outside tends to destroy the balance of the aura and to create waves, either centripetal or centrifugal, similar to those produced by a stone in the water of a pond. Wisdom consists in not intervening, in order to disturb it, in the formation of these waves that tend to adapt to the aura ones and therefore to incorporate themselves into our mental and organic life, in the guise of memories and reminiscences.' (Daudet 1928: 38–39)

72   'At night, in darkness and silence [...] you will perceive a sort of impalpable noise or, more exactly, firstly a rustle, comparable to the mixed dripping of time and space through an extraordinarily fine sieve', a 'particularly subtle and fleeting ecstasy, halfway between a vertigo and goosebumps.' (ibid: 31)

73   'Aura is therefore the manifestation of ambiance in the subjective experience through a subliminal aesthesia' that counts as '*prodrome*, the beginning of the critical transformation of an atmospheric balance.' (Carnevali 2006: 133)

74   The ideal of this cutaneous knowledge should in fact be seen in the orientation of flying birds and in telepathy, in poetical evocation, in love ecstasy (*interambiance*!) and in creative etymology (Daudet 1928: 33).

it suffices for us to find confirmation in the passive, affective and corporeal syntheticity attributed to atmosphere. Besides, we should not forget that it is precisely in Daudet that we find one of the first technical uses of the term 'aura'. It is used to refer to a) breeze, b) the archetypal atmospheric Petrarchan character (Laura → aura) and therefore a peculiar fusion of person, landscape and mood, c) the symptom preceding an epileptic crisis (Galen) and finally d) an exceptional pathological state, due to a fluid-luminous matter emanated from the soul (and even supposedly photographable)[75] to which all the explanations of the inexplicable – 'occult influences, mystical visions, hallucinations, unconscious impressions' (Carnevali 2006: 131) – should be referred to. The term comes to Benjamin maybe precisely through his reading of Daudet,[76] where he found a declination that merges Baudelaire's (prehistoric) *correspondances* and the mnestic-autobiographical ones of the *Recherche*. It is even too well known what the aura is in Benjamin: it is the unique and unrepeatable atmosphere, unwillingly (and also mnestically) perceived, of an instant of authentic life; it is the unrepeatable apparition of something distant and inaccessible that, in a way, returns our gaze, so that 'to perceive the aura of an object we look at means to invest it with the ability to look at us in return' (Benjamin 1973: 184). It is 'the unique phenomenon of a distance, however close it may be. If, while resting on a summer afternoon, you follow with your eyes a mountain range on the horizon or a branch which casts its shadow over you, you experience the aura of those mountains, of that branch' (ibid: 216). Here, too, the common traits of aura – whose decadence diagnosed by Benjamin seems today no less than controversial – and atmosphere are evident. Firstly, due to their common (antisemiotic, antiallegorical) extraneity to the 'trace', understood as the apparition of a nearness, however far its source may be, controlled by the subjective activity ('in the trace, we gain possession of the thing; in the aura it takes possession of us', Benjamin 1999: 447). But also because they both are pre-sentiments, ineluctable and unintentional,[77] that affectively and corporeally involve man from the outside, determining his emotional state – which is far from being under his control.

---

75 Which is what psychiatrist Baraduc aimed at. See Carnevali (2006: 131–132); Didi-Hubermann (2004); Link-Heer (2003).
76 See Agamben (1993: 44) and Carnevali (2006: 138–141).
77 'Aura cannot be sought nor deserved. It can only happen, surprise us and overwhelm us when we lest expect it.' (Carnevali 2006: 141)

2.7 From 'Affordances' to Emotional Design

The power of commercial goods is also well-known for being highly atmospheric, especially when (like today) their scenic value – prophesized by Benjamin (1999: 201) in the formula 'look at everything; touch nothing' – exceeds not only their use-value but also their exchange-value. The purchase, in fact, 'is less useful for goods and their aims than for social integration' (Hasse 1994: 27): it leads to a colonisation of the emotional life and of free time that is the more efficacious the more seductive the atmospheric power of the product, given to it by an increasingly sophisticated marketing in its emotional and polysensorial strategies. In a society of *Erlebnis*, finalised to the creation of potentially loyalizing 'scenarios',[78] design and marketing cooperate in ideating not only names of products and firms,[79] but also brand images and, indeed, atmospheres.[80] That is, 'a set of elements perceived by the customer that determine cognitive and/or affective reactions able to producing attitudes and behaviours that are favourable to the trader and purchase' (Bonaiuto *et al.* 2004: 91). Even the humblest shop-assistant knows that 'shopping areas should not address their customers on a logical-rational level, but rather emotionally involve them in a subliminal way. For this reason they are generally not set as storage rooms, but they are represented according to architectonic principles in the form of atmospheric spaces' (Hasse 2005: 350–351). It is the atmospheric finality that induces the planner of a shop to wonder from the very start, for instance, what lightings would be the most efficacious, and thus to ponder the relationship between light and shade, that between sunlight and artificial light, what reflections he wishes to produce over the objects, etc.[81]

This true compulsion to design, to the 'conscious production of atmospheres, the *mise-en-scène* of materials and by means of materials' (Böhme 2006a: 156), today affects every place. Especially for clubs, that 'by the means of lighting and voicing technique generate atmospheres of the greatest corporeal intrusiveness. Their aim is to generate a maximum degree of intensity of sensations, so to speak,

---

78 See Schulze (1992).
79 'Nesting today in trade names are figments such as those earlier thought to be hidden in the cache of "poetic" vocables.' (Benjamin 1999: 173)
80 See Babin-Attaway (2000).
81 See Zumthor (2006: 57–63).

"beyond" things' (Hasse 2000: 84). This also counts for hotels, museums, libraries, restaurants and cafes.

> Each cafe owner knows how to furbish his café in order to attract *that* audience he wants to attract. He will give the place such a shape that a certain audience will feel good in it [...] The commonality that here creates communication is already constructed in the place. Which means: the audience gathered here around something common feels good, because, in it, it is able to represent itself, already encountering this representation in the architectural form. (Lorenzer 1968: 78)

In this sense, accessing a place means moving to an (atmospherically) different world. For instance, there can be a warm atmosphere in which rusticity and genuineness invite us to rest in the space, to look around (local products, wooden shelves, aesthetising disposition of the goods, suffused lights, kindness of staff, minimisation of strictly economic elements like prices and counter, etc.); or a cold atmosphere, in which anonymity and serial production suggest, instead, to walk through it rapidly and with the sole purpose of the purchase (multinational brands, metal or Plexiglas shelves, disposition of the goods by price and target, central and direct lighting, detachment and impersonality of staff, visual highlighting of prices and counters, etc.). Each business ultimately aims at having a certain self-image and at creating a polysensorial atmosphere through a setting (array, layout, etc.) that – almost like a cinema scenic design or, mostly, like a theatre setting[82] – manages to evoke, with few traits, a certain historical and social climate and, in any case, a given lifestyle. A lifestyle that, if imitated, makes us loyalised to it to the point of making of it an identity *habitus* that 'distinguishes' us from not quite 'up-to-date' people – who, by making a true perceptive mistake, could consider a willingly 'casual' store as shabby. In the same way, today's polysensorial marketing brings to light the difficulties that would be met by anyone who tried to analyse atmospheres without resorting to the felt-body. In fact, it is evident that, ultimately, a place is warm and welcoming only because it expertly produces – thanks to (synaesthetic) cultural and natural characters such as temperature, brightness, smell, voicing, materials used, etc. – an atmospheric suggestion over

---

82 Böhme (2008).

the perceiver's felt-body. In the case of a business place, the preferred atmosphere is that of relaxation that notoriously favours purchases.[83]

And one should not delude oneself into thinking that one can contrast the atmospheric effect with the function, taking as a rule the fact that what, by ageing (instead of simply wearing itself out) loses its function[84] is compensated by an increasing atmospheric power. There are no rules: the good design of an object can be as atmospheric[85] as something openly dysfunctional, such as even the famous 'coffeepot for masochists'. One perhaps thinks of making it up for one's deficits by imitating the atmospheric power of other systems, like in the case of high speed trains that try to compensate for their limits (and often their unjustified costs) by means of a sport-like atmosphere borrowed from airplanes: 'welcome on board', 'the train conductor wishes you a good journey', narrowness of seats, limited or absent external view, hermetic closure of windows, etc. Yet from good design – not only founded on the behavioural and reflexive aspect but also on the 'visceral' one, largely referable to what we could define as pre-cabled mechanisms – to atmosphere, the distance is very short indeed.

> Pleasing objects enable you to work better [...] When you wash and polish your car, doesn't it seem to drive better? [...] When you bathe and dress up in clean, fancy clothes, don't you feel better? Emotions are judgmental and prepare the body accordingly. [...] Cognition interprets and understands the world around you, while emotions allow you to make quick decisions about it. Usually, you react emotionally to a situation before you assess it cognitively, since survival is more important than understanding. (Norman 2005: 10, 13)

---

83 For instance, both the customer's pace and her stay in the shop are apparently influenced by the background music.

84 'What is lacked by the public use of things fosters [...] the private sphere, atmospherically treasuring what went lost, in the form of pipsqueaks, of aesthetic correspondence.' (Knodt 1994: 13)

85 Guaranteeing a sufficiently precise affordance (affordances and constraints, whether natural or artificial) and a correct multistage process (visibility, constraints and affordances, natural mappings, feedback) (Norman 2002: 181).

2.8 And Art? From the Beautiful to the Atmospheric

'If only we could forget for a while about the beautiful and get down instead to the dainty and the dumpy!' One could also read in this wish of Austin's (1979: 183) the indisputable difficulty of identifying the atmospheric in the world of art. Unless of course one is not contented with saying, metaphorically, that the true work of art emanates a fresh morning air,[86] or that beauty is the specific atmosphere of works of art (they would all irradiate the same one, then!).[87] Although contemporary art compensates for the fictionalisation and virtualisation of the historic-social world, inviting the spectator to a pathic and physical comprehension of the works of art (that, at times, have to be touched, tapped, scratched on the surface), many regard the atmospheric approach as reductive. This is so for several reasons: for instance, because such an approach would fail to appreciate art's ontological revealing power and favour a superficial enjoyment (kitsch) instead of 'the effort from which only can authentic feeling spread out' (Bollnow 1956: 152); or because, hermeneutically requiring a feeling homogeneous to that felt during the *iter* of its genesis,[88] it would entail an undeserved psychologisation of art.

Then how can we justify an atmospheric theory of art? A first attempt could be that of considering atmospheric perception, capable of grasping a 'sensuosly and affectionally perceptible (and, in this respect, existentially significant) articulation of realized or *nonrealized* life possibilities' (Seel 2005: 92; my emphasis), a 'corresponsive' modality that is intermediate with respect to the purely contemplative one and the properly artistic one. Yet the fact that it consists in 'a sensual-emotional *awareness* of existential correspondences' (ibid: 93), circumscribing it to a conscious existential affinity, makes it *de facto* impossible to have a phenomenology that would find in atmospheres unforeseeable chaotic and pre-semantic situations. Then, a more promising attempt seems to be that of seeing in the atmospheric power of art a qualitative specificity of appearance, inexistent outside of the perception of the work of art and due both to the operative mode and to the chosen themes (extra-thing phenomena, intermittent apparitions that can be

---

86   'In every true work of art there is a place where, for one who removes there, it blows cool like the wind of a coming dawn.' (Benjamin 1999: 474)

87   It would make more sense to consider the beautiful as only one of the possible atmospheres (next to the sublime, the graceful, the grotesque, etc.).

88   Thus Geiger (2000: 177).

placed in museums only for banally documentary reasons). Thus, the canvases dedicated by Monet to Rouen's Cathedral – painted in different hours and climatic conditions, from 'the perspective of someone who is ravished [by it]', made so as to represent not so much the objects as their predualistic 'in between', namely 'the shell that embraces all things' (Mahayni 2002a: 63, 62) – are doubtlessly atmospheric. Yet, the identification of atmosphere, in this case the indistinction of subject and object, in only one of the possible themes of art makes it impossible *a limine* to atmospherically explain the whole philosophy of art. In the frame of this limitation, perhaps there is a more suggestive hypothesis: namely that artistic expressions are atmospheres when they are so self-referential that they induce us to ask what they show (or what their *mise-en-scène* is) rather than what they are, what their *actual fact* is (what the work irradiates) and not their *factual fact* (what the work is made of).[89] A potentially universal idea could be the one – which lies at the basis of George Dickie's and partly Arthur Danto's 'institutional theory' – that refers the whole 'world of art' to a theoretical atmosphere, but here atmosphere would irremediably lose its indispensable phenomenological and aesthesiological traits, and it could insist, at most, for instance, on the role of the museum as an ontological transformer (*ready made*, aesthetic differentiation, auraticity, etc.), or as a generator of atmospheres through the works exposed but also (if not mostly) – treasuring the fact that 'the expressions on the faces of people circulating in picture galleries shows an ill-concealed disappointment that only images hang there' (Benjamin 1979: 96) – through a cunning communicative strategy (polysensorial involvement, dramaturgic structure of the exhibition, care for the thresholds of perceptive saturation, etc.).

Hard to define on a theoretical level, the atmospheric is nevertheless easy to identify in art. For instance, in the bright installations by James Turrell, which are so much an extra-thing that they coincide with their 'optical presence, without being physically tangible' (Schürmann 2003: 350), or in the creative interventions of *land art*, for example in Richard Long.[90] Or in poetry, especially when one valorises its sentimental-synaesthesic halo, which transcends the 'consciousness of what is implied by meaning' (Empson 1966: 18), and which – while in the wait of a more mature 'phonosemantics orientated towards the felt-body' (Volke

---

89 Albers (1975), often referred to by Böhme (2010).
90 See Geiseler (2003).

2005: 120), capable of associating sound and figures well beyond the primitive cases of *maluma* and *takete*! – should be relatively analysable under the linguistic profile.[91] Or in cinema, which – thanks to music, characters, certain archetypal shots or sequences, the physiognomic potentiality of the close-up,[92] etc. – has been influencing for a century each experience of ours (in the most banal case, by making us familiar with places and situations never directly experienced), to the point of assuming an exquisitely psycho-geographical value.[93] And so forth. Provided that art is a perception that has come to thematise itself, we could claim that in it we can apprehend, in a privileged way,[94] – obviously with a quality influenced by the rank of the works – what an atmospheric perception is and how atmospheres (which are evidently also experienced otherwise) should be treated.[95] We could also learn how the affections of the felt-body, with its constraints and pleasures,[96] can be innocuously manipulated through works that actually 'communicate and express nothing' but in which 'one has experiences': such works 'do not expose atmospheres, as these are rather really present with and in works of art', almost as if they were 'tentative feeling[s]' (Böhme 1989: 148, 152–153).

Since we can only dwell here on one example of this atmospheric analysis of art, dutifully de-semanticised, let us take music (and not by chance). A musical aesthetics is, in fact, necessarily atmospheric if it is attentive to the 'tensive characterisation of the musical experience' and it conceives listening as 'a going out, moulded, formed, moved by sounds, voices, noises' and as 'an experience

---

91 Certainly not for the reasons brought about by Empson (1966: 21): 'though there may be an atmosphere to which analysis is irrelevant, it is not necessarily anything very respectable.'

92 See Balázs (1952: 54–55) and in general Somaini (2006).

93 For a first approach to an emotional cartography of films, see Bruno (2002).

94 'To the extent that the creations of art are intended to make perception itself perceptible – in short: to see the seeing – the work of art becomes the ideal perceptual field of atmospheres.' Or rather, 'art teaches us to see atmospheres, helping us strengthen our seeing, making of it a productive artistic activity.' (Bockemühl 2002: 219–221)

95 Böhme (1995: 16, 25). Jeff Koons, for instance, as a 'producer of atmospheres [and] manipulator of feelings' that rehabilitate advertising and kitsch, would manage to turn the audience itself into a ready-made, through 'an atmospheric technique, namely a technique of the influence of sensations.' (Hauskeller 2002: 174, 176)

96 'Though you may equip yourself easily to inhabit this form of digital space, you will neglect the socialities of bodily presence, its analog pleasures, at your peril' (Rykwert 2000: 157). Among these, there is also, perhaps in the art of the twentieth century, the self-pitying feeling of 'uselessness for the future.' (Nitschke 2002: 184, 188)

of perceptive dislocation able to give shape to a sensible space that marks the extension of our sensibility beyond the physical limits of our body' (Vizzardelli 2007: 152, 156–157). The effect of this atmospheric space, that deserves the name of 'soundscape' (Schafer 1977), is that of corporeal ecstasies which in the past, lacking better terms, were called 'spiritual' feelings,[97] and which (not by chance) were anti-introjectionistically compared to winds by the eighteenth-century doctrine of affections. These ecstasies feature the simply intensified affective and bodily (prototypically disquieting) charge of the sound, if not even of noise – to which, after all, every sound goes back to if it is not correctly separated from its environment.[98]

> All that can be observed, even just as the slipping trace of something getting closer, in the fear one feels at night in a frightening wood or in the peace of a pure morning mood – namely feeling in its originary presubjective form and yet unorganised around man – all that comes to us corporeally in music as an inscrutable enigma. (Schmitz 1978: 260)

Being thus the more disquieting the less they are identifiable as the effect *of* a known object, sounds seem to be atmospherically powerful first of all a) for their presence, which is impossible or at least rare in optics,[99] then b) for their contagious ability to arouse, through corporeal suggestions, definite behaviours precisely because they are pre-reflexive (think of the greater ease with which one moves backwards while dancing than without music).[100] But also c) for their immanent symbolic power and d) for their counting (intonation, 'grain' of the voice, tonality, etc.) as the *principium individuationis* of something, be it

---

[97] There is, for instance, 'a musically expressed spiritual atmosphere which precedes the hero, to effect a spiritual radiation felt from afar.' (Kandinsky 1946: 28)

[98] 'Only perspective constitutes noise, so that everything can become noise, even silence itself.' (Hauskeller 1995: 106)

[99] 'Colour is the attribute of a thing, sound is the effect of an activity', which is why 'in sound we have a presential event, in colour we grasp a being that is distant from us' (Straus 2005a: 39, 46). Which counts, though, only if one fails to appreciate the also chromatic ecstaticness of things: see Böhme (1995: 30; 2010: 131–144) and Griffero (2006b).

[100] 'Moving backwards in dance does not conflict with the dynamic impulses implied by the space; therefore it lacks that painful and difficult something that instead connotes moving backwards in the optical space.' (Straus 2005a: 63)

a person (whereas a portrait only regards the past) or a place.[101] Finally, if not most of all, e) for their paradoxically always more spatial than temporal character (headphones, ambient music, soundscape). For instance, the soundscape offered by the so-called 'hits' – namely the contagious tunes that, as real earworms, we cannot escape – is intentionally atmospheric. The same goes for shopping centres, art installations, cinemas but also bells (that emotionally mark everyday life) and certain emotionally antithetic noises – emblematically, the sound of helicopters over Belfast reassures the Protestants and threatens the Catholics.[102] And again the radio – truly responsible, in the first half of the twentieth century, for the 'affective rhythms of the home' (Tacchi 2003) – and, more recently, walkmans and iPods that, privatising or even derealising public space,[103] generate *de facto* unknown atmospheric potentialities.[104] The intense atmospheric charge of sounds, with utopian or dystopian outcomes which are in any case variable depending on their nature (continuous or intermittent, familiar and controllable or enigmatic, etc.),[105] thus ultimately derives from its implying, more than colour or form,[106] affectively connoted spaces, voluminous spaces[107] that are not dimensional or optical: think of the reassuring sound of house chores, of the topologically identifying sound of traffic, of the cosmopolite sound of an airport, etc.

In any case, this is certainly not the place – supposing that such an intent makes sense – to specify the atmospheric valence of every form of art. We shall therefore be contented with affirming that the work of art, if it is *moins un monde qu'une atmosphère de monde* (Dufrenne), it is so only because it selects and intensifies, also through its paratexts (environments, graphic layouts, etc.), atmospheric

---

101 And indeed, 'if you suddenly take away from a house these fundamental tones, it immediately becomes an unfamiliar environment.' (Schafer 1993: 16)

102 See Moore (2003).

103 See Thibaud (2003b).

104 The gaze of someone who listens to music through earphones (fleeting, but sometimes also more intense due to the acoustic isolation) is, for instance, the gaze of 'someone who looks at me, but in the same time takes care of himself.' (Knodt 1994: 14)

105 Sound 'enables individuals to create intimate, manageable and aestheticized spaces to inhabit but it can also become an unwanted and deafening roar threatening the body politic of the subject' (Bull-Back 2003: 1). On sound atmosphere see Böhme (2000), Mayr (ed. by) (2001) and the many works by Justin Winkler.

106 Ströker (1977: 28).

107 For a (certainly problematic) analogy between musical scale and sentimental scale, see Schmitz (1969: 199).

impressions that are already pre-existent in the extra-artistic environment. Which is to say, to use different terms, that 'a seductive atmosphere in a museum seduces us precisely as a seductive atmosphere would do elsewhere, and if it does not seduce us it is because it is no longer a seductive atmosphere' (Hauskeller 2002: 180).

2.9 Urban Seductions

It is hard to deny the atmospheric charge attributed to the city as an almost sacred landscape, walked through with unnerving slowness by the *flâneur*, the urban equivalent of the *promeneur*.[108] It is rather a common place to identify a city, and even its districts, with the atmospheric effect produced by their polysensorial image,[109] so much so that the townscape becomes a relevant psychotopic landmark. In this sense, the urban atmosphere (or character) can be said to be familiar when the city allows even newcomers to feel at home and to be better in control of their existence,[110] thanks for instance to a uniform reticular scheme. On the contrary, we could define as inhospitable the atmosphere of a city that is devoid of identity, urbanistically incoherent, counterintuitive in its road system, perceived only as a place of forced residence and work, etc. All these atmospheres, while deeply influencing the *habitus* of the inhabitants,[111] are rarely taken into account by those in charge of the planning. For instance, the fact that for some time Manhattan, 'offered its inhabitants the spectacle, inscribed in stone, concrete and steel, of a way of life obeying a very different program, one answering a question quite different from that of "housing"' (Damisch 2001: 110) led to results that were far from what was expected. In the same way, it is well known that a provincial atmosphere, although 'highly propitious for the quiet and placid development of creative talents' (Hellpach 1960a: 14 fn.) can even have 'pathological' consequences.

---

    108   Benjamin (1999: 42).
    109   See Hasse (2000: 168, 2002b, 2003, 2008a).
    110   Bismarck was told that people preferred the city because 'there one can "be sat outside" and listen to a band, drinking a beer in peace! Does this not seem to be a paradox? Is the desire to 'be sat outside' the reason for the exodus from the country and urbanism?' (Hellpach 1960a: 25)
    111   'Phenotypical transformations of the general *habitus* (and not simply of particular marks) cannot happen without leaving a trace in the psyche.' (Hellpach 1960b: 250)

Notwithstanding the fact that the image of the city 'was unsettled, not only as a result of the ever more apparent divorce between the forms and functions generally regarded as its own, but also because of the dissolution of traditional communitarian ties in the midst of the mob' (Damisch 2001: 14), each city continues to express 'a special character, a slang or dialect, a form of humour, which sometimes has a special label' (Rykwert 2000: 218), in other words an atmosphere. Far beyond its superficial look, urban atmosphere is still as ever 'a being that has bewitched us, from which we cannot be parted; we remain its children or its timid visitors' (Mitscherlich 1968: 32). It is overall an image that works, no matter how impressionistic, prejudicial, metaphorical or even merely virtual it is, as in the case of city views only known through cinema – emblematically, the Manhattan skyline seen from normally impossible frontal or aerial perspectives[112] and based, in any case, on the concealment of other parts. This urban atmosphere cannot be deemed less effective only because it derives from the superficial impressions of someone contemplating the city from a higher and distant perspective, rather than from the deeper one of someone really "experiencing" the city, perhaps finding even parallel cities by travelling all over it (by car or by foot) or immersing oneself into it, constructing authentic psychogeographies from it.[113] *De facto*, the atmosphere of a city quickly becomes a myth, so far from being uncertain that 'when we actually go to those places, we go there with the idea of doing some things and not others' (Marback-Bruch-Eicher 1998: 6); we are conditioned to do so by biotopes but also psychotopes, that is by 'points in which the soul quietens down [and that] constitute, for those who owe what they are to this city as well, a part of their self-certainty' (Mitscherlich 1968: 16).[114] In the city – arguably a secularised remnant of homeland[115] – 'each piece of world [is] increasingly subtracted from its sinister and little reassuring elements' (ibid: 120); this is also due to the effectiveness of

---

112 From other points of view, in fact, Manhattan 'juts out from a desert formed by industrial wreckage, rail tracks and fragmented city blocks.' (Knodt, 1994: 9)

113 Amin-Thrift (2001: 10–22) imagines an integration of the data emerging from *flânerie*, urban rhythms and footprints from the past.

114 'Psychic support [...] to which a uniform interest should be dedicated, towards which we should turn with constant affectivity.' (Mitscherlich 1968: 56)

115 Hasse (2000: 52).

an atmosphere,[116] the hypothetical organisability of which falls within the tasks of human sciences.

It is certainly not a recent discovery that the city expresses a specific atmosphere. Inaugurating a modality of description of the urban space from the point of view of the observer, and in opposition to the progressive anaesthetisation of modern urban planning (monotonous, unnatural and devoid of harmony), as early as 1889 Camillo Sitte chose the notion of 'effect' – unfortunately limited to the visual sphere and to public places,[117] dense with significance and sentiments (places of value)[118] – as the key concept in an organic-pictorial town planning inspired by late Impressionism. We can certainly speak of atmosphere also about the descriptions of lived urban spaces offered both by August Endell in 1909 and, more recently, by Kevin Lynch in his environmental enquiries founded on the notion of *imageability*, i.e. the urban quality perceived regardless of cartographic objectivity, resulting from the encounter between the subject and certain objective qualities. The identity atmosphere of a place – significantly absent in so-called 'gentrification' – is precisely the 'quality in a physical object which gives it a high probability of evoking a strong image in any given observer' (Lynch 1960: 9), influencing him and rooting itself spatially in his memory.[119] An atmosphere banally expressed by the ease with which one orientates oneself,[120] but also by more sophisticated qualitative performances (in Lynch: vitality-meaning-coherence-accessibility-control, plus two metacriteria such as efficiency and justice),[121] whose identity consequences – 'place identity is closely linked to personal identity "I am here" supports "I am"' (Lynch 1981: 132)[122] – confirm the privileged bond between the

---

116 'We do not know at all to what extent this very special vital aura affects in a determinant sense the biography of the citizens. It probably greatly affects it.' (Mitscherlich 1968: 33)

117 See Porfyriou (2005).

118 Venturi Ferriolo (2009: 172 ff.).

119 Atmospheric perception of mnemonic type (Melai, 1996: xxi) consists, like collecting, in welcoming things in our space, thus taking them away from broader contexts (see Benjamin 1999: 204).

120 'Even the most grasping developers will talk about "identity points", if only to allow a visitor to orient himself.' (Rykwert 2000: 132)

121 But we cannot exclude that an image of the city may positively derive from its inconsistencies and inaccuracies (ibid: 7).

122 'Cities have always been privileged sites, if in guises that are constantly changing, for interrogating the nature of the subject, for investigating just what markers it needs to keep its bearings in the milieu in which it is evolving.' (Damisch 2001: 16)

discourse on urban atmosphere and the neo-phenomenological investigation we started from, about how one feels in space. What matters there – obviously with variations according to nationality, climate, customs and traditions, etc. – is also the olfactory landscape ('smells make it possible to identify places and to identify oneself with places' (Böhme 1998: 50)) as well as the acoustic landscape, by which we mean the noise produced by the kind of pavement and vehicles travelling on it, by how one drives and by the music coming out of the houses, the languages spoken in them and the sound of pets, etc.[123]

As is often the case in this kind of work, here the risk is that the examples can get the better of theoretical argumentation. Yet some are really necessary. The atmosphere will be different if the town is historical, perhaps full of ruins capable of irradiating powerful suggestions[124] (the irreversibility of becoming, the revenge of nature over human actions, victory of chance over superb rational planning), or if it is a new town, perhaps rebuilt in its ancient form. If it has a true lively centre or only equivalent areas, satellite-neighbourhoods or even pleasant garden cities. If it is urbanistically compact or if it has been planned according to a high rate of zoning. If it isolates people in dull silos-like residential buildings, with a marked distinction between uptown and downtown, and even includes gated communities (possibly developed vertically: skyscrapers and penthouses), or if it allows those who inhabit it to live in constant proximity. The atmosphere will also be different if the city is made up of narrow streets and winding alleys resistant to vehicle traffic and thus apparently made for 'the people', or if it consists of large tree-lined avenues and freeways; if its buildings express a fascinating historical depth or if they are radically contemporary; if there is a main street (specific or standardised), maybe a Latin-style square, or only shopping centres; if there is a skyline of a symbolic value or not; if buildings are accessible to the audience or threateningly privatised;[125] if there is a museum able to 'create a public atmosphere of a new

---

123   According to Böhme (1998: 64) it is possible to acoustically distinguish even between the pedestrian areas of the various German cities.
124   See Hasse (2000: 95–121).
125   The atmosphere of the oldest skyscrapers in New York ('wide bases [...] riddled with semi-public and commercial spaces of various kinds', luxurious entry halls purposely designed to be on show) is different from that of the most recent ones ('security-guarded lobbies'), thus proving, today, the failure of the American egalitarian dream (Rykwert 2000: 273).

kind' (Rykwert 2000: 297), attracting the cult of the world religion of (also elite) tourism, or not.

Yet, is it legitimate to claim that the merely agglomerated city and therefore devoid of an identity, i.e. what today is called urban region, is *ipso facto* devoid of atmosphere? Can it not have, more simply, a negative one, characterised by the absence of a precise city centre and thus of a core of value? It is only in the name of a preconceived and nostalgic *Kulturkritik* that we could rule out the fact that an atmosphere can manifest itself 'even in the chimney of a factory, in a clay-coloured housing block, in a barracks-like hotel' (Klages 1940: 282). We thus admit that perceptions totally devoid of atmosphere can be pathological. For such perceptions 'the colours of things and the walls of the room [are] free of any atmospheric halo, perfectly sharp [...] What is most impressive is that [there is not] that layer that is normally barely lived and that for the moment I can only hardly explain. Things usually have a halo of details that sticks out also about their past and their future' (Fränkel-Joel 1927: 91 ff.).

In any case, as the result of urban self-representation, the inhospitability of the contemporary city is an atmosphere, although perhaps under the guise of a 'petrified nightmare' (Mitscherlich 1968: 29). This also holds true for the sad impression that 'each extra child makes the hope of escaping, once and for all, the rental barracks illusory', since 'every child born decreases the air space of a housing' (Hellpach 1939: 138, 140). Is it not true, after all, that even the suffocating courtyards and grimy urban alleyways found in Dickens exude their special atmosphere? Even the 'nervous exaltation' foretold by Simmel (1950: 36) is to all respects an atmosphere, whether it depends on a chromatic hegemony (of the exciting red-yellow),[126] on the impossibility – given the metropolitan coexistence of exterior proximity and interior distance – of 'sinking into an impression' (Hellpach 1960a: 123), or by a linguistic carelessness that touches the stenolaly and by the anaesthesia typical of the *blasé*. The functional climate of emotional indifference, explaining the impression of freedom that accompanies European urbanisation, and the subsequent 'greatest advance' of a super-personal 'objective culture' in which everything appears 'in an evenly flat and gray tone;

---

126 Green and blue 'are missing in the city, the more so the more it is widespread and the buildings are densely packed; in it, the eye cannot dwell neither on vast expanses of green nor on blue skies. Therefore the sedatives colours of the landscape are missing as impressions.' (Hellpach 1960a: 88–89)

no one object deserves preference over any other' (Simmel 1950: 422, 414), are ultimately the emergence of a new and specific atmospheric character we can call cosmopolitism. In it, confidentiality, indifference and psychic individualism are the price to pay for the undoubtedly beneficial emancipation from the prejudices and pettiness typical of rural life. In short, a landscape is such even when it is disfigured by artifice, and we can call atmospheric even the negative emotional and corporeal involvement that we feel in the most chaotic and anonymous city. We might say that the atmosphere is like the corporeal 'skin'[127] of the city.

> The city that can be lived with the felt-body becomes invasive in appearing sensible, which means that it is experienced not only as a visual space, but also as a tactile, olfactory, acoustic and gustatory space. The corporeal perception goes beyond the individual impressions and collects what sensibly appears in the feeling of the atmosphere, which becomes perceivable as something 'in itself'. (Hasse 2000: 46–47)

This urban atmospheric skin is also made up of cold and abstract places, (therefore, even of non-places). This is why 'a road with a long and stereotyped row of houses similar to one another is by no means a neutral road in terms of its form, but is on the contrary very effective on experience due to its exhausting monotony, that is felt and rejected as being cold, anonymous, absent and provokingly "place-less"' (Lorenzer 1968: 70).[128] And the same can be said for situations that are transitory both on the level of the perceived and on that of the perceiver.

> And as skin [atmospheres] are examples of dual living bodiliness, every time characterized by the transient. Atmospheres manifest on the one hand man's own corporeality, as he moves in the material space of the city and feels committed, being stimulated by it, to emotional situations. On the other hand, they manifest in a metaphorical sense the 'corporeality' of the city, which, with the chaotic

---

127 'The metaphor of the skin mostly leads to the awareness of one thing: it illustrates the difficulty *and* the necessity that one encounters when having to distinguish between the *physical space* (and between one's own *bodily existence in a physical sense*) and the *virtual space* (or one's *corporeal existence*)' (Hasse 2000: 118).

128 For the atmosphere of a road, see Hasse (2002a).

multiplicity (Schmitz) of the situations of its being and appearing as a city, narrates the life in (and of) the city. (Hasse 2000: 133)

2.10 The Magic of Dwelling

Part of the atmospheric power of the city also derives, of course, from its architectural character, from the 'mood (*Stimmung*), the sentimental tuning of the built space that is directly transmitted to the observers, inhabitants, visitors and even to the neighbourhood, propagating itself towards them' (Labs-Ehlert, in Zumthor 2006: 7). It derives, in other words, from an architecturally conditioned and, ever since childhood, interiorised spatial scheme, that of habitability: something that architecture should take into account especially if it is to offer, today, not only stories and philosophical utopias but 'lived experiences' (Janson 2005: 147), and if it wishes to create a *mise-en-scène* of expressive qualities (majesty, intimacy, coldness, merriness, etc.), in accordance with the belief that the '"experiential" measure of the quality of an environment or of an environmental element is "naïve" perception', addressed 'not only to functional aspects necessary to a building but also to emotional, communicational and symbolic aspects, typical of the relation between people and the physical-spatial structure' (Bonaiuto *et al.* 2004: 36, 9). That is, to aspects that are so atmospherically relevant that they lead even those who demolish a building to commit themselves to somehow preserve the spirit of the place.[129]

It is certainly possible to avoid this partly ideological (and overly postmodernist)[130] apology of the urban in the name of a more continuous and reflexive experience.[131] Nevertheless, it would be absurd if such planning did not consider 'how one feels' under the ecologic-social profile. For instance, it cannot underestimate the fact that even the shadow cast by a building, which invades the neighbouring space, determines a powerful aesthetic and corporeal effect (and

---

129   For instance re-using elements from the previous building (Koolhaas 1978).
130   See Durth (1988); Hasse (1994: 17 ff., 29, 72); Böhme (2006a: 175).
131   Zur Lippe (1987: 287 f.) distinguishes, for instance, between (biological) life, lived experience (emotional life) and experience *strictu sensu* (reflective re-elaboration).

therefore atmospheric):[132] from irritability to insomnia, to breathing difficulties and the aesthetic *diminutio* of the place, etc. Just like all external physical forms, buildings can also 'communicate to us only what we ourselves express with their qualities, [that is] relations of weight, hardness, etc., all the aspects that for us possess an expressive value [...], life's great feelings, *atmospheres*, that have as a premise the lasting condition of bodies' (Wölfflin 1985: 30; my emphasis). This also explains why, once recognised the organic-kinaesthetic effect of the optic, and especially of symmetry and asymmetry on breathing as 'the most direct organ of expression' (ibid: 35),

> powerful columns have on us the effect of powerful innervations, our breathing is determined by the vastness or narrowness of the environments; our muscles stiffen, as if we ourselves were these pillars, and we breathe deeply, as if our chest was as broad as these vaults, the asymmetry often provokes a kind of physical pain, as if we were missing an organ ourselves, or as if it were injured, and everybody knows the discomfort caused by the vision of a unbalanced balance. (ibid: 33)

Albeit a little primitive, theoretically feeble,[133] unfortunately still projectivistic[134] and at times even grotesque in its associations (weight-nostalgia, symmetry-wellbeing, windows-eyes, round arch-happiness, etc.), Wölfflin's approach correctly refers formal perception to an affective and corporeal situation.

> Seeing as such is not a sense for the being-in-something, it is rather a sense that sets differences and creates distances. But there is a specific sense for the being-in-something, the sense to which we give the name of affective situation.

---

132   With regard to the very controversial case of the installation of wind turbines, see Hasse (2005: 377–387). For an attempted integrated theory based on the atmospheric see also Wendorf *et al.* (2004).

133   Although 'an architectural style expresses the attitude and movement of the man of the time [...] the issue of whether it is the physical history of the human body that conditions the shapes of architecture or vice versa would take us too far for it to be discussed in this essay.' (Wölfflin, 1985: 73, 57)

134   'We *transpose* what we know of ourselves, the sensation that stretching out comfortably, peacefully relaxing brings to us, to this kind of distribution of masses and we enjoy the serene tranquillity that buildings of this type arouse in us.' (ibid: 54; my emphasis)

> In feeling ourselves we somehow feel the place in which we find ourselves. We experience our own presence and at the same time we feel the space in which we are present. (Böhme 2006a: 110)

By generating 'orientations, kinetic suggestions, markings' (ibid: 113), buildings thus produce a very wide range of atmospheres. Sometimes even by the virtue of their metaphorical sonority – 'there are buildings that resonate wonderfully, that tell me: I am safe, I am not alone' – or of their 'physical and most likely psychic' (Zumthor 2006: 33, 35) temperature: think for instance of the bureaucratic coldness suggested by a wholly interiorised office building (made of glass or granite), that rejects any connection with the urban tissue. In a humanistic architecture so far merely sketched,[135] atmospheres seem to play a central role. Being responsible for 'immediate understanding, immediate contact, immediate rejection' (ibid: 13), they are generated by 'everything, things, people, air, noises, tone, colours, material presences, structures, also forms' (ibid: 17) – in short, by everything that pathically modulates the corporeal space (new materials and technologies, extra-European styles, sophisticated lighting,[136] and so forth).

But it is now time to move into the front room. In fact, dwelling, which of course does not merely consist in having a roof over one's head, fosters a real culture of atmospheres, also by the virtue of the '"sentimental" operation' of literary narration, with its 'rhetoric of intimacy' and its 'epopee of small things' (Tarpino 2008: 22, 45, 98). It is a culture of feelings that mature within a space that is sharply and qualitatively (and once was also magically) separated from the outside like the house; a culture of atmospheres that, of course, change in time,

---

[135] 'The whole of architecture is, in fact, unconsciously invested by us with human movement and human mood [...] We transcribe architecture into terms of ourselves. This is the humanism of architecture' (Scott 1914: 213). 'Spatial structures in the corporeal experience, architectural forms as movements, architecture as configuration of the void – with concepts like these, from Wölfflin up to Endell, a potential was disclosed for architecture that has not yet been minimally exhausted.' (Böhme 2006a: 116; also 14–15, 151)

[136] Think of the overturning of the previous vertical hierarchical social order produced by lifts (Simmen-Drepper 1984), of the widespread use of glass and steel, or of the design of the space outside the building (Böhme 2006a: 86–87, 116–118) from which derives a synthesis between 'the shut body that isolates spaces within itself and the open body, that contains a portion of space connected to the infinite continuum' (Zumthor 1999: 22). See also Hasse (2008b).

depending, to give only one example, on the changing criterion for organising rooms, which were once linked to each other ('Grand Central Station atmosphere'), then were positioned around a corridor or hall (hence a more stable domestic atmosphere),[137] and were finally dissolved in today's large open spaces, with their illusionary atmosphere of vastness and freedom. Here it is obvious not only that aesthetics and atmospheric power do not always come together – 'many have had the experience of getting a room nicely arranged, only to find that conversation was impossible if the chairs were left nicely arranged' (Hall 1966: 111) – but also that 'residential satisfaction', as an 'evaluating response definable as the pleasure or gratification deriving from living and inhabiting specific place' (Bonaiuto *et al.* 2004: 47), should never be confused neither with domestic fetishism,[138] nor with the pathologic privilege of the front room as a formal space, since after all it could be nothing but a 'stately room with no castle behind it' (Mitscherlich 1968: 122). Now, it is clear that, regardless of its outcome, the culture of dwelling is a search for the right atmosphere, both protective and guaranteeing privacy, and capable of satisfying the inhabitants' socio-expressional needs.

Atmosphere and domosphere are thus inextricably linked, since 'dwelling is feeling in order to feel oneself, perceiving in order to perceive oneself' (Vitta 2008: 97): a felt-body disposition that, fusing *aisthesis* and *pathos*, largely derives from the given atmosphere and from signs (comfort, furniture, lighting, carpets, etc.) that are once again culturally variable. For instance, 'where the American would consider himself *outside* he has already entered the German's territory' given that 'the meanings of the open door and the closed door are quite different in the two countries' (Hall 1966: 133, 135).

2.11 Ecstasy of Materials

Why do we almost always prefer a wooden object to a plastic or metal one if not for its atmosphere? If not for its ability to evoke thus, for example, life (the tree with its roots), peace (the slow and regular life of the tree), strength (under large trees

---

137 Hall (1966: 104).
138 'Dazzling cleanliness is too often converted by us into tyranny.' (Mitscherlich 1968: 115)

we feel protected), sensuality (suggested both by touch and by smell), industry (which it urges us to), charm (also hypnotic, of its veins, for example) and the past (almost as if the wooden object preserved the memory of past environments)?[139] Perhaps, in general, for being a material whose stiffness is not at the expense of its 'warmth' and its certain rustic authenticity, which today – but only today, and what's more, only in certain cultural contexts – is so much desired?

The charm of materials therefore lies largely in their atmospheric potentiality. Being true passive syntheses, the perceptions of materials are 'integration processes that are based on syntheses directly proposed by the material,' suggested by the 'allusive capacity' or the 'hidden imagination' both of the materials themselves – as if there 'was hidden a potential of images that have to be actualised' (Piana 1979: 188, 157, 160) – and of their interaction with one another: in fact, 'they react with one another! The materials are in agreement with one another and arrive at an irradiation, and in this composition of materials there arises something unique' (Zumthor 2006: 25).

Here is something that has not yet been studied sufficiently, at least from the phenomenological point of view. And if 'the time is not far away when we will begin to scientifically study the influences deriving from the environment created by technology, such as rooms and furniture, home and atrium, road and square, roadway and vehicles, phenomena that can be defined as "tectopsychic"' (Hellpach 1960b: 20), it is precisely because we are beginning to recognize in the object, and in the material it is made of, not only the passive reflection of unfulfilled desires, but a quasi-subject whose point of view regards me and provokes me. Take an artefact degraded (though not especially atmospherically) from the prototype to the series.

> Suppose that the uniqueness of the aforementioned armchair lies in its particular combination of tawny leather, black steel, general silhouette and mobilization of space. The corresponding serial object will emerge with plasticized leather, no tawniness, the metal lighter or galvanized, the overall configuration altered and the relationship to space diminished. The object as a whole is thus destructured: its substance is assigned to the series of objects in imitation leather, its tawniness is now a brown common to thousands of other objects, its legs are

---

[139] Dichter (1964: 152–153).

indistinguishable from those of any tubular chair, and so on. The object is no longer anything more than a conglomeration of details and the crossroads of a variety of series. (Baudrillard 2005: 159–160)

Even more relevant reflections on the atmospheric charge (synaesthetic and social) of materials come from those who practice art history as history (social, symbolic but also phenomenological) of materials,[140] and especially by those who thematise the insubordination of materials with regard to the shape in contemporary art. A charge, once again, at times permanent and at times historically conditioned. If, in fact, it is always true that 'the blue of a carpet would never be the same blue were it not a woolly blue' (Merleau-Ponty, 2005: 365), the atmospheric qualities of the wool, instead, are not historically and geographically constant – besides, in the artistic use that can be made of them, they go far beyond the intentions of artists.[141]

The woodiness of the icon is, in fact, sometimes the indispensable sign of imperfection referring to transcendence[142] and sometimes, in the case of a contemporary installation, probably the concretistic and anti-fictional compensation of an era universally launched towards fiction.[143] The concrete, which 'in the first half of this century [the twentieth century] was given a positive and almost messianic value', is now 'reduced to a popular metaphor for flaws such as contempt for humanity, obtuseness and insensitivity' (Raff 1994: 15). However, whether you use them for their anonymous character (masonite, cement, plastic) or for their symbolic meaning (wood, marble, steel), it is a fact that the choice of materials always exceeds the functionalist-engineering dogma, namely that such choice aims at the 'quality of appearance' (Böhme 2006a: 157), from which it is hoped that the desired atmosphere can pour out. Materials are in fact 'bearers of magical messages; instead of a readable text they communicate feelings, they address the deeper layers of our perception' (Auer 1995: 19) and contribute significantly to the atmospheric power of the environment, enhancing the outside (the appearance aroused) at the expense of the inside (the substances actually used). Thus, paradigmatically, masonite works: it reveals to specialized observation (visual and haptic) the economic and transient nature of furnishings,

---

140 See Raff (1994); Böhme (2006a: 159).
141 Wagner (2001: 13, 15).
142 Florenskij (1993: 61).
143 Marquard (1994: 186–191).

while communicating to the majority of people the same atmospheric qualities of wood (warmth, friendliness, naturalness, hardiness, vital irregularities, etc.). Without even the disappointment of perception – we repeat – being completely non-atmospheric. It simply involves the transition from an atmosphere to another, perhaps even axiologically opposite.

Chapter 3

Atmospherology

'Are you in pain, dear mother? I think there's a pain somewhere in the room,' said Mrs Gradgrind, 'but I couldn't positively say that I have got it.'

Charles Dickens, Hard Times

3.1 History of a 'Sin': Introjection and Projection

However we get to atmosphere, i.e. a feeling whose peculiarity is that of being spatialised – whether we get to it from the aesthetics of empathy, from the philosophy of *Stimmungen* or even from mystics – it is worth reiterating that it is something 'all-embracing and all-permeating, that is supra-personal and, to this extent, is at the same time trans-objective or better pre-objective, not letting itself be "placed" in any circumscribed object'(Schmitz 1969: 102). Something that, while grasping us from an unspecified distance, possesses a peculiar voluminousness,[1] that in the preobjectual-adirectional dimension is empty (despair) or full (satisfaction), while in the objectual one (first directional and then local, see *supra* 1.6) may also be condensed, arbitrarily or not, into objects: 'the feeling itself is an atmosphere, which does not extend itself afterwards from the centre through an irradiating effect, but is simply condensed in it, organising itself in a form or constellation that would surely collapse without the centre' (ibid: 322).

> Even atmospheres, which are feelings, may be visible in the manner of a nimbus or a halo in determined objects, for example optical or tactile ones, and be thus subordinated to the same categories of spatial ordering as those objects. I speak therefore of *objective* feelings. These feelings – for example, the bliss of an evening sky, the bright darkness of a thundercloud, the horror of the silent and gloomy house of the killer entered by the woman who married him – are possibly

---

[1] The heat of an oven, for example, 'assumes a certain configuration. It has a sort of voluminousness, it is as if there was a thermal cap in front of our face.' (Katz 1969: 183)

in a relationship of local spatiality with the objects, which are not feelings as such, but are, however, feelings among one another, in the relation with which they fill the sentimental space, because this is not in itself a local space. (ibid: 368)

Atmospheric feelings – as we have seen on many occasions – are certainly felt in the isles of the felt-body:[2] concerns strangle the throat, sadness weighs down the heart, the object of admiration almost cancels the space that separates us from it, the object of awe pushes us to withdraw and leave it an adequate space of manifestation, the vaults of a Gothic cathedral induce us to bow, to lower our eyes and in any case to silence, and so on. But the genetic direction of such feelings – this is the tentative leitmotif of our work – goes from the outside to the inside: 'distress, for example, is something huge for the distressed, facing which he feels completely limited and absolutely passive, something like a huge black cloud that surrounds him, like a weight that oppresses him with its enormous strength' (Schmitz 1967: 32), in short, a *caligo* devoid of a circumscribed source and of closely objectual conditions.[3] The fact that these feelings infect the felt-body, that one sinks in them and is filled, captured and overwhelmed by them, suggests that we attribute an external and semi-objective existence not to all feelings, but certainly to the atmospheric ones, which are spatial in a non-metaphorical sense.[4] It suggests that we claim that they are therefore 'not a state' and, what is more, an interior one. They should rather be regarded as 'an antagonist of the person who is hit by them' (Schmitz 1969: 144), on the basis of an anti-introjectionist thought experiment that might not completely revolutionize 'the face of the world [...] and the way in which man understands himself' (ibid: xiv), but that explains that feelings are (phenomenologically) neither something we have and we dispose

---

    2 'There are no organic sensations, but rather corporeal motions; not totally determining feeling in the felt-body, they mark autonomous corporeal isles, joined together simply by an approximate spatial and temporal correspondence with what happens in the physical body of a man, present to us from the optical and tactile point of view.' (Schmitz 1969: 167–168)

    3 Unlike the atmosphere of relaxation, which shall cease once you leave, for example, the bathtub (ibid: 273–274, 97–98).

    4 A metaphoric character that, besides, would invalidate the whole thesis (Soentgen 1998: 105–106).

of, nor accidental properties of things: one cannot, in fact, 'be ravished by mere accidents'! (ibid: 406).

We do not know whether the anti-pathic myth,[5] with all its pathological consequences – if for the healthy things immediately mean something, 'in the patient the meaning has to be brought in from elsewhere by a veritable act of interpretation' (Merleau-Ponty 2005: 153) – really started in Greece in the second half of the Fifth century BC, with the transition from the more archaic daemonic culture (lyrical poetry, tragedians, some pre-Socratic philosophers, the *Iliad*)[6] to the ethical and rational one (the *Odyssey*, Plato, but also Aeschylus and Sophocles). But if a story is to be told, it is certainly this one.[7] That is, the story of a double sin: one is projectivistic, according to which atmospheres are nothing but inner feelings projected onto the outside. The projectivistic error was in turn derived from an earlier introjectionist error that can be summarized in the internalisation (with an apotropaic function) of feelings that are first widespread in the outside world, and thus of the more archaic intuition 'that tried to order the world through meaningful impressions typed on the model of the powers that one can feel in the felt-body' (Schmitz 2002b: 65).

It is, in other words, the story of the oblivion (justified as a practical-theoretical-pedagogical emancipation through self- and hetero-control) of a more archaic worldview, in which the more intense feelings, often incardinated in polarized cosmogonies, occurred precisely as atmospheres or exogenous powers. So Ares, Aphrodite, Eros, Dionysus, Eris, *phobos, orge, thymos, phthonos, pothos*, but also ambition, sadness, silence, etc.[8]: all the forces men are almost exclusively the side effects of,[9] and whose aggression the felt-body isles[10] (especially the diaphragmatic

---

5 'In the end, the ancients were pathic in their way of thinking.' (Klages 1921: 287)

6 'The Greek conception of feelings, even before the birth of philosophy, crosses two phases of genius: one in which Homer characterizes *eros* and oppressing affliction (*achos*) as enveloping atmospheres, whoever is hit by which is gripped every time in the felt-body, and one in which the archaic lyric significantly sets being affectively touched by feelings against the feeling itself as a power that attacks from the outside.' (Schmitz 1969: 506)

7 For a wide neo-phenomenological reconstruction of the archaic (not only Greek) concept of body see Rappe (1995).

8 See Schmitz (1969: 409 ff.; 1989).

9 Even more so if it were true that phylo- and ontogenetically the 'you' is older than the 'I' (Klages 1968: 34–36).

10 From whose 'local diversity and quality [derive] the many names of the pseudo-organs of the soul.' (Schmitz 1965: 440)

region) act as a sounding board of. The *thymos*, for example, does not indicate (at least before the *Odyssey*) neither the inner side of the person nor a unitary psychic organ, but 'the autonomous partner and the generator of drives, the true engine of the person' (Schmitz 1965: 378) – possibly also in conflict with her, as when we feel its aggression on the chest isle. Similarly, the Homeric *noos* is the 'outbreak or type of the corporeal drive in the chest isle of the material-physical body' (ibid: 424), since 'to the poet of the *Iliad*, a thought that it is not felt in our felt-body, in the same way as hunger or thirst, still seems unknown' (ibid: 426). The same applies to the Stoic notion of *tonos*,[11] etc.

We find a rather different version already in the *Odyssey*,[12] in which the concealment of the multiple corporeal dimension following the discovery of the spirit and the soul[13] implies precisely the solidification of a dualism that, while segregating experiences in the (presumed) interiority of the psyche (the successor to *thymos*), degrades the corporeal dimension to the merely physical,[14] and, simultaneously, reduces perception to merely physiological sensibility. In this process, firstly not yet devoid of ambiguity[15] – and describable if you accept Klages' pathos as the 'sacrifice of the being-woven into the multiplicity of images and the inexhaustible fullness of life in favour of a stateless uprooted spirituality separated from the world' (Klages 1998: 55) – the almost total internalisation of feelings is accompanied by 'the consolidation of personal autonomy with respect to gripping powers' (Schmitz 1969: 413). In the illusion of being able to (ethically) resist feelings, of being able to manipulate them, settling almost judicially any possible conflict between soul and body, the subject in a way generates himself

---

11 'In the conception of the unit that holds the world together as a whole and in its individual things, in the form of a tonic happening, a feeling of life manifests itself that is powered by the projection in the overall nature of experiences felt on the level of the felt-body one has.' (Schmitz 1965: 502)

12 'Odysseus also tells of his expressive countenance in the first person singular, without there being something equivalent in the *Iliad*.' (Schmitz 1969: 416)

13 'For the existence of the intellect and the soul are dependent upon man's awareness of himself.' (Snell 1953: ix)

14 'This development, in the interest of the emancipation of the personal I from the diktat of involuntary impulses, leads to the invention of the soul, to the introjection of feelings in the soul, to psychosomatic dualism and to the negation of corporeality, which, in virtue of an apparent analysis, is divided in a misleading and alternate way into a psychic side and a physical-bodily side.' (Schmitz 1965: 365–366)

15 In the same context a feeling is sometimes described as a goddess and sometimes as a quality of the subject.

through a reductionist and introjectionist abstraction.[16] That is, segregating the experienced *into* a fictional psychic container that, like a fortress, should face objective feelings of atmospheric nature.

> The figure of the Homeric man, who was characterized as an open field of forces and through whom feelings blew as winds and who was abandoned to the game of gods, but fully self-aware and capable of decisions, contributed to shaping his own destiny – this image turned into that of the Platonic rational man dominating his impulses and feelings [...] The atmospheric, which acted so powerfully in the *Iliad*, was introduced into an inner world that until today has been at the service of the philosophical ideal of control. (Rappe 1995: 271)

This new course was obviously not devoid of setbacks,[17] since no one really gave up the whole idea of the felt-body as a battlefield of impersonal-daemonic forces (*pneuma*, spirit, holy or not, god and the devil, the flesh and the sin, etc.).[18] But it certainly became hegemonic, thus ensuring control, on the one hand, over an external world reduced to quantity and, on the other hand, over an internal world reduced to a subjective sentimentality[19] that – especially since (from Plato

---

16 After the aforesaid pivotal turning point, 'man is no longer exposed to feelings as a being endowed with a felt-body, upset, impressed and dragged by a suprapersonal force of unknown origin, because, as states of the soul, feelings, as well as thoughts and sensations, now are nothing but the material available for the elaboration made by the by now emancipated person.' (Schmitz 1965: 467)

17 We mention here the Aristotelian, Stoic, and finally proto-Christian monism, the identification (James) of feelings and bodily motions (in short, we are sad because we cry and not vice versa), but also the cosmogonic polarities whose model are those of the felt-body (expansion / contraction): from the Christian mystic to the kabbalah (God's creation being the expansion of the previously contracted divine felt-body), from Jacob Böhme to Oetinger – for a summary see Griffero (2006c) – up to the dynamic construction of matter (the pre-critical Kant), consciousness (Fichte) or totality (Schelling), and Maine de Biran's conception, neither only psychic nor only physical, of the felt-body .

18 For Paul, 'it is not the flesh that is the body, but it is we that are in the flesh', that is, in a 'power that lets sinful passions pour out in the physical body' (Schmitz 1965: 510–11). And, besides, Paul's 'unlimited corporeality of being intensely affectively involved is very archaic' (ibid: 525): 'You [...] are [...] in the spirit, if the spirit of God dwells in you.' (Romans 8, 9)

19 'The internal and concretely felt part of the physical felt-body is misinterpreted, through a linguistic metaphorisation, in terms of a fictitious inner psychic part, a realm of intimate interiority.' (Schmitz 1965: 451–452)

onwards) psychicness has been interpreted as a dialogue of the soul with itself – paradoxically plays all the roles in the comedy.[20] A psychic self-referentiality that is not at all contradicted by today's media exhibitionism of one's intimate life, by an 'emotional capitalism' that supplants the public sphere, ignores the manipulated character of what it claims to be authenticity and transforms emotions, including the atmospheric ones,[21] in 'entities to be evaluated, inspected, discussed, bargained, quantified and commodified' (Illouz 2007: 109), thus generating an emotional freeze that is not a corrective, but is the unexpected 'commercial' outcome of the introjectionist illusion.[22]

As we have already mentioned, this anti-projectivistic and anti-introjectionistic conception of atmospheric feelings owes much to Klages' thesis according to which 'a feeling [...] is not something that I possess, because, if anything, it is the feeling that possesses me' (Klages 1976: 349). Thus, 'instead of "I'm sad", it would be better to say "Sadness overwhelmed me"' (Klages 1979: 449), especially if we avoid the misleading Indo-Germanic tendency to 'deal with the kinds of events as with kinds of doing' (ibid: 488). But it also owes much to the realistic-phenomenological principle that 'the sensible gives back to me what I lent to it, but this is only what I took from it in the first place' (Merleau-Ponty 2005: 249), in other words, to the refusal of projective associationism.

> Empiricism excludes from perception the anger or the pain which I nevertheless read in a face [...] Mental life withdraws into isolated consciousness devoted solely to introspection [...] Perception thus impoverished becomes purely a matter of knowledge [...] If on the other hand we admit that all these 'projections', all these 'associations', all these 'transferences' are based on some intrinsic characteristic of the object, the 'human world' ceases to be a metaphor and becomes once more what it really is, the seat and as it were the homeland

---

20 In considering the psyche as a stage, the actor but also the audience of the play (dialogue), 'it is as if someone wanted to say, the room speaks in the room to the room.' (Schmitz 1969: 11)

21 'For a long time the media have been taking care of the atmospheric character of our aspirations and enacting certain atmospheres of global participation in certain types of reportage.' (Knodt 1994: 7)

22 'The emotional climax we seek is all in the "oh!" pronounced before the desired object in the window, or in the "oh!" of relief when we ensure that someone else handles our family duties.' (Hochschild 2003: 11)

of our thoughts. [...] I perceive the grief or the anger of the other in his conduct, in his face or his hands, without recourse to any 'inner' experience of suffering or anger, and because grief and anger are variations of belonging to the world, undivided between the body and consciousness, and equally applicable to the other's conduct, visible in his phenomenal body, as in my own conduct as it is presented to me. (ibid: 27–28, 415)

Now, the argument that feelings 'seize us in the form of a power that comes from the outside, grab us, attack us, and we are possessed by them' (Haensel 1946: 83), i.e. that they are not our projections – 'it is clear that after caging psychical facts somewhere deep within the I and after re-defining them *ad hoc*, we can also hypothesize a similar projection. But none of us lives, in reality, such an experience' (Minkowski 1936: 247) – is undoubtedly a radical and relatively counterintuitive option.[23] We recall it here, however, without being contented with explaining the atmospheric externality in social terms,[24] in order to strategically oppose, first of all, the ubiquity of the contrary prejudice. We also wish to oppose the purely positional, basically idealistic, externalisation proposed by Husserl, according to whom if it is true that when 'in perception I see a landscape and it makes me sad [...] I need not think of me: the landscape itself lies there and has a certain mood as a property' it is also true that 'objects thus have their characters by the virtue of the setting acts referring to them' (Husserl 1973: 476–477).

We also wish to develop Heidegger's masterful, albeit unfinished, thematisation of the affective tone as a mode of being-in-the world, in our own terms as an atmosphere in which we are immersed and that pervades us,[25] before we know or want something, and of which we can say, exactly as for truth, that it floats around without really taking shape.[26] In this sense atmospheric feelings are not only the

---

23 See Croome (2003: 202). But it is doubtful that we can dismiss this option simply because it is not in line with Husserl's scholasticism, as naïve in its moving from a pre-reflective 'feeling' and in making the felt-body into a crypto-Cartesian subject (thus Waldenfels 2000: 267–284).

24 Hauskeller, in fact, refers the objectual immanence of the expressive characters to their 'huge social invariance' and the contrast between personal feeling and perceived atmosphere to that between 'different levels of subjectivity', particularly between how I should feel something and how I really feel it (Hauskeller 1995: 29–30, 45–46).

25 For some ideas on this, see Griffero (2008).

26 Heidegger (2008: 181; 1995: 67).

relational form but rather real quasi-things, 'no more subjective than highways are, only less easy to fixate' (Schmitz 1969: 87; see also 1964: 144).

Mind you: though endorsing this atmospheric externalisation and excluding *a limine* the possibility of an intentional 'bridge' (correspondentist and antisolipsistic, which as such would necessarily presuppose dualism and the Cartesian extra-worldliness of consciousness) the aesthetics of atmospheres does not need to accept *in toto* Schmitz's view. Neither do we deem possible or desirable to regress to a pre-introjectionist form of life – we are allergic to the philosophies that deduce everything from ancestral mistakes and oblivions! – which we can blame, in fact, both for disregarding the rights of the psychic,[27] and for relieving the emotional life of responsibility.[28] It is enough to enhance the hypothesis that atmospheres are the focus of a corporeal communication between man and the world that is anterior to splits and abstractions, thus trying to rebalance, with an adequate phenomenology of corporeal feeling, an ontological strabismus from which descend indisputable techno-scientific and pedagogical advantages (perhaps even evolutionary), but also a phenomenologically unacceptable one-sidedness, not least the intentionalist hypertrophy of Husserl's orthodoxy or the reductionist privatization of the psyche, now further 'reduced' to the brain.[29]

But it is time to clarify the ontological and non-metaphorical *status* of atmospheres.

3.2 Atmospheres: Not Metaphors but Quasi-things

We have been saying this many times by now: atmospheres are feelings poured out into space. They are modes of a corporeal predualistic communication that at times is supersubjective and superobjective – the calm before the storm, the fever of the limelight, the numinous, the wind, etc. – and at times is more dependent on the subject, or condensed into (or anchored to) preferential objects. In any case,

---

[27] 'Introjection is not at all a false theory, it is rather the adequate description of a certain form of organization of the human being. As such introjection cannot be refuted, at most it can be overcome in the perspective that it represents a very limited mode of the human being.' (Böhme 2003: 50, fn. 13)
[28] Vendrell Ferran (2008: 164).
[29] See Schmitz (2002b: 7).

they are quasi-things whose ecstasies are expressive characters or qualities, and whose extraneousness to the thingly dimension and to the predicative structure often leads to misleading metaphorical projectivist explanations – which, besides, are invalidated by the simple observation that with the elimination of the perceived (and precisely of *that* perceived) the atmospheric feeling disappears as such.

Freely borrowing Geiger's lexicon, we could define the atmospheres of the objectual lived experiences (or of 'sentimental character') as immanent: 'every object shows its own character precisely because it is this object. The knife we use to cut, the dress we wear are surrounded by a halo that only regards them and no other objects' (Geiger 2000: 172). Thus the following sophisticated (almost Fichtian) projectivist theory, according to which the perceived atmosphere is nothing more than the recoil of a previous emotional and unconscious projection, is rejected.

> The content of the sentimental disposition is even made immanent to the content of perception by means of an unconscious psychic activity. The content of feeling *seems* to come out of what is perceived [...] Only the result of this causal act of empathy presents itself to consciousness [...] But how does it happen that this sentimental expression is not felt by the contemplating subject as arising from the self [?] He skips, so to speak, his own I and makes the contemplated object offer him the feeling of his own product. (Volkelt 1927: 241–243; my emphasis)

Köhler's position is even more ambiguous, since for him the interest as a vector is 'what we really find. The vector is issuing there now phenomenally, it actually belongs to the object in question, just as before it putatively belonged to the self [although] in the phenomenal world demands often issue from objects really, *whatever previous history may be responsible for it*' (Köhler 1938, 93, my emphasis). The conclusion he draws is that 'qualities belong where we find them. And no explanation or theory can convince us that they were not where we found them' (ibid: 82). A conclusion that, while not being particularly consistent with the premise, converges with our commitment to conceive of atmospheres as external qualities that are irreducible to metaphors (i.e. externalised feelings). Once we admit that feelings are not necessarily and primarily internal states, besides, there is not even the transcendental condition (somatophobic dualism) of each metaphorisation, i.e. the distinction between the proper (literal) and the improper (figurative). The obviously not gravitational lightness of a bridge, the vitreous levity of a building, and even the common seductiveness both of a skilled adulator and of a sparkling morning spring (with a kind of sedative sweetness in both cases), etc., are therefore not at all projections of unextended and very private psychic states, just as the bright and the sharp, the dark and the strident, the rugged and massive, the heavy and the light, the hard and the soft are not metaphorical but corporeal atmospheric affections.

a) For example the empty atmosphere, in its allusion to a not axiologically nihilistic depersonalization, is not metaphorical:

> the mode of existence of the depersonalized *presents itself* as empty because it *is* empty. In these so-called images we do not have a mere transfer from the ontological sphere of the physical or the spatial to the psycho-spiritual sphere, hence not a metaphor in the true sense of the term, because the vacuum whose place is the ontological sphere of the body is identified in its general direction of meaning with the 'empty heart' or with the 'spiritual vacuum'. (Gebsattel 1937: 253)

This atmosphere thus indicates the failure to fill the space that we corporeally feel as a sensation of sinking[30] and that, as an emotional decentralization, can also deposit itself on individual objects emptying them of meaning.

b) Not even the atmospheric feelings we call superficial or deep are metaphorical. In fact they are such because this quasi-spatial determination is wholly immanent to them: we feel with the utmost precision, for example, that admiration is less deep than reverence and that aversion is less deep than despair.

c) A sad atmosphere breaks one down, that of shame leads to lower one's gaze and to contraction, that of hope raises, that of pain crushes, the euphoric one makes

---

30 'The representation of an endless fall into the abyss is particularly suitable to the empty feeling, because this atmosphere is diffused into the open space, yet without implying any compact and stable mass that can cushion a movement in this open space.' (Schmitz 1969: 228)

one jump for joy, i.e. it induces a levity that is not metaphorical for the mere fact that it is not quantitatively and metrically verifiable.[31] In all these cases we have corporeal correlates with outcomes that can be physical and paragravitational, quasi-objective and predimensional atmospheric feelings we have (i.e. we do not measure) 'in' us, but that do not come 'from' us. In short, 'he broke down' seems to be the fine corporeal description of a hopeless and resigned atmosphere rather than a metaphor, given that 'we remain physically upright not through the mechanism of the skeleton or even through the nervous regulation of muscular tone, but because we are caught up in a world. If this involvement is seriously weakened, the body collapses and becomes once more an object' (Merleau-Ponty 2005: 296, n. 18). Similarly, pride isomorphically involves the kinaesthetic fact that 'by straightening our backbones, we produce a muscular sensation akin to the attitude of pride, and thus introduce into our state of mind a noticeable element of bold self-sufficiency' (Arnheim 1966: 68).

d) The atmosphere of brightness, for instance, is not metaphorical either. While not being identifiable with the amount of solar irradiation,[32] it is a synaesthetic phenomenal quality – that is, it is given by optical, auditory, olfactive, climatic, corporeal, and also retentional and protentional, impressions – and we could possibly describe it as the opening of space to the free expansion of the felt-body.

e) This applies even more to silence. Precisely like noise, it signals a change in the external world and acts in an even more immediate, invasive and threatening way – being its source and vanishing point impossible to localise – than the visual impression,[33] and therefore it is far from being a mere privation.[34] In fact, it is normal to say 'there is such silence in here!' or 'a heavy silence fell' or even a 'deafening

---

31 Schmitz (1966: 31–32; 1969: 114–120).
32 The morning and a cool summer night are 'felt' as even brighter, respectively, both of midday and of the oppressive heat of a summer noon (Straus 1956: 223).
33 It is 'noise itself that turns the eyes of the listener. The agent in the proper sense is the noise and not the one who hears it.' (Hauskeller 1995: 111)
34 An intense silence, for instance, features 'synaesthetics characters (massive properties: size, weight, density) and, settled upon them, a powerful emotional atmosphere. It is not absence of sound pure and simple, but rather something that establishes with sound a varied relationship, but full of tension: in part as its opposite, and in part more intensely as the depth, ground or level from which the sound rises.' (Schmitz 1978: 229)

silence' that one could 'cut with a knife', and so on.[35] Be it serious, solemn, festive, oppressive,[36] threatening, more eloquent than many words (this concerns in particular the social dimension), or protective with respect to worldly cares (meditation, monastic atmosphere, a countryside dawn, etc.), silence always exists as expressively and situationally qualified in the motor corporeal suggestions.[37] In any case, in way that is far from being subjective and metaphorical.

f) Finally, when say we are suffocating it is certainly because the atmosphere is stuffy, but in most cases we refer not to the air in the physical sense, but rather to an indivisible and enveloping volumetric predimensional space, as far from being interior as the air or the heavy atmosphere preceding the storm, namely that 'something disturbing which is "in the air" in a unspecified width, that is skin-deep and yet boundless' (Schmitz 1967: 48).

In short, if 'the manner in which the perceiver feels corporeally affected corresponds at all times to the way in which the world presents itself to him' (Hauskeller, 1995: 82), then the metaphorical interpretation of the atmosphere turns out to be an unacceptable reductionist shortcut, incapable of understanding how it is possible that a primary and pre-epistemological language (the mother tongue) may achieve a realistic and intuitive description of the outside world. Such a language is undoubtedly concrete, but not metaphorical, if only because something that does not have a parallel literal sphere cannot be said to be metaphorical. Minkowski (1936: 81, 85–86) puts it well: 'is the bitterness of feeling less bitter than the bitterness of quinine? Nothing proves it. It is nothing but a preconceived idea [...] The bitterness is always the same [...] In both cases we stick to the letter.'

---

35 'If it would be absurd to want to smell the absence of odour, silence can be heard, as it is an acoustic phenomenon as corpulent as sound, which silence is able to meet and exceed by degree of intrusiveness.' (Schmitz 1969: 203)
36 'Understanding silence, hostile silence, benevolent silence, offensive silence or "eloquent" silence.' (Minkowski 1936: 175)
37 'Silence itself is sometimes presented as a feeling, which, due to its width, weight and density, has a spatial and material nature and [...] constitutes the from-where of a rapture' (Schmitz 1969: 208). See Minssen (2004: 201).

3.3 Sinaesthesias

Unmetaphorising the polymodal atmospheric character (sharp noises, bright sounds, sweet events and cool colours, etc.) obviously implies taking its synaesthetic nature seriously.[38] The atmospheric coldness of an environment – due to the type of furniture or sound quality, the colour of the walls[39] or the temperature, the unlived order, the placement of the lights, the sound of the voice of those who are there and so on – is thus not explainable only by means of the lexicalization of the metaphor. It is as intersubjectively effective, at least intraculturally, as social prestige is, being 'the secondary, ideological, level of reality' (Kreckel 1992: 90). It expresses an emotional and corporeal involvement, which cannot be traced to discrete cause-stimuli nor to the merging of the five specific senses, nor to the addition of an extra sense, nor even to an extrinsic faculty of association – why then would the latter weaken with age and civilization, and therefore precisely with the increasing of (even associative) experience?[40] – but it denotes the 'possibility of a significance that [gives itself] immediately on the sense level' (Hauskeller, 1995: 69). A sound can then be defined velvety, grinding, voluminous, earthy, cavernous, amber, polished, etc., in a way that is no more improper than calling it high or low (in which case one is still moving from space to sound),[41] in the light of an atmospheric synaestheticity that is so little arbitrary[42] that it can even be generated artificially.

---

38 Namely the 'spontaneous connection of two or more heterogeneous sensible qualities, regardless of the fact that these sensible qualities give themselves perceptually or in the representation.' (Werner 1966: 278)

39 As the choice of colours is 'not so much a question of blue and green as one of hot and cold.' (Baudrillard 2005: 35)

40 Werner (1966: 286); Böhme (1995: 92); Hauskeller (1995: 67).

41 Only in strictly objectual thought having 'a "heavy heart" does not establish any link between the body weight and the person's mood, and talking about "hot" colours does not establish a link between optical and thermal properties either, nor does the distinction between "high" and "low" tones connect the sound-thing with the dimensions of space' (Klages 1929–32: 385). For symbolic thought 'thus a high sound is not high only as a manner of speaking, but it really is so; as well as a harsh noise is really harsh, a hot colour is really hot, a sharp smell is really sharp.' (Klages 1921: 251–252)

42 'Let us talk about grave sounds [...] The "gravity" presents itself as a "value of gravity", therefore as an index of a synthetic direction of the imagination. In it, not only weight but also, for example, slowness, opacity, thickness are put into question; the idea of

It is in this spirit that, for Goethe, colour is not limited to evoking the moral element (the state of mind), but it directly refers to the moral element. Blue, for instance, is 'powerful [and] gives us an impression of cold. [...] The appearance of objects seen through a blue glass is gloomy and melancholy'. (Goethe 1840, §§ 758, 778–785). It therefore expresses emptiness and sadness[43] because it is precisely in this way that it acts on the felt-body. In fact, being 'that which prompts me to look in a certain way, that which allows my gaze to run over it in a specific manner', that is to say 'a certain field or atmosphere presented to the power of my eyes and of my whole body' (Merleau-Ponty 2005: 244), blue conveys a corporeal freshness, if not coldness, with even physiological (e.g. circulatory) consequences.

Obviously, the atmosphere of a colour[44] also derives from social-symbolic characters ('white-collar', 'white telephone films' etc.), as well as from the specific relationship it has with the shape of the thing, and even when it is only its casing: in the case of coffee, for example, 'the colour of the pack [...] develops expectations on the aroma of the content of the package itself and [...] these expectations, all other things equal, will affect the real taste of the food' (Dichter 1964: 392). The least that can be said, then, is that the atmospheric impressions suggested by colour choices – familiarity and conviviality, objectivity and sobriety, cheerfulness and coldness, authority and oppression, stimulus for consumption or meditation, etc. – far from being intellectual syntheses of associative processes, or performances of a higher (common) sense in which converge the others (with which the unresolved problem of mediation would arise again, taking place now among the other senses and this sixth sense), or arbitrary sensory trespassings, they are rather sensible qualities and meanings immanent to the object.

A discourse on synaesthesias might, and perhaps should, of course, be far more accurate.[45] We will just note here that, if 'feelings and evaluations, sympathy and antipathy, combinations, etc.' appear 'in the object, in the form of an objective

---

something massive, voluminous, possibly deep, and perhaps even obscure and dark.' (Piana 1979: 157)

43 Colours are 'energies that act upon us in a positive or negative way, whether we know it or not.' (Itten 1961: 16)

44   See Hauskeller (1995: 123–145).

45   We could talk about secondary synaesthesias (interference of two colours), submodal ones (interference of colour and form in the optical field), abstract ones ('the smell of sadness' for example), and so on (see Hauskeller 1995: 56). See also Mazzeo (2005).

precipitate' (Anschütz 1929: 14), it is because synaestheticity is an originary psychological phenomenon,[46] deeper and even more regular than ordinary perception.[47]

> Synaesthetic perception is the rule, and we are unaware of it only because scientific knowledge shifts the centre of gravity of experience, so that we have unlearned how to see, hear, and generally speaking, feel, in order to deduce, from our bodily organization and the world as the physicist conceives it, what we are to see, hear and feel. [...] One sees the hardness and brittleness of glass [...] One sees the springiness of steel, the ductility of red-hot steel, the hardness of a plane blade, the softness of shavings [...] The form of a fold in linen or cotton shows us the resilience or dryness of the fibre, the coldness or warmth of the material. [...] In the jerk of the twig from which a bird has just flown, we read its flexibility or elasticity [...] The form of objects is not their geometrical shape: it stands in a certain relation to their specific nature, and appeals to all our other senses as well as sight. (Merleau-Ponty 2005: 266–267)

In the very common activity of haptically seeing, for example, 'how honey sticks to everything it comes into contact with' (Schapp 2004: 16), the roughness or smoothness of things or the sweetness or sourness of things (of a fabric, for instance), we usually find a general tactile voyeurism, according to which 'even our taste, smell and touch have "eyes", just as, conversely, the eye can certainly touch as well' (Klages 1929–32: 192).[48] Just as it is thanks to their sound that we see the content of a container (if shaken) and the nature of a road (if taken),[49] so it is also thanks to the tactile quality of a food and a fabric that they exhibit their qualities. That is not surprising, given the ontological function of touch. There is,

---

46 See Wellek (1931).

47 'The stimuli of the *Umwelt* reach the consciousness not in the form of perceptions of objects, but in that of feelings conforming to expressions that fill the ego. In this layer it actually happens that sounds and colours are much more felt than perceived.' (Werner 1966: 297)

48 'The eye becomes a hand savouring the smooth and the soft, disconcerting for a sudden roughness, for an unexpected corner and then again calming down its anxiousness in the polished, only to rediscover around the corner the uncertain shadow and see, only by lifting up its gaze, an unexpected new reflection.' (Mazzocut-Mis 2002: 14)

49 See Klages (1929–32: 192); Schapp (2004: 28).

in fact, 'something tactile in every perception, since what distinguishes perception from other mental faculties, such as thought, abstraction or imagination, is the very fact that it makes us "touch the ground"; it makes us "touch" what in the world is substantial and perceptible [...] Touch [...] determines the mode of being of all that is' (Minkowski, 1936: 179–180).

Is the atmosphere masterfully described by Zola in *The Belly of Paris* not a synaesthetic atmosphere of fat?

> In spite of the excessive cleanliness, fat oozed everywhere; it sweated between the tiles, glistened on the red surface of the floor, put a greyish sheen on the stove, and gave a varnished appearance to the edges of the chopping block. In the midst of the ever-rising steam, the continuous evaporation from the three big pots, in which pork was boiling and melting, there was not a single nail from floor to ceiling that was not dripping with grease. (Zola 2007: 78)

In this direction, once again Husserl cannot be helpful. His distrust towards the actual perceptibility of tertiary polysensorial qualities[50] is at least in part comparable to that shown by physicalists, for whom, ironically,

> how should there be any power in lightning and in thunder? How any tenderness in a spring day? [...] There are no such things in nature. To be sure, properly speaking there are no such things even in human perception; people are foolish and cannot resist the temptation to project upon their wholly indifferent environment what is so clearly nothing but their own emotional reaction to such neutral percepts. (Köhler 1938: 14)

On the contrary, escaping the predictable objection of a pathetic fallacy (Gombrich), atmospheres turn out to be similar, also in their synaesthetic nature,

---

50 'The smoothness we see in paper, or the roughness we see in the file is not a properly perceived smoothness or roughness. Yet we do indeed see them, on the visually appearing thing (more precisely, in its properly appearing front side) [...] The roughness seen [...] is in a certain sense there in the proper appearance, but yet it is only detected, almost as if seen and yet not seen.' (Husserl 1998: 62)

to characters, expressive or tertiary qualities and lived essences;[51] in fact, they are so immanent to the experienced facts that they constitute a 'reality independent of conscience' (Klages 1929–32: 385) and certainly not projectively externalised ingredients.[52] Even when what expresses an atmospheric-synaesthetic halo are simply names,[53] maybe of places.

> But names present to us – of persons and of towns which they accustom us to regard as individual, as unique, like persons – a confused picture, which draws from the names, from the brightness or darkness of their sound, the colour in which it is uniformly painted, like one of those posters, entirely blue or entirely red, in which, on account of the limitations imposed by the process used in their reproduction, or by a whim on the designer's part, are blue or red not only the sky and the sea, but the ships and the church and the people in the streets. The name of Parma, one of the towns that I most longed to visit, after reading the *Chartreuse*, seeming to me compact and glossy, violet-tinted, soft, if anyone were to speak of such or such a house in Parma, in which I should be lodged, he would give me the pleasure of thinking that I was to inhabit a dwelling that was compact and glossy, violet-tinted, soft, and that bore no relation to the houses in any other town in Italy, since I could imagine it only by the aid of that heavy syllable of the name of Parma, in which no breath of air stirred, and of all that I had made it assume of Stendhalian sweetness and the reflected hue of violets. (Proust 2010: 467)

---

51 'That same red, with which in the previous formulation the being-hot is expressed, is not the objective red but the appearance of an essence.' (Klages 1929–32: 388)

52 'The ancients knew the genius loci, the nimbus, the aura, and we still talk ourselves of the "atmosphere" of a person, a house, a place. Now, this "atmosphere" – which so-called sensitive natures capture and the refined ones feel, while remaining unknown to more robust minds – is a reality that acts, by giving and increasing or by absorbing and weakening, by wrapping up and heating or by digging and cooling down, by soliciting and exciting or by braking and damping down, by expanding or compressing, by encouraging or paralysing, and its action is essentially different from the touching of bodies.' (Klages 1929–32: 1103)

53 See the rather imaginative phonetic analysis proposed by Jünger, according to whom, for example, 'A is verticality and width, O is height and depth, E is emptiness and sublimity' etc. (Jünger 1997: 79).

To make another example, 'The word "hard" produces a sort of stiffening of the back and neck, and only in a secondary way does it project itself into the visual or auditory field and assume the appearance of a sign or a word. [...] Words have a physiognomy because we adopt towards them, as towards each person, a certain form of behaviour which makes its complete appearance the moment each word is given' (Merleau-Ponty 2005: 273–274). This is doubtlessly a consideration endowed with a polymodal validity.

> The vital freedom that we have in our relationship with the world can be constrained or unconstrained [...] by the different senses. Brightness and spaciousness with it, the cool and the lively, the allegro in the musical sense, the gay: all of them release us from constrains. Vivid smells are fleeting, brightness increases with slipperiness and thinning. The filthy, however, persecuting us and remaining stubbornly stuck on us, restricts our freedom of life. A spring wind brings to us with its blow the whole vastness of the world. A violent storm that roars above us and crashes us to the ground does not have the breadth and brightness of the delicate blow. (Straus 1956: 223)

In short, to feel the atmospheric always means to co-perceive (precategorically, synaesthetically, kinaesthetically) our affective corporeal situation and to ascertain how we feel in a certain place, through a bilateral perception that has nothing metaphorical about it: 'on the one hand, [there is] the environment that irradiates a qualitatively specific mood, on the other hand [there is] me, who, by feeling a certain way, participate in this mood and realize that I am here now' (Böhme 1995: 96). If they were metaphors, atmospheres would thus be as much external and conceptually ineffable as 'absolute' metaphors are:[54] similarly to the latter, they pathically possess us – 'reality can only be endured!' (Klages 1929–32: 861)[55] –

---

54 Which are in correspondence with those 'supposedly naïve, in principle unanswerable questions whose relevance lies quite simply in the fact that they cannot be brushed aside, since we do not *pose* them ourselves but find them already *posed* in the ground of our existence.' (Blumenberg 2010: 14)

55 'An emotion, whatever it is, is not owned by me, but owns me [...] I cannot command the emotion to come and stay, or to fade away' (Klages 1976: 349). And 'emotions are all the wealth of men, but the poverty of the gods.' (Klages 1944: 286)

more than we possess them. A given space enlarges our heart, but – let us restate it – this happens kinaesthetically and not metaphorically:

> we experience the feeling of a general extension [...] when, entering a forest of tall trees or unexpectedly walking into a beautiful room, we breathe freely. Without wanting to, we expand the thorax and increase in size, as if we wanted to adapt to the immensity of the environment and prove to measure up to it. By dilating and expanding in this way, we make a vital experience of conquest of space and power extension. (Strehle 1954: 45)

3.4 'All Out': Atmospheric Ontology

Without further exploring the generating characters of atmospheres,[56] it is now time to explain how and to what extent man capitulates before atmospheres as quasi-things.

a. *Atmospheres appear and disappear, but we cannot sensibly ask ourselves where they have gone and how they have existed in the meantime.*[57] While being legitimate about two temporally different appearances of one thing, this question is absurd, although highly instructive, with regard to atmospheric[58] and climatic intermittency (what does the wind do when it stops blowing and where was it before it blew?). Similarly, it makes no sense to wonder what happened before or after the events narrated in an imaginative sequence, such as a fairy tale, or to ask ourselves what a bistable figure 'really' is, since it is a form that changes with its material elements being the same. This issue, though tainted by a thingly ontology

---

56 I refer to the excellent analysis by Gernot Böhme (2001): a) social characteristics (power, elegance, etc..), b) synaesthesias (hot, cold, rough, etc..), c) moods (happy or sad scenes, etc..), d) communicational characteristics (facial expressions, gestures, physiognomy) d) motor affordances (kinaesthetic architectural, plastic and broadly formal suggestions).
57 See Schmitz (1990: 216; 1998: 188).
58 Provided that we do not rigidly identify (see Spinicci 2008: 184) the real experience with evenemential continuism.

that is perhaps evolutionarily conditioned,[59] appears hard to overestimate. Not least because it focuses on a promising affinity between atmosphere and other ontologically heterodox dimensions – for example, the spirit that (in the Christian view) blows where and when it wants – implying a phenomenal disappearance that has little in common with the trivial perspective blockage of this or that side of the object.

b.   *Atmospheres do not act as the causes of the influence, but are the influence itself.* Eschewing the traditional separation between noun (cause) and verb (effect), they are events in which action and effect coincide. The fact that they are neither the external manifestation of something interior nor a trace of something other than oneself[60] undermines any approach based on an etiological and distancing 'why': it is somewhat artificial to trace the atmosphere of wind back to a cause-substrate (the air moved), since, when it attacks us, it is rather an influence experienced in the felt-body (as well as in the physical).

c.   *Atmospheres are not the property of some object, but, as quasi-things, they coincide with their own phenomenic character,*[61] which also consists of unpredictable aggregations of objects. Twilight, for example,

> cannot be listed among things. However, it belongs to the intuitive image of a flag fluttering in the twilight, but the fluttering flag is also part of the intuitive image of the twilight in question! [...] The manifestation of the flag would no longer be what it is without the fluttering, the fluttering would not be the same without the flag, the fluttering flag would not be it without the twilight, and the

---

59   It is natural for superior hunting animals to be interested in 'things', that is 'in stable supports of meaning that one can also search for once they have disappeared from the field of perception.' (Spranger 1944: 237)

60   'In the midst of a hurricane, the idea of "trace" does not yet come to our mind. At that moment, the noise of the uprooted trees and the sinister creaking of the roof of a house are mixed with the hurricane [...] And it is only later, after the storm, that we will find, on the threshold of the house, the desolate landscape.' (Minkowski 1936: 224)

61   'Quasi-things are absorbed in their manifestation, in the sense that they are bound to their character; and blowing is part of the character of the wind, talking is part of that of the voice. Conversely, things have learned, so to speak, to be above their character: they may change it.' (Schmitz 1978: 147)

twilight would not be the same without the fluttering of the flag [...] The unity of meaning we call 'flag fluttering in the twilight' forms an intuitive totality that could not be made up of the significant content of the twilight, the fluttering and the flag, just as it could not be broken down into these three or any other number of 'properties'. (Klages 1929–32: 177)

In spite of the traditional ontological thingness – modelled upon enclosed beings carrying accidental, although relatively constant, properties – atmospheres at the very most condense into objects, whose contours, however, are no less nuanced than those of tasting compared to attentive seeing. They are *qualia* that are not possessed by situations, but that show themselves through and coincide with situations, possibly also expressive abstractions – in the sense of the noticeable affinity, for example, between all that, for various reasons, 'shines' – that are liable to become pathological only when they are exclusive, as in the case of extrapersonal voices which the hallucinated feels attacked by.

d. *Atmospheres are an 'in-between', made possible by the (corporeal but also social and symbolic) co-presence of subject and object.* So far we have insisted on the extra-subjective existence of the atmospheric. Which, however, exists – in the sense of being perceived – only for a perceiver, of course, thus situating itself 'at the threshold between biography and world of facts, things and situations', in 'an imaginary "in-between" that extends from the object to the observer and, vice versa, from the observer to the object' (Hasse 1994: 58, 81). The atmospheric thus exists 'between' the object, or rather the environmental *qualia*, and the subject, or rather his felt-body. Nevertheless, the 'in-between' – the assumption of inter-corporeal communication – is not reified to the point of counting as 'a third element which, as a membrane, is interposed between the two margins' (Schmitz 2002b: 71): this would lead to the strengthening of the dualism that we are willing to avoid. In a holistic joyful atmosphere, the joy is not so much my joy, but rather a joyous situation, in which the subject and the object are not independent and isolable parts.

Atmospheres also represent a challenge to classical ontology in this respect. While such ontology allows for relations only as by-products of related substances,[62] an aesthetics of atmospheres aims at recognising in relations the same autonomy that it is not difficult to see in the Japanese mindset. Whether it is the *ma*, namely the necessary symbolic and spiritual interval between things (but also the place together with the subjective way one experiences it),[63] or the *engawa*, i.e. the veranda as an element that is both outside and inside the house (because it has a cover); whether it is the *ki* – i.e. the soul or breath in the air that grabs the bystanders,[64] namely an 'elementary atmospheric contact' (Tellenbach 1968: 58) that makes it possible both to feel at home in a certain situation and to experience immediate hetero-understanding[65] – or the interpersonal *aïda*, which is not a relationship between separate lives, but the originary common place which self and otherness derive from; or, again, the *keshiki* as a cosmological atmosphere and landscape space:[66] well, all of those, in any case, are always notions that (indicating a fundamental dimension precisely because it is antidualistic and ephemeral)[67] are very similar to that of atmosphere. It is not surprising, therefore, that Oriental painting has such a strong interest in atmospheric elements, the psycho-climatic nuances that dematerialise the physical landscape.[68]

> It is not the depth of the mountains and valleys that the Chinese have painted, but the life of the air and the weather surrounding mountains and valleys, the twilight of the evening and the shadows of the morning, the intertwine of the seasons, indicating in all these things the breath, the heart and the heartbeat of the mountain [...] Before the senses of the Chinese, images of a surface hover one after the other, and, opened up between them, waves the unlimited atmosphere

---

62 For a critical look on the ontology of relations see Böhme (2001: 54–55) and Schmitz (2005a: 33–50).

63 'In the West, man perceives the objects but not the spaces between. In Japan, the spaces are perceived, named, and revered as the ma, or intervening interval.' (Hall 1966: 75). See Janson (2005: 161, fn. 18 with bibl.)

64 See Kimura (1992), Böhme (2006a: 37).

65 We could probably 'translate' the opposition between the physical body and felt-body into that between the tangible manifestation (cosmic-vital) of the *ki* and its invisible manifestation (desires and states of consciousness) (Linck 2005: 122).

66 Sasaki (2006).

67 On the aesthetics of the ephemeral, see Böhme (1989: 166–189). For an analysis of Böhme's *anima naturaliter japonica*, see Müller (1998).

68 Lehmann (1986: 226).

(*Atmosphäre*); indeed from this atmosphere, as from a mother's womb or the boundless sphere of dreams, come and alternate images which then fall back into it. This atmosphere, not perceptible in itself and therefore exclusively virtual, is the real space of the Chinese landscape, and its peculiar dimension is not the depth we experience during a movement, based on our feeling of the place and of the physical body. (Fischer 1943: 140, 142)

Attentive more to the predimensional atmosphere than to the directional and local one, the Oriental painter is therefore eminently atmospheric, sometimes even in representing a single object (a branch, a rock), to the extent that he 'forces us to feel with him the atmospheric space' (Lehmann 1986: 138).

e. *Unlike other phenomena considered invariable by naïve physics, atmospheres are relatively (perceptually) amendable, i.e. they are cognitively penetrable, if only on the level of common sense.* It is ordinary experience that the atmospheric perception could mutate even in the absence of a change in the physical elements that generate it. When we discover, for example, that we have mistakenly interpreted an atmosphere of tension as an atmosphere of tacit euphoria, all its expressive qualities change sign. This also happens when a prosaic noise in the church contradicts the religious atmosphere,[69] when death gives to a past atmosphere of happiness a melancholic tone, when knowing that in other cultures black means joy makes it (*contra* Wertheimer) immediately a little less atmospherically lugubrious and when a (however slight) alteration of the provisional optimal condition to which we owe the atmosphere alters its expressive quality. The appearance of a doubt – due to the discrepancy between the different sensory channels, the temporal change, an additional knowledge or the undesired re-emergence of the objectual base – thus always involves a revision, or at least a local one, of the first atmospheric impression, generating at times an atmosphere of a different, even opposite, sign; at times, with the loss of the organic nature of the perceived, an atmosphere whose charge is perhaps so weak that it is not even detectable. Still, the constitutional atmospheric vagueness is epistemically unamendable: I might say that 'I see' the stick unbroken in the water (if I resorted

---

69 For a literary example, see Tellenbach (1968: 77 ff.).

to the factive scope of verb 'to see'), but it would not be possible to ever feel the atmosphere differently from the way I feel it here and now.

f.   There is no entity without identity. Right. Then, *if atmospheres are quasi-things, they must have some kind of identity*. This is proved by the fact that, in a way, one can be mistaken both in perceiving them and in producing them. Would it not be frankly wrong, to make a few examples, to try and arouse an atmosphere of cheerfulness in a foggy, damp and ghostly lake sunset, or to create an atmosphere of seductive gluttony by giving a pastry shop too cold and hygienic a look?[70] There are also atmospheres that are so identical that they remain perfectly recognisable as a memory trace: it is the case of the specific synaesthetic maternal atmosphere, in which as it were lies the essence of one's mother, and which results into a pre-reflective state of trust in others that, like a 'protective aura' (Tellenbach 1968: 154), is an indispensable prerequisite of a successful education to adulthood.[71]

g.   *Atmospheres never exist, if not in a very inappropriate way, as purely potential states.*[72] The thesis, entirely consistent with a healthy 'phenomenological positivism which bases the possible on the real' (Merleau-Ponty 2005: xix), must be at least differentiated. At first glance, in fact, it sounds improper to speak of an oppressive atmosphere that does not oppress anyone here and now.[73] This suggests that atmospheres are pure phenomena (or acts), whose existence only coincides with their appearance,[74] unlike properties that exist even if they are only thinkable. Knowing that a square has certain geometric properties is independent of our perception of it *hic et nunc,* whereas perceiving atmospheres means experiencing

---

70   Only a furniture rich in warm tones seems to 'convey a sense of indulgence to people, making them feel that to indulge in something sweet is perfectly legitimate', and it therefore is not 'contradictory to the olfactory, gustatory, sensory enticement and seduction which the candy displays should have achieved.' (Dichter 1964: 390, 429)

71   'The lack of a clear and unambiguous atmosphere does not allow for the development of a climate of confidence in which the child could develop a sure flair for the behaviour of others towards him.' (Tellenbach 1968: 97)

72   See especially Böhme (2001).

73   Hauskeller (1995: 14); Ströker (1977: 53).

74   In the sense in which, for Merleau-Ponty (2005: 338), in the mythical and childish world (which for him is pathological!), 'every "apparition" (*Erscheinung*) is [...] an incarnation, and each entity is defined not so much in terms of "properties" as of physiognomic characteristics.'

phenomena behind which one should not look for any cause,[75] and in respect of which the only permitted dimension of possibility belongs, if anything, to the content (in the sense that there is undoubtedly an atmosphere of broken dreams).[76]

But all this only holds for the perceived atmosphere: not for its retentional and protentional context, and even less for the processes that generate it. Firstly, in fact, the atmospheric in act undoubtedly also depends on the co-perception of past and / or expected atmospheres that are not in act, such as when, for example, the atmosphere of a hospital is tense precisely because we anticipate the situation to follow (the visit, the diagnosis, etc..) and we remember earlier ones (further waits, etc..). Secondly – and on this point we shall linger a bit – the atmospheric in act may also be the result of a design so hypothetical that it justifies the fact that we can counterfactually reason about it. Returning to the example of the hospital, we can certainly imagine the conditions under which its atmosphere could be less tense (with positive effects on convalescence if not even on complete recovery): if, for example, the structure of the building were focused not on the technical equipment but on people, stimulating their socialisation but not at the expense of privacy; if the aspects of medicalisation were reduced to the minimum to the benefit of the family nature of the environments. To go into detail,[77] there should be more sunlight and fresh air, an adequate air conditioning and a lower presence of disturbing smells (medicines and disinfectants), a greater space between the beds and consequently more privacy, less cold materials than plastic and metal, pleasant views and green areas, not centralised lighting (which is anonymous and aesthetically cruel) focused on limited spaces and objects, warm colours and services (newsagents, bars) that avoid the impression of segregation, and so on.

A reflection upon the potential atmospheric character is decisive even in intensive care units, where the atmosphere, normally not suited to the patients' needs and yet felt on the skin by them, could improve the quality of the hospital

---

75 'The voice [...] is not "behind" its manifestation, just as the fire is not behind its burning or a man looking is not behind his gaze: it resolves into it, like the wind does in blowing. Just as one cannot ask the corresponding question with respect to the wind, so one cannot ask, with respect to the voice, what it does when it does not resonate.' (Schmitz 1978: 120)

76 Only in this way does it make sense to state that 'atmosphere is a sensuously and affectionally perceptible (and, in this respect, existentially significant) articulation of realized or *nonrealized* life possibilities.' (Seel 2005: 92; our emphasis)

77 See Bonaiuto *et al.* (2004: 55 ff.)

stay, if it were different. While maintaining the unavoidable conditions for such departments – technological coldness, perennial lighting, absolute sterilisation and isolation, constant sense of alarm, attention to the merely physical body[78] – would it be really impossible, allowing for a certain variability of responses,[79] to create a more positive atmosphere? One could still offer these special patients a view of green spaces, order the staff to speak softly, move slowly and convey serenity to the patients (through looks, gestures, etc.), design spaces devoid of unwanted sounds and noises, choose positive and harmonious colours for the walls and furniture, etc.. Therefore, all the atmospheres which the aesthetic work applies to are ultimately almost entirely potential.

h.   Despite being neither a substance nor an accident, and in *Gestalt* terms neither mere background nor mere figure,[80] *the atmosphere has*, as we have seen, *a sui generis spatiality* (which is, prototypically, pre- or extra-dimensional). And then *it could also have boundaries*, beyond which its efficaciousness actually ceases to be.[81] And, in this case, would those be *fiat* boundaries, i.e. established by our cognitive activity, or *bona fide* boundaries, due to an immanent qualitative and spatial discontinuity?[82] The mereological interpretation is perhaps more complicated: atmospheres, although unitarily nominated, might be *fiat* wholes, but formed by the aggregation of discontinuous *bona fide* parts and – perhaps due

---

78   'In the Cartesian type of relationship that doctors have with their patients, the social character of atmosphere is manifested very clearly [...] The patient, as *homo patiens*, is completely passive and captured by this atmosphere.' An inevitably asymmetrical atmosphere: 'through the constant presence of devices the relationship is reified and functionalised, the patient is more and more considered as a machine. Which is especially true for the state of coma.' (Monke 2007: 25)

79   'Depending on the degree of supervision of patients, the same technological devices generate either the ecstasy of safety or the ecstasy of a disturbing and misunderstood aspect.' (ibid: 27)

80   'When we say, for example, that a man emanates purity or perhaps *freshness*, we are thus expressing a judgement we are entitled to by an instance that much anticipates all the criteria for formal determination, such as, for example, expression or physiognomy. The atmospheric [...] is neither figure nor background but, if anything, an irradiation of the surrounding field, the very reflection of which can also be emanated by the things present.' (Tellenbach 1968: 61)

81   Like smell, 'the atmosphere of a thing extends as far as its presence makes a difference.' (Hauskeller 1995: 33)

82   For a first approach, in this sense, to the atmosphere of the landscape, see Griffero (2005b).

to the occlusion (intentional or otherwise) – of internal or contiguous dystonic elements, as when the impression depends on the ignorance of certain continuities that are not immediately perceptible.[83] That is to say, atmospheres might have *fiat* boundaries that, rooted on boundaries that are initially and perceptually *bona fide* (using the example of the horizon in the optical field),[84] are destined, after ceasing to be transient, to become once again *bona fide* boundaries, as when an initially anonymous situation acquires such a constant salience that it is then perceived as natural. The atmosphere, in short, could be an ecological niche intertwined with *fiat* boundaries: those are dependent on the perception situational character but hinged on *bona fide* boundaries (i.e. dependent on qualities that are inherent in the perceived). In other words, a whole whose identity, as we have already seen, is very delicate: in fact, while, for example, a football team remains the same despite the replacement of all its players, an atmosphere may be threatened even by the change of the slightest detail.

i.   We have already mentioned how unorthodox and Heraclitean the 'n-dimensional' ontology of the atmospheric is:

> Not only the poets, writers and artists, but all without exception have experienced thousands of times that one and the same object, such as a certain section of landscape, gives rise to a 'state of mind' that is totally different at dawn and dusk, in fog or under the moonlight, in the storm and the rain or in the blue sky in full summer. It thus shows us a different 'face' every time and makes it seem for us that there always appear other and different characters. (Klages 1942: 46)

For the moment, however, it will be enough to point out that, *along with transient atmospheric qualities, there are relatively persistent atmospheric qualities*. The bright, olfactive etc. atmosphere of an alpine landscape, which obviously varies depending on the weather, is one thing; the atmosphere of sublimity it arouses (almost) regardless of weather conditions is another thing. It is not by chance that such a distinction presents itself, although burdened by

---

83   Like when in Rousseau (1783) the initial wild atmosphere is neutralised by the unexpected perception of human presence: see Griffero (2005b: 24–25).
84   Smith (2002: 62, 66).

projectivistic prejudices that must be here dismissed,[85] already in Alexander von Humboldt. If the physiognomy of nature, as 'mysterious communion with the spiritual life of man', through 'thought and sentiment' (Humboldt 1850: 154; 1845 I: 53) always irradiates a universally calming atmosphere, the 'many and different impressions' that affect 'those who are capable of surveying nature with a comprehensive glance, and abstract their attention from local phenomena' (Humboldt 1850: 217) can certainly modify that background atmosphere. And again, if 'the vague feeling of the natural local character' and the 'impression of any one region' (ibid: 217, 218) can persist, the atmospheres can vary according to the relatively mutable topological collocation of the perceiver: in fact, 'who is there that does not feel himself differently affected beneath the embowering shade of the beechen grove, or on hills crowned with a few scattered pines, or in the flowering meadow where the breeze murmurs through the trembling foliage of the birch? A feeling of melancholy, or solemnity, or of light buoyant animation is in turn awakened by the contemplation of our native trees' (ibid: 219).

j. *There are, then, things and situations that stably arouse certain atmospheres, and others that occasionally take charge of them.* That is to say, (as we has already said with respect to amendability), depending both on the constellation they became part of (covariance) and the mood of the person who considers them (retentional and protentional influences). A wild atmosphere, for example, ceases to be such when, sensorially perceived components being equal, its origin is ascertained to be artificial. The strong atmospheric power irradiated by the most minute things is such only during periods of poverty or incomplete socio-psychic development.[86] The murderer is disturbing especially when he 'moves softly and speaks with a velvety voice' (Arnheim 1966: 67). It is well known, in fact, that even the most prosaic things irradiate an atmosphere of familiarity on someone travelling through a non-place: 'for him, an oil company logo is a reassuring landmark; among the supermarket shelves he falls with relief on sanitary, household or food products validated by multinational brand names' (Augé 1995: 106). Precisely the possibility that a non-place could (again) become a place – as in the case of the

---

85   'Impressions change with the varying movements of the mind, and we are led by a happy illusion to believe that we receive from the external world that with which we have ourselves invested it.' (Humboldt 1866 I: 26)

86   Minssen (2004: 7).

subway, which has become in time and with changes of scale an 'exemplary public space' (Augé 2008: 65)[87] – or that a place, by wearing itself out, could become a non-place, seems to prove conclusively that in addition to stable atmospheres there are also contingent atmospheres.

3.5 Principles of a Phenomenology of Atmospheres

Now let us leave aside the ontological character of atmospheres and assess the mode of their phenomenological manifestation. Before this, however, we must say something about the predictable objection with regard to their subject-dependence. While being rooted in objectual elements that are completely indifferent to what we think of them and hear in them, of course they mean something only for those who perceive them: for someone who, even if only momentarily, escapes the process (perhaps even ontogenetic)[88] of disintegration of that originary experience that does not yet abstract the objectual nature from the subjective form with which it is perceived – for example, the colour quality from its sentimental-atmospheric effect. However, if bays only exist for those who sail, beaches and mountains only for those who may land on the first or find a visual impediment in the latter;[89] that is, if our ontological-phenomenological segmentation is perspectively conditioned first of all in a species-specific way and then also in a socio-ideological way, then the salience detected every time is by no means the result of an illusory projection devoid of objective roots, as is evidenced by the fact that a bay can only be a

---

87   The metro 'is not a non-place, in any case, not for me, nor for those who regularly make the same journey with it. In the metro, they have memories and habits, they recognize faces and entertain with the space of certain stations a kind of bodily intimacy measurable in the rhythm of their descent down the stairs, in the precision of the gesture with which they introduces the ticket into the slot of the turnstile or in the acceleration of the pace when they identify, from its noise, the arrival of the train at the edge of the track.' (Augé 2008: 31–32)

88   It seems that even a three year old child, for example, perceives colours in a polymodal way, so that for him certain objects have a red or green smell, etc. (Werner 1966: 287).

89   By 'mountain' we indicate, in fact, 'a certain mountainous profile that limits the human horizon; its meaning is fulfilled by the sensations and intentions of a living being with relatively short legs and limited forces. There is mountain climbing only for those who climb them up, only for man' (Rothacker 1964: 66), while, for example, for the Homeric (gigantic) gods, mountains would be but lower surfaces of no impediment.

portion of land-sea that has certain characteristics. This being said, it is time to consider, without deflationary scruples, the possible atmospheric effects and offer, as much as is possible, a comprehensive phenomenology of them.

a.   Often 'the serenity of a landscape is not the serenity of my feeling, it is something in the landscape, just as I can have an experience quite at odds with my personal subjective feelings (proper of my ego). In this sense, the space endowed with an emotional tone is also an objective space' (Ströker 1965: 53). This happens in the case, which is prototypical for all our work, of the ingressive atmosphere: being refractory to any more or less conscious attempt at a projective re-interpretation or reflective reductionism, it gives life to a successful process that, generating an almost unavoidable corporeal and affective involvement in the perceiver, completely reorients his emotional situation.[90] It emotionally affects anyone who comes within its range of influence[91]: be it the harmlessly oppressive atmosphere of the lift – 'the hands are kept at the side or used to steady the body by grasping a railing. The eyes are fixed on infinity and are not brought to bear on anyone for more than a passing glance' (Hall 1966: 118) – or the melancholic or joyful atmospheres from which derive, respectively, a corporeal contraction and an expansion; be it the sacral atmosphere, so engaging that it captures even those who walked into the church only to steal, or that of joy, that 'in a "pub" or at a party may "infect" the newcomers, who may even have been depressed beforehand, so that they are "swept up" into the prevailing gaiety' (Scheler 2008: 15). What is produced, in cases like these, is an authentic atmospheric overpowering.

> One who is affected by it is delivered to it as to a power that completely fills the man with suffering and terror, with horror and despair, with anxiety or disgust. You can see how this power uniformly gives the same colour to the self and to the world, thus dissolving, though often only in a provisional way, the global situations and the previous relations of reference. (Tellenbach 1968: 115)

---

90   Hellpach (1960a: 120, fn. 48).
91   A phenomenon associable to suggestion, which has always been studied by natural magic (Griffero 2003) and social psychology since the the time (1895) of le Bon (2009).

While in various shades and degrees of sensitivity, it is indeed likely that the atmosphere of mourning irradiated by a funeral, provided, of course, that it be recognized as such, should influence the behaviour of all those present, even more so if 'every atmosphere corresponds to a motor style that can be found in all those who are emotionally touched by this atmosphere' (Thibaud 2003a: 291). When 'a place that has been the scene of a crime appears sinister' with the same tenacity with which the 'stick immersed in water [...] appears bent' (Metzger 1941: 33), it is because an ingressive atmosphere resists any reflective change (judgement), inducing an assessment that is the more certain the more it is cognitively deficient. An assessment which in fact:

> does not even imply the recognition of the object in its entirety, but simply the assessment of some of its important aspects. The fear of the bear does not require the recognition of the bear and of all of its zoological features, but simply the recognition of its potential danger, which depends on the perception and the combined evaluation of very simple elements such as shape, size, proximity, type of motion made by the animal, sound signals emitted by it and so on. (Galati 2002: 267)

b.   The second possibility is that the atmosphere is syntonic thanks to the coincidence between the form of perception, i.e. the state of mind with which we perceive, and its content, namely the external mood perceived. Even this atmosphere of solidarity is a sufficient proof that there are also (and, from our point of view, especially) quasi-objective atmospheres, and that the receptive (cultural, historical and individual) variability should not be overestimated. In short, it is not true that ten different people, arrived at the same time in the same station, will perceive ten different atmospheres.[92] And anyhow, the fact that the perception of an atmosphere is not perfectly identical in two different people does not prove the subjectivity and privacy of the atmosphere – at least no more than the fact that one shelters oneself with an umbrella and the other lets himself be hit by it – does not proves the subjectivity of the rain.[93] The impressive entrance hall of a major banking institution will express a mood of power for those who venture there in

---

92   Blume (2003: 75).
93   Thus Schmitz (1969: 216; 2003: 202–203).

search of a loan (whence perhaps the impulse to leave the centre of the room to take refuge in protective nooks and crannies) while expressing, on the contrary, a mood of proud belonging for an employee who has developed a strong *esprit de corps*. And yet – note this – what generates both moods (fear and love) is still the same spatial-sentimenental-atmospheric quality of intimidating vastness.

c.   In other cases, the atmospheric perception is instead even antagonistic. Just as it is possible to discover new landscape values in the same place, it is undoubtedly possible to feel an atmosphere relatively different from the one expected (and that maybe has become a cliché). Walking through Paris, I could not feel at all the Parisian atmosphere made famous by books, films and paintings; also while travelling through Italy the atmospheric expectations instilled in me by figurative culture could also be disproved by direct experience (this is what famously happened to Goethe). But what is significant is that, once again, the supposed atmosphere of the place is understood by us in any case, whether to adapt to it or to escape it. So to speak, it can be read physiognomically in the external situation, so that we can define it and describe it to others without being truly touched by it; a bit like Faust, who perceives the atmosphere 'of order, peace and contentment' in Gretchen's 'small neat room' (Goethe 1962: 263), without sharing it, if not as one who grasps the painful atmosphere of others, but through a dystonic form like joy.

One might also use here the distinction[94] between a) the mere conventional knowledge of external atmospheres, b) the corporeal understanding of the atmosphere felt by others, and that *we should* analogously *feel*, and finally c) the actual com-passion (in the original sense of the term) of the present atmosphere. Or, better yet, one could resort to the even subtler articulation made by Moritz Geiger. He distinguishes first between the contemplation of a mood (e.g. of a landscape) as something extraneous and the receiving, on the basis of which 'we do not just look at the sentimental character [...] but we sink into it. We take part in it inwardly' (Geiger 2000: 175).

> We can contemplate the mood of the landscape so as to regard it as something totally extraneous [...] Our consciousness opens up to let the sentimental

---

94   See Scheler (2008) and Hauskeller (1995: 50–52).

> characters act on us; we internally behave in a completely passive way in order to incorporate within ourselves everything that the object radiates. It is as a fluid that springs out of the object and inundates me. And yet I remain in a purely contemplative attitude – I am here and there is the object. One could define this atmosphere of a sentimental character that irradiates upon me a feeling, a mood. It seems to me that such definitions are not correct. Try to compare a genuine feeling of happiness with an irradiation of joy of colour in my consciousness, and you will notice a clear difference with respect to a mood. (ibid.: 176)

That is to say, the passive exposure to the external atmosphere has to be followed by its active absorption, which comes to the point of permeating the (maybe recalcitrant) details of the object itself.

> It is no longer a simple irradiation of the sentimental character on me. Something in me must emerge of that oppression, of that gloom. I have to look at things with such eyes that they will appear to me in this oppressive and gloomy light. So there will no longer exist the separation between the sentimental character and my life, though the sentimental character will be clearly read as something objective. (ibid: 178–179)

It is certainly problematic to make a distinction between this receptive state and the 'sentimentalistic' one, in which 'the object only provides the starting point and the support for my mood [...] I let myself be simply overwhelmed by my mood, just as the object brings it to me, without an interest in its details' (ibid: 180). Then, it seems even inconsistent that, in order to explain empathy in the strict sense, we should rehabilitate the projectivistic hypothesis, apparently already ruled out by the assertion that it is 'the object [that] elicits a certain mood which, in turn, invests the object' (ibid: 181).

> Everyone knows the effect that a cheerful or a gloomy room, the presence of sun or rain, have on our mood. On the other hand the mood itself gives objects certain sentimental tones. So a gloomy landscape will make me gloomy and this gloomy mood will make the landscape look gray to me [...] The object arouses in me a mood *that I experience as coming from the object*. At the same time, the

tendency is born in me to relive this mood as something that comes from me, to produce it spontaneously by myself [...] These are not separate experiences: the atmosphere and the mood emanating from the object and those produced spontaneously by me are one single experience. (ibid: 169, 183, my emphasis)

Contra Geiger we must reiterate, however, that we experience atmosphere *as if it came* from the object only because *it actually comes* from the object! Although it can certainly return to it, potentiated. When this atmospheric empathy or corporeal tuning between object and perceiver[95] is replaced by an atmospheric empathy that is so subjectively conditioned that, being anxious to express itself in the object, it only finds 'what one's mood lends to the object' (ibid: 186, see also Geiger 1911b: 64–65), then we are beyond even the simple atmospheric dystonia. Unless we also wish to regard as atmospheric the pathologically extra-situational moods of the cyclothymic, who sees everything black, or of the millenarian, who sees a revolutionary and / or eschatological atmosphere even in the most anodyne aspect of reality.

Although it is rare to be completely indifferent to the atmospheres that permeate a certain space, it is not wrong to make a distinction, not so much between the atmosphere and the personal feelings,[96] but between the atmosphere that is superficially perceived – typical of those who are 'pleased because they have been given a present, sad because they are at a funeral, gay or sad according to the countryside around them, and, on the hither side of any such emotions, indifferent and neutral' (Merleau-Ponty 2005: 441) – and the atmosphere that really involves the felt-body.[97] That is to say, one can recognise the objective roots of an atmosphere, but it does not necessarily manage to capture the form

---

95 Schmitz (1966: 91), embraces, *contra* Robert Vischer, the idea that empathy, as claimed by Lipps (1903: 122), is the proper transfer in the place promoting empathy, while criticizing, however, the absence of the notion of felt-body and the resulting conception of such transfer in merely mechanical-physiologic if not even only projective and mimetic terms.

96 As claimed by Hauskeller (1995: 13).

97 Perhaps this explains why 'one can plan the assignment of atmospheres to an architectural space but not of moods' (Hasse 2005: 370), so of feelings whose direction is from outside to inside and not of those which proceed instead from the inside to the outside (Fuchs 2000: 215).

in which it is perceived, and even less so in a coercive manner.[98] And indeed, this very resistance, maybe even conditioned by the inability to let oneself go[99] or even by a pathological protest,[100] can in turn create a qualitatively different and even antithetical atmosphere,[101] as it happens when an atmosphere of joy is so dull and conventional that, rather than making us rejoice, it ends up making us even sad. So there are certainly atmospheres arising from the dissonance and the discrepancy between what we feel and what we would expect to feel, and even from indifference,[102] but this does not make it legitimate to reduce atmospheres to a mere product of subjectivity that forgets its own unconscious projection of an expectation over them.[103] The intensity of the atmospheric protest is indeed the best proof of the objective effectiveness of the atmosphere we react to: an atmospheric-personal reaction by virtue of which the perceiver sometimes scatters the encountered atmosphere and sometimes feels his previous atmosphere accentuated, such as when our sadness is exacerbated by the atmosphere of joy we come across, which is evidently not contagious and felt as inappropriate.

---

98   'No one' can be 'forced to the recognition of their states (i.e. atmospheric states).' (Tellenbach 1968: 60)

99   'About the rapture, then, what decides is not only the corporeal feeling, but also the form and the way in which the person relates – in their level of personal emancipation – to this being corporeally involved, or (through a personal regression with respect to this level) is carried away, possibly to immerse themselves completely in the rapture.' (Schmitz 2002b: 74)

100   'Certain types of excretory behaviour, for example certain forms of spit, vomit, sudden defecation or diarrhoea, enuresis, have the character of an atmospheric protest; perhaps even certain forms of retention, such as the refusal of food or defecatory retention, may have the sense of a rejection of the atmospheric tuning.' (Tellenbach 1968: 53)

101   'We all know from experience that our melancholy can be dispersed by the serenity of the environment (by irradiation), but it can also re-sharpened by contrast.' (Hellpach 1939: 120, fn. 48)

102   Man 'perceives in principle everything he has receptive organs for and everything he finds in the images as a whole, so not only in stimulating and threatening essences, but even in indifferent ones, which simply express themselves and, in a way, speak to him.' (Klages 1964: 391)

103   'It is therefore not an objective expression of the landscape that is opposed to subjective feeling, but it is the way I should perceive the landscape (i.e., as serene, having previously perceived it this way) that is set against the way I actually perceive it (i.e. as sad).' (Hauskeller 1995: 46)

d. It is true that the atmosphere prototypical for us is the one suggested by the first impression. But the second (and third, fourth...) impression also gives rise to a less intense atmosphere, as emerges from the already considered question of their relative amendability (see *supra* 3.4). As a dynamic and chronologically structured process, atmospheric perception could very well change sign and colour for various reasons. Let us consider see some of them.

It may change, for example, because of an even slight change in the perceptual space.[104] Or because of a change in the climatic conditions, such as when the atmosphere of sadness suggested by a shaded space brightens up when the cloud disappears, or when the atmosphere of a fully illuminated landscape turns into a different one when it appears to us in the backlight. But also due to an additional cognition,[105] such as when the growing doubts of the subordinates gradually turn the charismatic atmosphere of their leader into an atmosphere of inadequacy if not even worthlessness, or when the discovery of the fictional or even manipulative character[106] of the proposed atmosphere reflexively cancels its effect, at least in part. Or perhaps because of a perception of the atmospheric situation outside of the sensory illusion it normally feeds on,[107] or due to a purely personal experience, such as when the atmosphere of the hospital ceases to be anxious because after despairing for a long time we finally find a doctor, or because, working there, we feel like it is a sort of second family to us.

Sometimes it is a new salience that re-tonalises the whole situation, which was previously anonymous:

---

104 'In every single moment,' in fact 'there is a new overall situation unified in itself.' (ibid: 42)

105 The (perceived) lightness, refinement and elegance of the London Eye are spoiled, for example both by the memory 'of the heavy bulk of concrete' that had to be poured into to river to support the structure, and by the thought that a structure born to be transient was made permanent (Rykwert 2000: 265).

106 'No one is left without help in this atmospheric pressure: there is always the possibility to look at the fictional as-if of presence itself and to reject in this way its affective influence.' (Hauskeller 1995: 197)

107 The atmospheric effect of the mountains, for example, cannot but change if we ascertain by means of photography that they are less and less steep than it appears or than we might imagine, or that in any perceptual framework the left is always optically privileged (Thibaud 2003a: 294).

> A very confusing part of town, a warren of streets I had avoided for years, all of a sudden became clear to me when one day somebody I loved went to live there. It was as if a searchlight installed in her window now carved the district up with its beams. (Benjamin 1979: 74)

In other cases the different impact of the spatial (relational) context suffices, as when 'an apartment which is barely adequate becomes uninhabitable to some people at the exact moment that a rising apartment house next door cuts off the view' (Hall 1966: 171). Or it could be sufficient to experience a variation of the perceptive distance, as when the atmosphere of magnificence of a building resolves, at a close distance, in an atmosphere of decay. Or, even more simply, a change in the physiological conditions: in fact, 'when our stomachs are "out of sorts" they can cast a pall over all things. What would otherwise seem indifferent to us suddenly becomes irritating and disturbing' (Heidegger 1979: 99).[108]

Atmospheric perception – as has already been pointed out – is at least partly cognitively penetrable and not totally deterministic.[109] In fact, 'who had ever seen that the shadows on the snow are blue before a painter found out? Who had seen the sparkling pearly colours flickering in the summer air in Paris before the Impressionists?' (Lehmann 1986: 141). Who had ever felt certain atmospheres (of places and people) before some cult film made them popular? How could one feel 'chills of fear and sublimity' seeing the Gropius' room in Herculaneum style before the discovery of Pompeii and Herculaneum (Benjamin 1999: 405)? Mind you: this is not to sanction here, with a coarse culturalism, a direct effect of the historical and social conditions over perception, but to admit some changes in the ability to 'note' other aspects within the same framework of perception. The acceleration of life in the metropolis, for example, 'certainly does not produce an increase in the strength of perception but only a shift: the farmer with his healthy senses sees several other things for which the city-dweller no longer has any "organ"' (Hellpach 1960a: 121). This is a variability – the atmosphere is the object of a natural perception, but it is filtered through the ideas and evaluations of the

---

[108] Since 'we are not first of all "alive," only then getting an apparatus to sustain our living which we call "the body," but we are some body who is alive', then 'every feeling is an embodiment attuned in this or that way, a mood that embodies in this or that way.' (Heidegger 1979: 99–100)

[109] See Wendorf *et al.* (2004).

perceiver – that common sense advises us to admit. But without ever embracing *in toto* projectivistic relativism.

And the reason is always the same: if by observing an atmosphere we *ipso facto* altered it, no atmosphere could ever overwhelm us and affect us. What happens is, rather, that our atmospheric perception can change in time.[110] An initially indeterminate atmosphere can specify itself, centring on a specific anchor point and generating a field of condensation, such as when you perceptually realize that the overall atmosphere of nervousness is actually the irradiation of a single person. Or it can spill over, creating improper anchor points and fields of condensation, thus also infecting objects that are *per se* irresponsible (hence, perhaps, the illusory intentionality of atmospheric feelings),[111] such as when the atmospheric fear of a visit to the dentist spreads a negative aura on every visible object, on the gossip magazines in the waiting room as well as on the dentist and the tools he uses.

The atmosphere changes even more, however, when it is the provisional and fragile outcome of non-homogeneous sub-atmospheres,[112] of variable charge and perhaps in conflict with the whole. This explains the possible semantic variations engendered by the association of the colour with this or that element (shapes, objects, other colours, etc.),[113] or the situations in which, similarly to what happens in bistable figures, we perceive this or that atmosphere depending on the anchor point (but never both atmospheres together): a group photo, for example, suggests perhaps an atmosphere of collective joy if we look at the whole, and a melancholic, if not desperate, atmosphere if we pay attention to details, especially to a student that is slightly secluded and not really smiling like the others. This is not too surprising, considering that, just like every other experience

---

110 One limitation of Schmitz's analysis is perhaps that he underestimates the *status nascendi* and the possible time course of atmospheres (Soentgen 1998: 114).

111 Schmitz (1969: 312).

112 'Every perceptual space is the intersection of a plurality of atmospheric ecstasies arising from the heterogeneous regions we can isolate within this space. Since not every atmospheric ecstasy acts with the same intensity or can act on the basis of the specific disposition of the subject [...], the overall character of the perceptual space is generally more strongly marked by some ecstasies than by others [...] All phenomic characters are ordered in a single perceptive character that marks the atmospheric space as a totality.' (Hauskeller 1995: 40)

113 Just one example: the redness of the dress, a colour that is normally not sad, accentuates the sadness, detected otherwise, of the figure (contrast effect), whereas a melancholic colour would decrease it (Kandinsky 1912: 79–80).

in act, atmospheric perception (unlike the remembered one which is qualitatively sketched and characterised by the loss of internal distinctions and nuances, simplified borders, an uncertain relationship with the environment, etc.) imposes its own data (hence the passivity of the synthesis) but still 'in a context of open possibilities', because 'in the present I can always do something' (Piana 1979: 80). For instance, returning to the example of the hospital, you can change, at least in part, the initial atmosphere of tension by reading, talking with other patients and perhaps, with a certain sadism, trying to console yourself with the (hopefully more serious) diseases of others.

e.   Let us try to summarise what we have been saying. An atmosphere can overwhelm us, it can find us in tune with it, it can be recognised without being really felt, it can elicit a resistance that pushes us to change it, it may (for various reasons, also absolutely idiosyncratic) be perceived differently in the course of time, and it may be so dependent on the perceptual (subjective) form that it concretises itself even in materials that normally express other moods. This is why we can grieve even because of a clear and serene sky, or feel oppressed and threatened (as in horror films) by the joyful laughter of children, that we can get to 'hate all seven days of creation' (Raabe), or to think that April is 'the cruellest month' (T.S. Eliot). But even in this case, the felt atmosphere is such only because it is opposite to the expected one which, in some way, is still evidently perceived.

At times, the subject-dependence can impede even the mere sensorial-affective observation of the atmosphere one is in, thus causing an embarrassing atmospheric inadequacy for oneself and for others, such as when one euphorically joins a community where a tragic atmosphere hovers or when, in general, one unexplainably feels out of place, perhaps even just because one is extraneous to the specific cultural declination of this or that atmosphere.

f.   Having made the atmosphere into a kind of corporeal (unintentional) bridge between perceived and perceiver allows us to uphold the atmospheric unintentionality. As much as the erotic atmosphere of a person may be just a special instance of the sexual atmosphere that permeates the whole of existence,[114] and as much as it is totally wrong, of course – as well as the result of endless

---

114   Thus Merleau-Ponty (2005: 200).

misunderstandings rightly punished in the era of political correctness – to consider such irradiation as deliberate, the person in question is still the objective source of this atmospheric feeling (which is by no means only subjective-projective), at least as the condensation point of a more extensive atmosphere.[115] It turns out, paradoxically, that the condensation or anchor point of an atmosphere might even ignore the atmospheric mood that it (unintentionally) radiates. This means not only that, of course, the blissful sky of a summer evening does not feel the bliss it inspires, but also that, for example, those who commit shameful acts might not feel in any way the atmosphere of shame they are responsible for.

Precisely the case of the atmosphere of shame deserves a more careful analysis. 1) It can happen, first of all, that those who are responsible for it will feel attacked by an atmosphere of external shame, delocalised and emblematically embodied in a kind of anonymous gaze; even when he is certain that he was not caught, 'far from disappearing with [the] first alarm, the Other is present everywhere, below, above, in the neighbouring rooms, and continue[s] to feel profoundly [his] being-for-others; it is even possible that [his] shame may not disappear' (Sartre 1969: 301). This is atmospheric shame as a personal feeling which, in fact, is often accompanied by repentance. But shame may also 2) not be felt by those who are responsible for it, by their associates and in special cases even by anyone (except in retrospect). In other circumstances it is instead 3) felt by others, obviously without resulting in repentance, in the form of an atmosphere so objectively diffused in the extradimensional space that it can be opposed only with extreme difficulty.

It is this atmosphere, and not the person who radiates it, that attacks the bystanders[116]: whether we are ashamed 3a) *for* him, such as when we suffer because of the image he gives of himself, or – and it is not the same – 3b) *of* him, as when obviously we are not emotionally tied to him, well, in any case, the atmosphere of shame involves the felt-body, even overflowing into its physical prosthesis, as is demonstrated by the fact that whoever is ashamed of what he sees involuntarily tightens his eyes, as if he did not want to see: he is overwhelmingly led to move away, to sink or hide.[117] That atmosphere of shame (but also that of courage,

---

115 The same can be said of the loved person (Schmitz 1969: 321; 2003: 177).
116 Fuchs (2000: 84).
117 Here I am following the objection made by Schmitz (see Blume 2003: 82 and fn. 24) to the hypothesis that those who assist to something shameful do not feel shame but mere awkwardness.

gratitude, etc.) is certainly very special, because, unlike natural ones, it only exists if there is someone who is ashamed of or for someone; as well as that of courage is present if there is someone who senses the courage of another, in short if there is someone who – apparently also in this case of extreme subject-dependence of the qualities inherent to the phenomenon – feels what in his view 'should' be felt also by the person who is responsible for the atmosphere. While the latter person, more often than one might think, comes to know something of his own situation only thanks to the others' reaction to his involuntary atmospheric power.

Conclusion

The analysis, both ontological and phenomenological, of the atmospheric experience – as is not hard to imagine – could be more sophisticated than this. Even more so if one were to accept the argument that, just as we always necessarily are in a certain mood,[1] we are forever and always atmospherically involved. Seemingly extra-atmospheric situations – that are not to be confused with impersonal and anonymous atmospheres – are perhaps solely so because their atmospheric charge is too weak to be detected. And it is from here, from the universality of the atmospheric, that atmospherology (of which we have only sketched the outlines) should start. At the centre of atmospherology – we repeat – there is the conviction that atmosphere, at least the prototypical one, lies not so much in the eye of the perceiver, but it is rather a relatively objective (intersubjective) feeling we encounter in the external space. A feeling in whose production various professions (stage set design, event organisation, rhetoric, marketing, museum settings, interior design, architecture, urban planning, personal training, etc.) participate, whose competence – now legitimated by handbooks and academia – consists in manipulating certain physical and psychological situations and statistically hypothesising their atmospheric effect. However, several questions remain open: here are some of them.

a.   While sympathising with the philosophical discourses that are the more striking the more they are counterintuitive, we have not embraced *in toto* the campaign of desubjectification of feelings (even of atmospheric ones) promoted by Schmitz. Nor did we intend to radically set his position (according to which the only authentic atmospheres are those totally independent of man and things)[2]

---

1   'A certain mood can switch to another determined mood, but it is a passage that still leads only to a new mood, yet never outside of the collocation of man within some kind of mood'. At most it can lead to a state of emotional indifference, which turns out, however, to be 'not indifferent to the mood, but remains essentially bound to it in the form of a broken and not reconstituted mood.' (Bollnow 1956: 61–62, 64, 130)

2   Schmitz (1965: 343; 1998: 188; 1999b: 285 ff.).

against that of those who, like Böhme, try instead – by mitigating the overly random nature of atmospheres – to bind them as far as possible to objectual poles which they allegedly are the ecstasies of,[3] possibly even with evolutionary purposes.[4] We preferred to admit that there are various types of atmospheres: they can be prototypic (objective, external and unintentional), derivative (objective, external and intentionally produced) and even quite spurious in their relatedness (subjective and projective).

b. While reiterating the transitivity of atmospheric perception, sometimes intransitivity (non-thetic character) seems to better explain this particular experience, namely that, in this case, rather than perceiving something (even if it were the atmosphere), we perceive 'according to' something. From this perspective, atmospheres would not be perceived quasi-things but rather contextual conditions of perception,[5] a sort of horizon that tinges everything it hovers on and is 'comparable to goggles, which you do not see when you look through them' (Bockemühl 2002: 221). It is in this sense that Minkowski understands

> the spiritual atmosphere in which both the man and the world around him are immersed [, where] the important thing is not the actual presence of the man, with his physical and moral properties, but the presence of a breath of humanity, that in certain moments exhales from the man, without ever converging onto a specific point [...] This breath, in fact, creates a unique spiritual atmosphere and incorporates inside of it, *beyond concrete objects and beyond men,* the whole that it itself describes. (Minkowski 1936: 257, my emphasis)

This would be consistent with considering atmospheres, being the ecstasies of things, as purely contextual qualities;[6] not as close and discrete forms but, as we have said many times, as relatively chaotic situations with which we communicate

---

3 But see also zur Lippe (1987: 515): 'something is never merely enclosed into its borders. It gives off heat like an oven and cold like ice.'
4 Böhme (1995: 30).
5 'We do not perceive an atmosphere, but rather perceive in accordance with the atmosphere.' (Thibaud 2003a: 293)
6 We can speak, in fact, of the 'atmospheric "contributions" of things to the overall contexts in which they appear.' (Buchholz 2002: 73–74)

corporeally and that are beyond the distinction (it does not matter now if the source is language or not)[7] between substance and accidents.

c. But the possibility that we might perceive 'according to' an atmosphere does not exclude that other times, far from finding in people and things only occasions to manifest themselves, atmospheres are exactly the expressive way in which things call for us or even look at us.

> The world watches me. Everything watches me: it watches out of itself; it 'looks out". To appear is a basic ontological mode of the being of things; they are in all respects 'appearance' [...] To appear is really a form of seeing. The originary way of seeing, with which things are in a sense born to the world. It founds my seeing related to them. The seeing of man is a response, an adherence to the gaze of the things themselves. Gaze-of-response. (Rombach 1987: 185)

Which is what happens, not coincidentally, in the atmospheric irradiation of the gaze of others,[8] which can 'be given [...] when there is a rustling of branches, or the sound of a footstep followed by silence, or the slight opening of a shutter, or a light movement of a curtain' and suddenly 'I am no longer master of the situation [since] the appearance of the other [...] causes the appearance in the situation of an aspect which I did not wish, of which I am not master, and which on principle escapes me since it is *for the other*' (Sartre 1969: 281, 289). Speaking and acting in public, for example, 'we never lose sight of the fact that we are looked at, and we execute the ensemble of acts which we have come to perform in the presence of the look; better yet we attempt to constitute a being and an ensemble of objects for this look' (ibid: 305).

---

    7 Heidegger derives both options from a more originary source: 'is the structure of the simple declarative sentence (the nexus of subject and predicate) the mirror image of the structure of the thing (the union of substance and accidents)? Or is it merely that, so represented, the structure of the thing is a projection of the structure of the sentence?' (Heidegger 2002: 6)
    8 Which famously can 'punish, encourage, or establish dominance; the size of the pupils can indicate interest or distaste.' (Hall 1966: 65)

d.   We also recall the distinction suggested by Gernot Böhme between the atmospheric, i.e. more reified situations independent from the I, and the atmosphere, that is, the feeling more dependent on the subject.[9] He distinguishes, for example, between the night as an objective atmospheric quality and the atmosphere of this-night-for-me, or between a vague threat and the localization of the threatening agent.[10] The increase of subjectivisation entailed by the atmosphere easily explains the certifiable variety of atmospheric perceptions, but it excessively overestimates – and it is the reason why we have considered instead the two terms as basically interchangeable – the individualisation and relativisation[11] of the spatialised feelings. After all, they are mostly interesting because they are extremely invariant, at least with respect to the long time of evolution, and as such they are also presupposed by the personalistic declination they would face in the atmosphere. In other words, a bright April morning can appear to me in a cruel atmosphere because the expected atmosphere, which I somehow note in its objective corporeal components, should be entirely different.

e.   We have already dwelt on the possibility of making a mistake in producing an atmosphere and sometimes clumsily generating an unwanted one – like when an advertisement that wants to convey authority produces laughter instead,[12] or when a strict anti-globalisation movement furbishes its headquarters in the style of a flashy and bombastic shopping centre. This is the truly emblematic case of the open-space office: invented in order to encourage socialisation in the workplace, it soon turned out to be responsible at least for 'an increase in the perception of stress caused by an enhancement of distractions, noise and the sense of crowding,

---

9   But the choice of words is already controversial, since it appears just as likely to define (*contra* Böhme 2001: 59 ff.) the atmospheric as the most subjective sphere (Croome 2003:198).
10   Böhme (2001: 45 ff., 168–172).
11   If it is true that 'selective screening of sensory data admits some things while filtering out others' it is not true that 'experience as it is perceived through one set of culturally patterned sensory screens is *quite different* from experience perceived through another.' (Hall 1966: 2, our emphasis)
12   By suddenly coming out of the tank, for example, the presidential candidate Dukakis (1988) looked ridiculous and did not evoke the prospect of a serious policy of national defense (Pratkanis-Aronson 2001: 173).

combined with a lower perception of privacy, due to the easier visual and auditory accessibility of the worker at his workplace' (Bonaiuto et al. 2004: 77).

On the other hand, it is much more difficult to determine whether one can be mistaken in perceiving an atmosphere. This is so for obvious reasons: would the mistake consist in being unknowingly affected by it? Or in resisting it? In declining it in an entirely subjective direction? Or perhaps in not perceiving it at all? Nor is it helpful to distinguish between real atmospheres and apparent atmospheres, both because the only existing atmosphere (in the proper sense) is precisely the apparent one in act, and because it could be illusory only if it could be assessed in the light of an external criterion. Such a criterion is absent here, as it can be neither the intention of those who created it, nor an improbable view from nowhere on the surrounding reality. And resorting – with an inevitably normative approach – to a socially and culturally ideal-typical atmosphere as the legitimate one to perceive, not only is not interesting for us, but perhaps poses more difficulties than it solves.

f.   Also, we should admit that, despite being intuitive, the definition of atmospheres as an 'in-between' – between subject and object, but also prior to this very distinction – does not entirely solve the main problem in every discourse on the atmospheric, namely that of the objective or subjective nature of the atmosphere. The fact that it is obviously impossible to wonder what the atmospheric charge of a situation is in the absence of an observer does not mean that an atmosphere, at least a prototypical one, depends in all respects on his perceptual presence. Even if one wanted to make the atmosphere into an agentive function ('x counts as y in c'),[13] such 'counting as' would have, in this case, almost nothing arbitrary or conventional about it, rather relying on a specific and largely unchangeable objectual and corporeal component, which would somehow encourage, promote and suggest precisely *that* (and not another) emotional tone. So here is all that can be reasonably attributed to the subject: the ability to detect the atmospheres he encounters, which determine the way he 'feels' in their presence far more than they can act as an expressive pretext for the subjective feelings he may want to project in them. In atmospheres – we repeat – there is something similar to the phenomenon of expressiveness, namely that it 'is directly supported by the constellation of observable events which identifies its position in space, i.e. it depends on them and

---

13   Searle (1995).

is located where they are' (Bozzi 1998: 115). This is demonstrated once and for all by the fact, very banal but shamefully underrated, that with the disappearance of the localized events the perceived atmosphere inevitably disappears as well.[14]

In conclusion, any strategy that seeks to exclude the atmospheric *prius* from the fundamental ontological catalogue[15] seems, therefore, doomed to failure. Such strategy acts almost as though we could afford the luxury of neutralising and distancing any emotional intuitiveness on the level of apophantic reflexivity. Even if an ontology of atmospheres irritated the taste for desert landscapes typical of every deflationism *à la* Quine, it would be sufficient to point out – noting a serious phenomenological underestimation in the metaphor – that the desert is full of life, and if you forgive the joke, even of atmospheres.[16] Therefore, it ultimately seems that atmospheres can withstand all kinds of reductionist and reistic strategies. They can resist the brutal one of eliminativism, forced to downgrade our whole perceptual-affective life to a millennial collective deceit, but also the more subtle one of dispositionalism, which is all in all not very convincing in declassing atmospheres to adverbs of objectual poles[17] and in making the atmospheric into the perception of a mere possibility – thus emphasising only the hypothetical-schematic approach of those who produce atmospheres, or of those debating on 'how they would affect us if we were different from whom we are (today)' or 'how they affected us when we were different at one time' (Seel 2005: 218, fn. 60).

Like other elusive qualitative entities, marginalised by the hegemonic reism (holes, shadows, clouds, void, waves, perceptive phantoms, fumes, etc.), atmospheres should also be taken seriously, both aesthetically and ontologically.[18] Precisely because – as sentiments embodied in a certain space, and thus as quasi-things – they constitute, in their prototypical value, the *prius* of the passive synthesis and the material *a priori* about whose contagious effect (possibly also on rational choices) little or nothing can be done by the necessarily subsequent rational distinctions. Whether their perception is due or not to the very rapid

---

14 See Zumthor (2006: 17).
15 See Griffero (2006b).
16 See Banham (1982: 222 ff.).
17 See the rather suggestive hypothesis brought forward by Matteucci (2005: 55).
18 A little bit as Casati and Varzi (1994) do for holes.

reactions of the so-called emotional brain (amygdala and anterior insula)[19] – but locating a function, all the more so in the era of neuromania, does not mean having its meaning explained![20] – what is evident is that the emotional-atmospheric dimension always knows more than we do. In fact, we cannot break free from the (atmospheric) passivity just because we want to. And besides, it is not obvious that it should be preferable to get rid of it: a healthy aesthetic experience, duly sceptical with respect to Stoic imperturbability, is in fact always a fluid oscillation between taking and being taken,[21] and it happily welcomes the discovery that no one is entirely in control. Namely, the discovery – to finish by paraphrasing Freud – that perhaps 'where the I was there shall atmospheres be'!

---

19   'At the neocortical level stimuli are known as objects, at the level of the hippocampus they are placed in their proper context, at the level of the amygdalae they are evaluated solely for their positive or negative value.' (Galati, 2002: 202)

20   Thus already Köhler (1938: 32).

21   We must 'learn to be attacked, touched, hit, crushed, to explode and be dismembered and, in a word, to [have] the courage [...] to expose ourselves in the world even to dangerous encounters, to welcome the rise of all the "daemons".' (Dürckheim 2004: 101)

Bibliography

Agamben, G. (1993) *Stanzas: Word and Phantasm in Western Culture*, Minneapolis: Minnesota UP.

Albers, J. (1975) *Interaction of Color: Revised Edition*, Yale: Yale University Press.

Amin, A. and Thrift, N. (2001) *Cities: Reimagining the Urban*, Cambridge: Polity Press.

Andrews, M. (2005) 'The Autoroute and the Picturesque', *Rivista di Estetica*, XLV, n.s. 29, 2005, pp. 91–104.

Anschütz, G. (1929) *Das Farbe-Ton-Problem im psychischen Gesamtbereich. Sonderphänomene komplexer optischer Synästhesien («Sichtgebilde»)*, Halle: Marhold.

Aristotle (1907) *De Anima*, Cambridge: Cambridge University Press.

Arnheim, R. (1966) *Toward a Psychology of Art: Collected Essays*, Berkeley: University of California Press.

Assmann, J. (1989) 'Der schöne Tag. Sinnlichkeit und Vergänglichkeit im altägyptischen Fest', in Haug, W. and Warning, R. (eds) *Das Fest*, München: Fink, 1989, pp. 3–28.

Auer, G. (1995) 'Editorial', *Daidalos*, 56 (Magie der Werkstoffe), pp. 18–19.

Augé, M. (1995) *Non-Places: Introduction to an Anthropology of Supermodernity*, London: Verso.

—— (2008) *Le métro revisité*, Paris: Seuil.

Austin, J.L. (1979) *Philosophical Papers*, Oxford: Oxford University Press.

Babin, B.J. and Attaway, J.S. (2000) 'Atmospheric Affect as a Tool for Creating Value and Gaining Share of Customer', *Journal of Business Research*, 49, pp. 91–99.

Bachelard, G. (1994) *The Poetics of Space*, Boston: Beacon Press.

Baensch, O. (1924) 'Kunst und Gefühl', *Logos*, XIII, 2, pp. 1–28.

Balázs, B. (1952) *Theory of the Film (Character and Growth of a New Art)*, London: Dennis Dobson.

Banham, R. (1982) *Scenes in America Deserta*, Layton (UT), Gibbs M. Smith, Inc.

Barbaras, R. (2004) 'Pulsione e percezione', *Aut aut*, 324, pp. 62–74.

Battisti, A. (2006) 'Atmosfera e "beni culturali"', in Goldoni, D., Rispoli, M. and Troncon, R. (eds) *Estetica e management nei beni e nelle produzioni culturali*, Bolzano-Trento-Vienna: Il Brennero, pp. 19–30.

Baudrillard, J. (2005) *The System of Objects*, London: Verso.

Baudelaire, Ch. (2008) *The Flowers of Evil*, Oxford: Oxford University Press.

Becking, G. (1928) *Der musikalische Rhythmus als Erkenntnisquelle*, Augsburg: Filser.

Begg, I. and Denny, J.P. (1969) 'Empirical Reconciliation of Atmosphere and Conversion Interpretations of Syllogistic Reasoning Errors', *Journal of Experimental Psychology*, 81, pp. 351–354.

Benjamin, W. (1973) 'On Some Motifs in Baudelaire', *Illuminations*, London: Fontana, pp. 152–190.

—— (1979) *One-Way Street and Other Writings*, Thetford, Norfolk: Lowe and Brydone Printers Limited.

—— (1996) *Selected Writings*, Volume 1, 1913–1926, Cambridge (MA): Harvard University Press.

—— (1999) *The Arcades Project*, Cambridge (MA): Harvard University Press.

Bianchi, I. (2005) 'Condivisibilità dell'esperienza e "qualità" della struttura percettiva: contributi della Fenomenologia Sperimentale della percezione', *Nuova civiltà delle macchine*, 1, pp. 94–102.

Binswanger, L. (1933) 'Das Raumproblem in der Psychopathologie', *Ausgewählte Vorträge und Aufsätze*, vol. 2, Bern: Francke 1955, pp. 174–225.

Bizzozzero, V. (1997) *L'univers des odeurs. Introduction à l'olfactologie*, Ginevra: Georg Editeur.

Blankenburg, W. (1998) *La perdita dell'evidenza naturale*, Milano: Raffaello Cortina Editore.

Bloom, P. (2004) *Descartes' Baby: How the Science of Child Development Explains What Makes Us Human*, New York: Doubleday Basic Books.

Blume, A. (2003) *Scham und Selbsbewusstsein. Zur Phänomenologie konkreter Subjektivität bei Hermann Schmitz*, Freiburg-München: Alber.

—— (ed.) (2005) *Zur Phänomenologie der ästhetischen Erfahrung*, Freiburg-München: Alber.

Blumenberg, H. (2010) *Paradigms for a Metaphorology*, Ithaca (NY): Cornell University Press.
Bockemühl, M. (2002) 'Atmosphären sehen. Ästhetische Wahrnehmung als Praxis', in Mahayni (ed.) 2002b, pp. 203–222.
Böhme, G. (1985) *Anthropologie in pragmatischer Hinsicht*, Frankfurt am Main: Suhrkamp.
—— (1989) *Für eine ökologische Naturästhetik*, Frankfurt am Main: Suhrkamp.
—— (1995) *Atmosphäre. Essays zur neuen Ästhetik*, Frankfurt am Main: Suhrkamp.
—— (1998) *Anmutungen. Über das Atmosphärische*, Ostfildern vor Stuttgart: Tertium.
—— (2000) 'Acoustic Atmospheres. A Contribution to the Study of Ecological Aesthetics', *Soundscape*, I, 1, pp. 14–18.
—— (2001) *Aisthetik. Vorlesungen über Ästhetik als allgemeine Wahrnehmungslehre*, München: Fink.
—— (2003) 'Leibliches Bewusstsein', in Hauskeller (ed.) 2003b, pp. 35–50.
—— (2006a) *Architektur und Atmosphare*, Fink: Munchen.
—— (2006b) 'L'atmosfera come concetto fondamentale di una nuova estetica', in Griffero and Somaini (eds) 2006, pp. 5–24.
—— (2008) *The Art of the Stage Set as a Paradigm for an Aesthetics of Atmospheres* (http://www.cresson.archi.fr/elements/FAIREamb8/AMB8-conf GBohme-eng.pdf).
Böhme, H. (1988) *Natur und Subjekt*, Frankfurt am Main: Suhrkamp.
Bollnow, O.F. (1956) *Das Wesen der Stimmungen*, Frankfurt am Main: Klostermann.
—— (2004) *Mensch und Raum*, Stuttgart: Kohlhammer.
—— (1964) *Die pädagogische Atmosphäre. Untersuchungen über die gefühlsmäßigen zwischenmenschlichen Voraussetzungen der Erziehung*, Heidelberg: Quelle & Meyer.
Bonaiuto, M., Bilotta, E. and Fornara, F. (2004) *Che cos'è la psicologia architettonica*, Roma: Carocci.
Bourdieu, P. (1984) *Distinction: a Social Critique of the Judgement of Taste*, Cambridge (Ma): Harvard University Press.
Bozzi, P. (1998) *Fisica ingenua. Studi di psicologia della percezione*, Milano: Garzanti.

Bruno, G. (2002) *Atlas of Emotions: Journeys in Art, Architecture and Film*, London: Verso.

Buchholz, K. (2002) 'Hans Christiansen: die Villa in Rosen', in Mahayni (ed.) 2002b, pp. 71–84.

Bull, M. and Back, L. (2003) *The Auditory Culture Reader*, New York: Berg.

Buytendijk, F.J.J. (1956) *Allgemeine Theorie der menschlichen Haltung und Bewegung*, Berlin-Göttingen-Heidelberg: Springer.

Carnevali, B. (2006) '"Aura" e "ambiance": Léon Daudet tra Proust e Benjamin', in Griffero and Somaini (eds) 2006, pp. 117–141.

Casati, R. and Varzi, A.C. (1994) *Holes and Other Superficialities*, Cambridge (MA): The MIT Press.

Chapman, L.J. and Chapman, A.P. (1959) 'Atmosphere Effect Re-examined', *Journal of Experimental Psychology*, 58, pp. 220–226.

Conrad, K. (1958) *Die beginnende Schizophrenie*, Stuttgart: Thieme.

Corbin, A. (1988) *The Foul and the Fragrant: Odor and the French Social Imagination*, Cambridge (MA): Harvard University Press.

Croome, D. (2003) *Gefühl und Erkenntnis*, Darmstadt: Books on Demand.

D'Angelo, P. (2001) *Estetica della natura*, Roma-Bari: Laterza.

—— (2009) (ed.) *Estetica e paesaggio*, Bologna: Il Mulino.

Damisch, H. (2001) *Skyline: The Narcissistic City*, Stanford: Stanford University Press.

Danto, A. (2001) 'Symposium: The Historicity of the Eye. Seeing and Showing', *The Journal of Aesthetics and Art Criticism*, 59:1, Winter.

Daudet, L. (1928) *Mélancholia*, Paris: Grasset.

De Certeau, M. (1984) *The Practice of Everyday Life*, Berkeley: University of California Press.

Dewey, J. (1989) *The Later Works, 1925–1953*, vol. 12, ed. by J.A. Boydston, Carbondale: Southern Illinois University Press.

Dichter, E. (1964) *Handbook of Consumer Motivations: The Psychology of the World of Objects*, New York: McGraw-Hill.

Didi-Hubermann, G. (2004) *Invention of Hysteria: Charcot and the Photographic Iconography of the Salpêtrière*, Cambridge, MA: The MIT Press.

Douglas, M. and Isherwood B. (1966) *The World of Goods: Towards an Anthropology of Consumption*, London: Routledge.

Dufrenne, M. (1991) *L'œil et l'oreille. Essai*, Paris: Jean-Michel Place.

Dürckheim, K.G. von (1932) 'Untersuchungen zum gelebten Raum. Erlebniswirklichkeit und ihr Verständnis. Systematische Untersuchungen II', in Hasse, J. (ed.) *Graf Karlfried von Dürckheim: Untersuchungen zum gelebten Raum*, Mit Einführungen von Hasse, J., Janson, A., Schmitz, H. and Schultheis, K., Frankfurt am Main: Institut fur Didaktik der Geographie 2005.

—— (2004) *Der Alltag als Übung*, Bern, Göttingen, Toronto, Seattle: Huber.

Durth, W. (1988) *Die Inszenierung der Alltagswelt. Zur Kritik der Stadtgestaltung*, Vieweg: Braunschweig.

Eckstein, L. (1937) *Psychologie des ersten Eindrucks*, Leipzig: Barth.

Edinger, L. (1911) *Vorlesungen über den Bau der nervösen Zentralorgane des Menschen und der Tiere*, Leipzig: Vogel.

Empson, W. (1966) *Seven Types of Ambiguity*, New York: New Directions Publishing.

Endell, A. (1908) *Die Schönheit der großen Stadt*, Stuttgart: Strecker & Schroeder.

Evans, J.S., Newstead S.E. and Byrne R.M.J. (1993) *Human Reasoning: The Psychology of Deduction*, Hillsdale NJ: Lea.

Fischer, O. (1943) *Chinesische Landschaftsmalerei*, Berlin-Wien: Neff.

Florenskij, P. (1993) *Le porte regali. Saggio sull'icona*, Milano: Adelphi.

Fränkel, F. and Joel, E. (1927) 'Beiträge zur experimentellen Psychopathologie. Der Haschisch-Rausch', *Zeitschrift für die gesamte Neurologie und Psychiatrie*, 11, pp. 84–106.

Franzini, E. (2006) 'L'atmosfera simbolica del mondo della vita', in Griffero and Somaini (eds) 2006, pp. 69–83.

Friedrich, C.D. (1989) *Scritti sull'arte. Con testimonianze di Tieck, Goethe, Kleist, Brentano, Arnim*, Milano: SE.

Fuchs, Th. (2000) *Leib, Raum, Person – Entwurf einer phänomenologischen Anthropologie*, Stuttgart: Klett-Cotta.

—— (2003) 'Briefwechsel über Gefühle', in Schmitz (2003), pp. 175–205.

Galati, D. (2002) *Prospettive sulle emozioni e teorie del soggetto*, Torino: Bollati Boringhieri.

Gebsattel, V.E. Freiherr von (1937) 'Zur Frage der Depersonalisation. Ein Beitrag zur Theorie der Melancholie', *Der Nervenarzt*, 10, pp. 169–178; 248–257.

Geiger, M. (2000) 'Sul problema dell'empatia di stati d'animo', in Besoli, S. and Guidetti L. (eds) *Il realismo fenomenologico. Sulla filosofia dei Circoli di Monaco e Gottinga*, Macerata: Quodlibet, pp. 153–188.

Geiseler, M.L. (2003) *Zeit/Raum/Natur-Erfahrung im Werk von Richard Long*, diss., Berlin.

Giammusso, S. (2008) *La forma aperta. L'ermeneutica della vita nell'opera di O.F. Bollnow*, Milano: Franco Angeli.

Gibson, J.J. (1986) *The Ecological Approach To Visual Perception*, London: Routledge.

Goethe, J.W. von (1840) *Theory of Colours*, London: John Murray.

—— (1866) *Goethe's Minor Poems*, London: Pitman.

—— (1962) *Faust*, New York: Random House.

—— (2005) *Conversations of Goethe*, Whitefish: Kessinger Publishing.

Goffman, E. (1956) *The Presentation of Self in Everyday Life*, Edinburgh: University of Edinburgh Press.

Goodman, N. (1968) *Languages of Art: An Approach to a Theory of Symbols*, Indianapolis: The Bobbs-Merrill Company, Inc..

Graf, B. (2006) '"Atmosphäre" in der Stadt. Denkansätze für einen psychologisch reflektierten Städtebau', *Wolkenkuckusheim. Internationale Zeitschrift zur Theorie der Architektur*, 10, 1 (http://www.tucottbus.de/theo/Wolke/deu/Themen/themen051.htm#7).

Griffero, T. (2003) *Immagini attive. Breve storia dell'immaginazione transitiva*, Firenze: Le Monnier.

—— (2005a) 'Corpi e atmosfere: il "punto di vista" delle cose', in Somaini, A. (ed.) *Il luogo dello spettatore. Forme dello sguardo nella cultura delle immagini*, Milano: Vita & Pensiero, pp. 283–317.

—— (2005b) 'Paesaggi e atmosfere. Ontologia ed esperienza estetica della natura,' *Rivista di Estetica*, XLV, n.s. 29, pp. 7–40.

—— (2005c) 'Apologia del "terziario": estetica e ontologia delle atmosfere', *Nuova Civiltà delle macchine*, XXIII, 1 (Grammatiche del senso comune), pp. 49–68.

—— (2006a) 'Nessuno la può giudicare. Riflessioni sull'esperienza dell'atmosferico', in Chiodo, S. and Valore, P. (eds) *Questioni di metafisica contemporanea*, Milano: Il Castoro, pp. 80–112.

—— (2006b) 'Quasi-cose che spariscono e ritornano, senza che però si possa domandare dove siano state nel frattempo. Appunti per un'estetica-ontologia delle atmosfere', in Griffero and Somaini (eds) 2006, pp. 45–68.

—— (2006c) *Il corpo spirituale. Ontologie 'sottili' da Paolo di Tarso a Friedrich Christoph Oetinger*, Milano: Mimesis.

—— (2008) 'Quasi-cose. Dalla situazione affettiva alle atmosfere', *Tropos*, I, n.s. (L'apertura del presente. Sull'ontologia ermeneutica di Gianni Vattimo), pp. 75–92.

—— (2009a) 'Atmosfericità. "Prima impressione" e spazi emozionali', *Aisthesis*, 1, pp. 49–66.

—— (2009b) 'Vincoli situazionali', in Di Monte, M. and Rotili, M. (eds), *Vincoli* (Sensibilia 2-2008), Milano: Mimesis, pp. 199–227.

—— (2010) 'Il ritorno dello spazio (vissuto)' in Di Monte, M. and Rotili, M. (eds), *Spazio fisico – Spazio vissuto* (Sensibilia 3-2009), Milano: Mimesis, pp. 207–239.

Griffero, T. and Somaini, A. (eds) (2006) (Atmosfere), *Rivista di estetica*, XLVI, n.s. 33.

Grossheim, M. (1994) *Ludwig Klages und die Phänomenologie*, Berlin: Akademie Verlag.

Gusman, A. (2004) *Antropologia dell'olfatto*, Roma-Bari: Laterza.

Haensel, C. (1946) *Das Wesen der Gefühle*, Überlingen: Wulff.

Hall, E.T. (1966) *The Hidden Dimension*, New York: Doubleday.

Hasse, J. (1994) *Erlebnisräume. Vom Spass zur Erfahrung*, Wien: Passagen.

—— (2000) *Die Wunden der Stadt. Für eine neue Ästhetik unserer Städte*, Wien: Passagen.

—— (2002a) 'Die Atmosphäre einer Straße. Die Drosselgasse in Rüdesheim am Rhein', in Hasse, J. (ed.) 'Subjektivität in der Stadtforschung', *Natur – Raum – Gesellschaft*, 3, pp. 61–113.

—— (2002b) *Zum Verhältnis von Stadt und Atmosphäre*, ibid, pp. 19–40.

—— (2003) 'Stadt als erlebter und gelebter Raum – kein Sein ohne Handeln?', in Döring, M., Engelhardt, G., Feindt, P. and Oßenbrügge, J. (eds) *Stadt-Raum-Natur: Die Metropole als politisch konstruierter Raum*, Hamburg: Hamburg University Press, pp. 174–218.

—— (2005) *Fundsachen der Sinne: Eine phänomenologische Revision alltäglichen Erlebens*, Freiburg/München: Alber.

—— (2006) 'Atmosfere e tonalità emotive. I sentimenti come mezzi di comunicazione', in Griffero and Somaini (eds) 2006, pp. 95–115.

—— (2008a) 'Die Stadt als Raum der Atmosphären. Zur Differenzierung von Atmosphären und Stimmungen', *Die alte Stadt*, 35, 2, pp. 103–116.

—— (2008b) 'Licht und Atmosphäre. Zur Dämmerungs- und Dunkelästhetik der Altstadt', *Licht*, 60, 6, pp. 506–511.

Hauskeller, M. (1995) *Atmosphären erleben. Philosophische Untersuchungen zur Sinneswahrnehmung*, Berlin: Akademie Verlag.

—— (2002) 'I could go for something Koons. Neue Ästhetik und kommunikative Kunst', in Mahayni (ed.) 2002b, pp. 173–182.

—— (2003a) 'Das unbeweisbare Dogma von der Existenz des Nachbarn. Über die Wahrnehmung des anderen', in Hauskeller (ed.) 2003b, pp. 157–156.

—— (2003b), (ed.) *Die Kunst der Wahrnehmung. Beiträge zu einer Philosophie der sinnlichen Erkenntnis*, Kunsterdingen: Die Graue Edition.

Hauskeller, M., Rehmann-Sutter, C. and Schiemann, G. (eds) (1998) *Naturerkenntnis und Natursein. Für Gernot Böhme*, Frankfurt am Main: Suhrkamp.

Heidegger, M. (1966) *Discourse On Thinking*, New York, Harper & Row.

—— (1977a) 'The Origin of the Work of Art', in *Basic Writings*, New York: HarperCollins 1977, pp. 139–212.

—— (1977b) 'Building Dwelling Thinking', ibid, pp. 343–364.

—— (1979) *Nietzsche*, vol. 1, New York: Harper & Row.

—— (1995) *The Fundamental Concepts of Metaphysics: World, Finitude, Solitude*, St. Bloomington: Indiana University Press.

—— (2002) *Off the Beaten Track*, Cambridge: Cambridge University Press.

—— (2008) *Being and Time*, New York: Harper Perennial Modern Classics.

Hellpach, W. (1960a) *Geopsyche: die Menschenseele unter dem Einfluss von Wetter und Klima, Boden und Landschaft*, Leipzig: Engelmann.

—— (1960b) *Mensch und Volk der Grossstadt*, Stuttgart: Ferdinand EnkeVerlag.

Henning, H. (1916) *Das Geruch*, Leipzig: Barth.

Hilger, W. (1928) *Die Suggestion*, Jena: Fischer.

Hippius M.T. (1936) 'Graphischer Ausdruck von Gefühlen', *Zeitschrift für angewandte Psychologie und Charakterkunde*, 51, pp. 257–336.

Hochschild, A.R. (2003) *The Commercialization of Intimate Life: Notes from Home and Work*, Berkeley: University of California Press.

Humboldt, A. von (1850) *Views of Nature, or, Contemplations on the Sublime Phenomena of Creation: With Scientific Illustrations*, London: Henry G. Bohn.

—— (1866) *Cosmos: A Sketch of a Physical Description of the Universe*, New York: Harper & Row.
Huppertz, M. (2003) 'Die Kunst der Wahrnehmung in der Psychotherapie', in Hauskeller (ed.) 2003b, pp. 177–200.
Husserl, E. (1973) *Zur Phänomenologie der Intersubjektivität. Texte aus dem Nachlass*, Erster Teil. 1905–1920, Leiden: Nijhoff.
—— (1977) *Experience and Judgment*, Evanston: Northwestern University Press.
—— (1982) *Ideas Pertaining to a Pure Phenomenology and to a Phenomenological Philosophy*. First Book, New York: Springer.
—— (1990) *Ideas Pertaining to a Pure Phenomenology and to a Phenomenological Philosophy*. Second Book, New York: Springer.
—— (1991) *On the Phenomenology of the Consciousness of Internal Time* (1893–1917), New York: Springer .
—— (1998) *Thing and Space: Lectures of 1907*, New York: Springer.
Illich, I. (1987) *H$_2$0 und die Wasser des Vergessens*, Hamburg: Reinbeck.
—— (2002) 'The cultivation of conspiracy', in Hoinacki, L. and Mitcham, C. (eds) *The Challenges of Ivan Illich. A Collective Reflection*, Albany, NY: Suny Press, pp. 233–242.
Illouz, E. (2007) *Cold Intimacies: The Making of Emotional Capitalism*, Cambridge: Polity Press.
Itten, J. (1961) *Kunst der Farbe*, Ravensburg: Otto Maier Verlag.
Janson, A. (2005) 'Einführung in den Beitrag von Graf Karlfried von Dürckheim aus der Perspetive der Architektur. Ein Scherzo in Zitronenholz', in Dürckheim (1932), pp. 147–171.
Jünger, E. (1997) *Elogio delle vocali*, in Id., *Foglie e pietre*, Milano: Adelphi, pp. 43–80.
Kandinsky, W. (1946) *On the Spiritual in Art*, New York: Solomon R. Guggenheim.
Kant, I. (2006) *Anthropology from a Pragmatic Point of View*, Cambridge: Cambridge University Press.
Katz, D. (1969) *Der Aufbau der Tastwelt*, Darmstadt: Wissenschaftliche Buchgesellschaft.
Katz, D. and Katz, R. (1960) *Handbuch der Psychologie*, Basel-Stuttgart: Schwabe.
Kimura, B. (1992) *Ecrits de psychopatologie phenomenologique*, Paris: Presses Universitaires France.
Klages, L. (1998) *L'uomo e la terra*, Milano: Mimesis.

—— (1921) *La natura della coscienza*, in Klages (1940), pp. 199–364.
—— (1979) *Dell'eros cosmogonico*, Milano: Multhipla.
—— (1923) *L'essenza del ritmo*, in Klages (1940), pp. 7–90.
—— (1927) *Preludio alla caratterologia*, in Klages (1940), pp. 91–198.
—— (1929–32) *Der Geist als Widersacher der Seele*, 3 vol., Leipzig: Barth.
—— (1940) *L'anima e lo spirito*, Milano: Bompiani.
—— (1942) *Ursprünge der Seelenforschung*, Leipzig: Reclam.
—— (1944) *Rhythmen und Runen*, Leipzig: Barth.
—— (1964) *Ausdruckskunde*, Bonn: Bouvier (SW 6).
—— (1968) *Ausdrucksbewegung und Gestaltungskraft*, München: Heinrich Härtle (Selbstverlag).
—— (1974) *Philosophische Schriften*, Bonn: Bouvier (SW 3).
—— (1976) *Charakterkunde I*, Bonn: Bouvier (SW 4).
—— (1979) *Charakterkunde II*, Bonn: Bouvier (SW 5).
—— (2005) *La realtà delle immagini*, Milano: Marinotti (partial translation, pp. 1251–1415, of Klages 1929–32).
Knodt, R. (1994) *Atmosphären und das Fest. Über einige vergessene Gegenstände des guten Geschmacks*, Norderstedt: Grin.
Köhler, W. (1938) *The Place of Value in a World of Facts*, New York: Liveright Publishing Corporation.
—— (1992) *Gestalt Psychology: An Introduction to New Concepts in Modern Psychology*, New York: Liveright Publishing Corporation.
Koffka, K. (1922) *Perception: An Introduction to the Gestalt-theorie*, Psychological Bulletin, 19, pp. 531–585.
—— (1999) *Principles of Gestalt Psychology*, London: Routledge.
Koolhaas, R. (1978) *Delirious New York. A Retroactive Manifesto for Manhattan*, New York: Monacelli Press.
Koubek, J. (2000) *Soziokulturelle Konstruktion virtueller Lernräume*, Vortrag in Dagstuhl.
Kozljanič, R.J. (2004) *Der Geist eines Ortes. Kulturgeschichte und Phänomenologie des Genius Loci*, 2 vol., München: Albunea.
Kreckel, R. (1992) *Politische Soziologie der sozialen Ungleichheit*, Frankfurt am Main, New York: Campus.
Kuhlmann, D. (1998) 'Der Geist des (W)ortes', *Wolkenkuckucksheim*, 2 (http://www.tucottbus.de/theo/Wolke).

Kunz, H. (1946) *Die anthropologische Bedeutung der Phantasie*, 2 vol., Basel: Verlag fur Recht und Gesellschaft.
Lakoff, G. and Johnson, M. (1999) *Philosophy in the Flesh*, London: HarperCollins.
Landweer, H. (2004) 'Phanomenologie und die Grenzen des Kognitivismus', *Deutsche Zeitschrift für Philosophie* 52, 3, pp. 467–486.
Langeveld, M.J. (1968) *Studien zur Anthropologie des Kindes*, Tübingen: Niemeyer.
Le Bon, G. (2009) *Psychology of Crowds*, Southampton: Sparkling Books.
Le Breton, D. (2006) *La Saveur du monde. Une anthropologie des sens*, Paris: Éditions Métailié.
Leeuw, G. van der (1938) *Religion in Essence and Manifestation: A Study in Phenomenology*, London: Macmillan.
Lehmann, H. (1986) *Essays zur Physiognomie der Landschaft*, Wiesbaden-Stuttgart: Steiner.
Lessing, Th. (1926) *Prinzipien der Charakterologie*, Halle: Mahrhold.
Lethen, H. (2005) 'Nervosität und Literatur im ersten Drittel des 20. Jahrhunderts oder wie Herzflattern und Reizbarkeit in den Text der Kultur gerieten', in Blume (ed.) 2005, pp. 143–158.
Linck, G. (2005) *Qigong mit dem Pinsel. Zur Körper- und Leibverbundenheit der chinesischen Kalligraphie*, in Blume (ed.) 2005, pp. 121–142.
Link-Heer, U. (2003) 'Aura Hysterica or The Lifted Gaze of the Object', in Gumbrecht, H.U. and Marrinan, M. (eds) *Mapping Benjamin: The Work of Art in the Digital Age*, Stanford: Stanford University Press, pp. 114–123.
Lipps, H. (1977) *Die menschliche Natur*, Frankfurt am Main: Klostermann.
Lipps, Th. (1903) *Ästhetik*, vol. 1, Hamburg-Leipzig: Voss.
—— (1908) *Estetica*, in Pinotti (ed.) 1997b, pp. 177–217.
Lorenzer, A. (1968) 'Städtebau: Funktionalismus und Sozialmontage? Zur sozialpsychologichen Funktion der Architektur', in Berndt, H., Lorenzer, A. and Horn, K. (eds) *Architektur als Ideologie*, Frankfurt am Main: Suhrkamp, pp. 51–104.
Löw, M. (2001) *Raumsoziologie*, Frankfurt am Main, Suhrkamp.
Luhmann, N. (2000) *Art as a Social System*, Stanford: Stanford University Press.
Lynch, K. (1960) *The Image of The City*, Cambridge, MA: The MIT Press.
—— (1981) *Good City Form*, Cambridge, MA: The MIT Press.

Mahayni, Z. (2002a) 'Atmosphäre als Gegenstand der Kunst. Monets Gemäldegalerie der Kathedrale von Rouen', in Mahayni (ed.) 2002b, pp. 59–69.

—— (ed.) (2002b) *Neue Ästhetik. Das Atmosphärische und die Kunst*, München: Fink.

Marback, R., Bruch, P. and Eicher, J. (1998) *Cities, Cultures, Conversations. Readings for Writers*, Boston (Mass.): Allyn & Bacon.

Mark, D. and Smith, B. (2003) 'Do Mountains Exist? Towards an Ontology of Landforms', *Environment and Planning B (Planning and Design)*, 30 (3), 2003, pp. 411–427.

—— (n.d.) *A Science of Topography: From Qualitative Ontology to Digital Representations* (http://ontology.buffalo.edu/smith/articles/topography.pdf).

Marquard, O. (1986) *Apologie des Zufälligen*, Stuttgart: Reclam.

—— (1994) *Estetica e anestetica*, Bologna: Il Mulino.

Massironi, M. (1998) *Fenomenologia della percezione visiva*, Bologna: Il Mulino.

—— (2000), *L'osteria dei Dadi Truccati. Arte, psicologia e dintorni*, Bologna: Il Mulino.

Mattenklott, G. (1984) 'Geschmackssachen. Über den geistigen Zusammenhang von sinnlicher und geistiger Ernährung', in Kamper, D. and Wulf, C. (eds) *Das Schwinden der Sinne*, Frankfurt am Main: Suhrkamp, pp. 179–190.

Matteucci, G. (2005) *Filosofia ed estetica del senso*, Pisa: ETS.

Mayr, A. (ed.) (2001) *Musica e suoni dell'ambiente*, Bologna: Clueb.

Mazzeo, M. (2005) *Storia naturale della sinestesia. Dalla questione Molyneux a Jakobson*, Macerata: Quodlibet.

Mazzocut-Mis, M. (2002) *Voyeurismo tattile. Un'estetica dei valori tattili e visivi*, Genova: Il Melangolo.

Melai, R. (1996) 'Vita e opere di Kevin Lynch', in Lynch (1996): XVII–XXIX.

Merleau-Ponty, M. (1964) *The Primacy of Perception*, Evanston: Northwestern University Press.

—— (2005) *Phenomenology of Perception*, London: Routledge.

Mersch, D. (2002) *Ereignis und Aura. Untersuchungen zu einer Ästhetik des Performativen*, Frankfurt am Main: Suhrkamp.

Metzger, W. (1941) *Psychologie. Die Entwicklung ihrer Grundannahmen seit der Einführung des Experiments*, Dresden und Leipzig: Steinkopf.

Minkowski, E. (1936) *Vers une cosmologie. Fragments philosophiques*, Paris: Aubier.

Minssen, M. (2003) 'Wahrnehmungen auf See', in Hauskeller (ed.) 2003b, pp. 88–107.

—— (2004) *Hinter der Dornenhecke. Spröde Liebschaften mit Dingen und Materialien*, Kunsterdingen: Die Graue Edition.

Mitscherlich, A. (1968) *Il feticcio urbano. La città inabitabile, istigatrice di discordia*, Torino: Einaudi.

Monke, S. (2007) *Die neue Ästhetik und die Atmosphäre Intensivstation*, Norderstedt: Grin.

Moore, P. (2003) 'Sectarian Sound and Cultural Identity in Northern Ireland', in Bull and Back (eds) 2003, pp. 265–279.

Müller, R.W. (1998) 'Gernot Böhme – *Anima naturaliter japonica*', in Hauskeller, Rehmann, Sutter and Schiemann (eds) 1998, pp. 323–337.

Nietzsche, F. (2005) *Thus Spoke Zarathustra: A Book for Everyone and Nobody*, Oxford: Oxford University Press.

Nitschke, A. (2002) 'Eduardo Chillida: Itsasoratu II. Die Zeitmuster des Körpers und das Meer', in Mahayni (ed.) 2002b, pp.183–201.

Norberg-Schulz, Ch. (1980) *Genius Loci: Towards a Phenomenology of Architecture*, London: Academy Editions.

Norman, D. (2002) *The Design of Everyday Things*, New York: Doubleday Basic Books.

—— (2005) *Emotional Design: Why We Love (Or Hate) Everyday Things*, New York: Doubleday Basic Books.

Osborne, P. (2000) *Travelling Light: Photography, Travel and Visual Culture*, Manchester: Manchester University Press.

Otto, R. (1936) *The Idea of the Holy: An Inquiry Into the Non-rational Factor in the Idea of the Divine and Its Relation to the Rational*, Revised with additions, Oxford: Oxford University Press.

Palágyi, M. (1925) *Wahrnehmungslehre*, Leipzig: Barth.

Pallasmaa, J. (2005) *The Eyes of the Skin. Architecture and the Senses*, Chichester: John Wiley & Sons.

Petzold, H. (1991) *Integrative Therapie. Modelle, Theorien und Methoden für eine schulenübergreifenden Psychotherapie. Ausgewählte Schriften*, vol. 2, Padernborn: Junfermann.

Piana, G. (1979) *Elementi di una dottrina dell'esperienza*, Milano: Il Saggiatore.

Piattelli Palmarini, M. (1995) *L'arte di persuadere*, Milano: Mondadori.

Pinotti, A. (1997a) 'Arcipelago empatia. Per una introduzione', in Pinotti (ed.) 1997b, pp. 9–59.

—— (ed.) (1997b) *Estetica ed empatia*, Milano: Guerini.

—— (2005) Introduzione in Straus and Maldiney (2005), pp. 7–34.

Plessner, H. (1999) *The Limits of Community: A Critique of Social Radicalism*, New York: Humanity Books.

Porfyriou, H. (2005) 'Camillo Sitte und das Primat des Sichtbaren in der Moderne', in Semsroth, K., Jormakka, K. and Langer, B. (eds) *Kunst des Städtebaus. Neue Perspektiven auf Camillo Sitte*, Wien: Böhlau, pp. 239–256.

Pratkanis, A. and Aronson, E. (2001) *Age of Propaganda: The Everyday Use and Abuse of Persuasion*, New York: Macmillan.

Pretor-Pinney, G. (2006) *The Cloudspotter's Guide: The Science, History, and Culture of Clouds*, London: Penguin.

Proust, M. (2010) *In Search of Lost Time: Swann's Way*, New York: Random House.

Putnam, H. (1999) *The Threefold Cord: Mind, Body and World*, New York: Columbia University Press.

Raff, T. (1994) *Die Sprache der Materialien. Anleitung zu einer Ikonologie der Werkstoffe*, München: Deutscher Kunstverlag.

Rappe, G. (1995) *Archaische Leiberfahrung. Der Leib in der frühgriechischen Philosophie und in außereuropäischen Kulturen*, Berlin: Akademie Verlag.

Ratzel, F. (1905) *Glücksinseln und Träume*, Leipzing: Grunow.

Révész, G. (1938) *Die Formenwelt des Tastsinnes*, vol. I., Den Haag: Nijhoff.

Rombach H. (1987) *Strukturanthropologie*, Freiburg-München: Alber.

Rothacker, E. (1934) *Geschichtsphilosophie*, München: Oldenbourg.

—— 1948, *Probleme der Kulturanthropologie*, Bonn: Bouvier.

—— 1964, *Philosophische Anthropologie*, Bonn: Bouvier.

—— 1966, *Zur Genealogie des menschlichen Bewusstseins*, Bonn: Bouvier.

Rousseau, J.J. (1783) *The Confessions of J.J. Rousseau: With The Reveries of the Solitary Walker*, London: J. Bew.

Rudert, J. (1964) 'Die persönliche Atmosphäre', *Archiv für die gesamte Psychologie*, 116, pp. 291–298.

Rumpf, H. (1994) 'Mit allen Sinnen lernen?', *Musik & Bildung* 2, 1994, pp. 5–9.

—— 2003, 'Vom Bewältigen zum Gewärtigen. Wahrnehmungsdriften im Widerspiel', in Hauskeller (ed.) 2003b, pp. 228–260.

Rykwert, J. (2000) *The Seduction of Place: The History and Future of the City*, New York: Pantheon Books.

Sartre, J.P. (1969) *Being and Nothingness*, London: Routledge.

—— (2002) 'Intentionality: A Fundamental Idea of Husserl's Phenomenology', in Moran, D. and Mooney, T. (eds), *The Phenomenology Reader*, London: Routledge.

Sasaki, K.I. (2006) 'Landscape as Atmosphere. An Aspect of Japanese Sensibility', in Griffero and Somaini (eds) 2006, pp. 85–94.

Schafer, R.M. (1977) *The Tuning of the World*, New York: Knopf.

—— (1993) 'Soundscape – Design für Ästhetik und Umwelt', in Langenmaier, A.V. (ed.), *Der Klang der Dinge*, München: Schreiber, pp. 10–27.

Schapp, W. (2004) *Beiträge zur Phänomenologie der Wahrnehmung*, Franfurk am Main: Klostermann.

—— (1976) *Erinnerungen an Edmund Husserl. Ein Beitrag zur Geschichte der Phänomenologie*, Wiesbaden: Heymann.

Scheler, M. (1973) *Formalism in Ethics and Non-Formal Ethics of Values: A New Attempt Toward the Foundation of an Ethical Personalism*, Evanston: Northwestern University Press.

—— (2008) *The Nature of Sympathy*, Piscataway (NJ): Transaction Publishers.

Schivelbusch W. (1986), *The Railway Journey*, Berkeley: University of California Press.

Schmitz, H. (1965) *System der Philosophie*, vol. II.1, Der Leib, Bonn: Bouvier.

—— (1966) *System der Philosophie*, vol. II.2, Der Leib im Spiegel der Kunst, Bonn: Bouvier.

—— (1967) *System der Philosophie*, vol III.1, Der leibliche Raum, Bonn: Bouvier.

—— (1969) *System der Philosophie*, vol III.2, Der Gefühlsraum, Bonn: Bouvier.

—— (1977) *System der Philosophie*, vol III.4, Das Göttliche und der Raum, Bonn: Bouvier.

—— (1978) *System der Philosophie*, vol III.5, Die Wahrnehmung, Bonn: Bouvier.

—— (1990) *Der unerschöpfliche Gegenstand*, Bonn: Bouvier.

—— (1992) *Die entfremdete Subjektivität. Von Fichte zu Hegel*, Bonn: Bouvier.

—— (1994) 'Wozu Neue Phänomenologie?', in Grossheim, M. (ed.) 1994, *Wege zu einer volleren Realität: Neue Phänomenologie in der Diskussion*, Berlin: Akademie Verlag, pp. 7–18.

—— (1995) *Selbstdarstellung als Philosophie: Metamorphosen der entfremdeten Subjektivität*, Bonn: Bouvier.

—— (1996) *Husserl und Heidegger*, Bonn: Bouvier.

—— (1998) 'Situationen und Atmosphären. Zur Ästhetik und Ontologie bei Gernot Böhme', in Hauskeller, Rehmann, Sutter and Schiemann (eds) 1998, pp. 176–90.

—— (1999b) *Der Spielraum der Gegenwart*, Bouvier: Bonn.

—— (2002a) 'Der Sogenannte Brutus', in Mahayni (ed.) 2002a, pp. 127–137.

—— (2002b) with Marx, G. and Moldzio, A., *Begriffene Erfahrung. Beiträge zur antireduktionistischen Phänomenologie*, Rostock: Koch (Schmitz, pp. 13–211).

—— (2003) *Was ist Neue Phänomenologie?*, Rostock: Koch.

—— (2005a) *Situationen und Konstellationen: Wider die Ideologie totaler Vernetzung*, Freiburg-München: Alber.

—— (2005b) 'Einführung in den Beitrag von Graf Karlfried von Dürckheim aus philosophischer Perspektive', in Dürckheim (1932), pp. 109–115.

—— (2006) *I sentimenti come atmosfere*, in Griffero and Somaini (eds) 2006, pp. 25–43.

—— (2007) *Der Leib, der Raum und die Gefühle*, Bielefeld, Locarno: Sirius.

Scholz, G. (1992) 'Significatività. Sulla storia dell'origine di un concetto fondamentale della filosofia ermeneutica', *Discipline filosofiche*, 1, pp. 13–28.

Schulze, G. (1992) *Die Erlebnisgesellschaft. Kultursoziologie der Gegenwart*, Frankfurt am Main-New York: Campus-Verlag.

Schürmann, E. (2003) 'So ist es, wie es uns erscheint. Philosophische Betrachtungen ästhetischer Ereignisse', in Hauskeller (ed.) 2003b, pp. 349–361.

Scott, G. (1914) *The Architecture of Humanism: A Study in the History of Taste*, Boston/New York: Houghton Mifflin Company.

Searle, J.R. (1995) *The Construction of Social Reality*, New York: The Free Press.

Seel, M. (2005) *Aesthetics of Appearing: Cultural Memory in the Present Series*, Palo Alto: Stanford University Press.

Sells, S.B. (1936) 'The Atmosphere Effect: An Experimental Study of Reasoning', *Archivia Psycologica*, 29, pp. 3–72.

Simmel, G. (1987) 'Exkurs über die Soziologie der Sinne', in Stahnke, A., Winkler, P., Immelmann, K., Vogel, C. and Scherer, K.R. (eds), *Psychobiologie. Wegweisende Texte der Verhaltenforschung von Darwin bis zur Gegenwart*, München: DTV, pp. 538–550.

—— (1950) 'The Metropolis and Mental Life', in Wolff, K. (ed.) *The Sociology of Georg Simmel*, New York: Free Press, pp. 409–424.

—— (1997) *Simmel on Culture: Selected Writings*, London: Sage.

—— (2007) 'The Philosophy of Landscape', *Theory, Culture & Society*, December 24, pp. 20–29.

Simmen, J. and Drepper, U. (1984) *Der Fahrstuhl. Die Geschichte der vertikalen Eroberung*, München: Prostel.

Smith, B. (2002) 'Oggetti fiat', *Rivista di estetica*, n.s. 20, XLII, pp. 58–86.

Smuda, M. (1986) 'Natur als asthetischer Gegenstand und als Gegenstand der Ästhetik. Zur Konstitution von Landschaft', in Smuda, M. (ed.) *Landschaft*, Frankfurt am Main: Suhrkamp, pp. 44–69.

Snell, B. (1953) *The Discovery of the Mind; the Greek origins of European Thought*, Oxford: Blackwell.

Soentgen, J. (1998) *Die verdeckte Wirklichkeit. Einführung in die Neue Phänomenologie von Hermann Schmitz*, Bonn: Bouvier.

Somaini, A. (2006) 'Il volto delle cose. "Physiognomie", "Stimmung" e "Atmosphäre" nella teoria del cinema di Béla Balázs', in Griffero and Somaini (eds) 2006, pp. 143–162.

Spinicci, P. (2008) *Simile alle ombre e al sogno. La filosofia dell'immagine*, Torino: Bollati Boringhieri.

Spitz, R. (1965) *The First Year of Life: A Psychoanalytic Study of Normal and Deviant Development of Object Relations*, New York: International Universities Press.

Spranger, E. (1944) *Die weltanschauuliche Bedeutung der modernen Biologie*, in Id., *Gesammelte Schriften*, VI, Tübingen: Niemeyer, 1980, pp. 236–244.

Straus, E. (1956) *Vom Sinn der Sinne*, Berlin-Gottingen-Heidelberg: Springer.

—— (1980) *Phenomenological Psychology*, New York & London: Garland Publishing Inc..

—— (2005a) 'Le forme della spazialità. Il loro significato per la motricità e per la percezione', in Straus, E. and Maldiney, H., *L'estetico e l'estetica. Un dialogo nello spazio della fenomenologia*, Milano-Udine: Mimesis, pp. 35–68.

—— (2005b) 'Paesaggio e geografia', ibid, pp. 69–79.
Strehle, H. (1954) *Mienen, Gesten und Gebärden*, München: Reinhardt.
Ströker, E. (1977) *Philosophische Untersuchungen zum Raum*, Frankfurt am Main: Klostermann.
Székely, L. (1932) 'Uber den Aufbau der Sinnesfunktionen', *Zeitschrift für Psychologie*, 127, pp. 227–264.
Tacchi, J. (2003) 'Nostalgia and radio sound', in Bull and Back (eds) 2003, pp. 281–295.
Tarpino, A. (2008) *Geografie della memoria. Case, rovine, oggetti quotidiani*, Torino: Einaudi.
Tellenbach, H. (1968) *Geschmack und Atmosphäre*, Salzburg: Müller.
Thibaud, J.P. (2003) 'Die sinnliche Umwelt von Städten. Zum Verständnis urbaner Atmosphären', in Hauskeller (ed.) 2003b, pp. 280–297.
—— (2003b) 'The Sonic Composition of the City', in Bull and Back (eds) 2003, pp. 329–341.
Uexküll, J. von (2010) *A Foray Into the Worlds of Animals and Humans with a Theory of Meaning*, Minneapolis: University of Minnesota Press.
Vendrell Ferran, I. (2008) *Die Emotionen. Gefühle in der realistischen Phänomenologie*, Berlin: Akademie Verlag.
Venturi Ferriolo, M. (2009) *Percepire paesaggi. La potenza dello sguardo*, Torino: Bollati Boringhieri.
Verhoog, H. (2003b) 'Biotechnologie und die Integrität des Lebens', in Hauskeller (ed.) 2003b, pp. 130–156.
Vitta, M. (2008) *Dell'abitare. Corpi spazi oggetti immagini*, Torino: Einaudi.
Vizzardelli, S. (2007) *Filosofia della musica*, Roma-Bari: Laterza.
Volke, S. (2005) 'Lautsymbolik und Synästhesie – Beiträge zu einer leiborientierten Phonosemantik', in Blume (ed.) 2005, pp. 92–129.
Volkelt, J. (1927) 'Teoria dell'empatia estetica', in Pinotti (ed.) 1997b, pp. 229–260.
Volz, P. (1910) *Der Geist Gottes und die verwandten Erscheinungen im Alten Testament und im anschließenden Judentum*, Tübingen: Mohr.
Wagner, M. (2001) *Das Material der Kunst. Eine andere Geschichte der Moderne*, München: Beck.
Waldenfels, B. (2000) *Das leibliche Selbst. Vorlesungen zur Phänomenologie des Leibes*, Frankfurt am Main: Suhrkamp.

Walther, G. (1955) *Phänomenologie der Mystik*, Freiburg im Breisgau: Olten.

Watsuji, T. (1961) *Climate and Culture: A Philosophical Study*, Westport: Greenwood Press.

Wellek, A. (1931) 'Zur Geschichte und Kritik der Synästhesieforschung', *Archiv für die gesamte Psychologie*, 79, pp. 325–384.

Welsch, W. (1997) *Undoing Aesthetics*, London: Sage.

Wendorf, G., Felbinger, D., Graf, B., Gruner, S., Jonuschat, H. and Saphörster O. (2004) 'Von den Qualitäten des Wohnumfeldes zur Lebensqualität? Das Konzept des "Atmosphärischen" als Ausgangspunkt einer integrierten Theorie', Discussion paper Nr. 11/04, Zentrum für Technik und Gesellschfaft der TUB, Berlin.

Werner, H. (1966) 'Intermodale Qualitäten (Synästhesien)', in Metzger, W. (ed.) *Handbuch der Psychologie*, vol. 1.2, Göttingen: Hogrefe, pp. 278–303.

Whitehead, A.N. (2010) *Process and Reality*, corrected edition, New York: Simon and Schuster.

Willis, J. and Todorov, A. (2006) 'First Impressions: Making Up Your Mind After a 100-Ms Exposure to a Face', *Psychological Science*, 17, pp. 592–598.

Wölfflin, H. (1886), *Psicologia dell'architettura*, Venezia: Cluva 1985.

Woodworth, R.S. and Sells, S.B. (1935) 'An Atmosphere Effect in Formal Syllogistic Reasoning', *Journal of Experimental Psychology*, 18, pp. 451–460.

Zola, E. (2007) *The Belly of Paris*, Oxford: Oxford University Press.

Zumthor, P. (1999) *Architektur denken*, Basel-Boston-Berlin: Birkhäuser.

—— (2006) *Atmosphären. Architektonische Umgebungen. Die Dinge um mich herum*, Basel-Boston-Berlin: Birkhäuser.

Zur Lippe, R. (1987) *Sinnesbewußtsein*, Hamburg: Reinbeck

Index

Numbers in italics refer to the notes

Aeschylus, 103
Agamben, G., *78*
Albers, J., *83*
Amin-Thrift, N., *88*
Andrews, M., *22, 23*
Anschütz, G., 115
Aristotle, *15*, 44
Arnheim, R., 15, *16*, 18, 48 and n., 111, 128
Aronson, E., *146*
Assmann, J., 72
Attaway J.S., *79*
Auer, G., 98
Augé, M., *21*, 22 and n., *23, 44*, 128, 129 and n.
Augerau, P.F.C., 29
Augustine, 1
Austin, J.L., 82

Babin B.J., *79*
Bachelard, G., 37, 42 and n.
Back, L., *86*
Baensch, O., *61*
Balázs, B., *84*
Banham, R., *148*
Baraduc, H., *78*
Barbaras, R., *14*
Battisti, A., *3*
Baudelaire, C., 65 and n., 76, 78
Baudrillard, J., *2*, 98, *113*
Becking, G., *47*
Begg, I., *4.*
Benjamin, W., 25, 31, *44*, 57, 66, *67*, 78, 79 and n., *82*, 83, *87, 89,* 137
Bianchi, I., *54*
Binswanger, L., 37, *38, 42*
Bismarck, O.L.E. von, *87*
Bizzozzero, V., *66*

Blankenburg, W., *68*
Bloom, P. *9*
Blume, A., *131, 140*
Blumenberg, H., *118*
Bockemühl, M., *84,* 144
Böhme, G., *3, 4, 6, 7, 20, 28, 44,* 58, 59, 64, 68, 70, 76, 79, *80, 83,* 84 and n., *85, 86,* 90 and n., *93,* 95 and n., 98 and n., *108, 113,* 118, *119, 122, 124,* 144 and n., 146 and n.
Böhme, H., 14
Böhme, J., *105*
Bollnow, O.F., 1, 20, 27, 37, 41 and n., *51,* 52, 57 and n., *58,* 59, *61,* 72, 82, *143*
Bonaiuto, M., 79, 93, 96, *125,* 147
Bourdieu, P., 72
Bozzi, P., 53, 148
Bruch, P., 88
Bruno, G., *84*
Buchholz, K., *144*
Bull, M., *86*
Buytendijk, F.J.J., *35*, 49

Caravaggio, M. Merisi da, 1 9
Carnevali, B., *65,* 75, 76 and n., 77 and n., 78 and n.
Carpenter, W.B., 49
Casati, R., *148*
Chapman, A.P., *4*
Chapman, L.J., *4*
Conrad, J., 4
Conrad, K., 52
Conte, P., 22 and n.
Corbin, A., *66*
Croome, D., *60, 107, 146*

Damisch, H., 87, 88, *89*
D'Angelo, P., *60, 62*
Danto, A., *12,* 83

Daudet, L., *3*, 10 and n., *30*, 60, 64, 65 and n., 76, 77 and n., 78
De Biran, M., *105*
De Certeau, M., 44 and n.
Denny, J.P., *4*
Descartes, R., 44
Dewey, J., 19, 34
Dichter. E., 2, *97*, 114, *124*
Dickens, C., 91, 101
Dickie, G., 83
Didi-Huberman, G., *78*
Douglas, M., *71*
Drepper, U., *95*
Dürckheim, K. von, 37, 39 and n., 40, *149*
Dufrenne, M., *12, 86*
Dukakis, M., *146*
Durth, W., *93*

Eckstein, L., 30 and n.
Edinger, L., *66*
Eicher, J., 88
Eliot, T.S., 139
Empson, W., 83, *84*
Endell, A., 89, *95*
Evans, J.S., *4*

Fichte, J.G., *105*
Fischer, O., 123
Florenskij, P., *98*
Fränkel, F., 91
Franzini, E., *3*, 6
Freud, S., 149
Friedrich, C.D., 62
Fuchs, T., 17, 18, *134, 140*

Galati, D., 3, 131, *149*
Galen, 78
Gebsattel, V.E., 110
Geiger, M., *3, 82,* 109, 132, 134
Geiseler, M.-L., *83*
Giammusso, S., *72*
Gibson, J., 50, 51 and n., 60, 61 and n.
Goethe, J.W., 6, 75 and n., 114, 132
Goffman, E., 71
Gombrich, E., 117
Goodman, N., 13
Graf, B., *3*

Griffero, T. *11, 29, 31, 38, 54, 60, 76, 85, 105, 108, 126, 127, 130, 148*
Gropius, W., 137
Großheim, M., 24
Gusman, A., 63, *66*

Haensel, C., 107
Hall, E.T., 23, *37, 64,* 66, *67, 71,* 96 and n., *122,* 130, 137, *145, 146*
Hasse, J., *3,* 7, *30, 40, 45,* 79, 80, *87, 88, 90,* 92 and n., 93 and n., *94, 95,* 121, *134*
Hauskeller, M., *3,* 6 and n., *11, 20,* 22 and n., *51,* 53, *54,* 58, *64, 66,* 68, *69, 84, 85,* 87, *107,* 112 and n., 113 and n., *114, 115, 124, 126, 132, 134, 135, 136, 138*
Heidegger, M., 15, 20, 34, *35,* 37, 38 and n., *75,* 107, *108,* 137 and n., *145*
Hellpach, W., 21, 47, 55, 56, *59,* 60 and n., 62 and n., *68,* 87 and n., 91 and n., 97, *130, 135,* 137
Henning, H., *68*
Hilger, W., 50
Hippius, M.T., *55*
Hochschild A.R., *106*
Homer, *103*
Humboldt, A. von, 128 and n.
Huppertz. M., *16*
Husserl, E., 13, *16,* 23, *24,* 36 and n., 107 and n., 108, 116 and n.

Illich, I., 65 and n.
Illouz, E., 106
Isherwood, B., *71*
Itten, J., *114*

James, W., *105*
Janson, A., 93, *122*
Joel, E., 91
Johnson, M., *48*
Jünger, E., *117*

Kandinsky, W., *85, 138*
Kant, I., 44, 67 and n., *105*
Katz, D., *51, 101*
Kimura, B., *122*

Klages, L. *10*, 13 and n., 14, 19, 24 and n., 25 and n., 26 and n., 29 and n., *30*, 38, 48 and n., *49,* 63 and n., 91, *103,* 104 and n., 106, *114,* 116 and n., 117 and n., 119 and n., 121, 127, *135*
Knodt, R., *81, 86, 88, 106*
Koffka, K., 15, *48,* 53
Köhler, W., 2, 29 and n., 109, 117, *149*
Koolhaas, R., *93*
Koons, J., *84*
Koubek, J., *72*
Kozljanič, R.J., 74, *75*
Kreckel, R., 113
Kuhlmann, D., 75
Kunz, H., *25*

Labs-Ehlert, B., 93
Lakoff, G., *48*
Landweer, H., 55
Langeveld, M.J., 53
Le Bon, G., 30, 70, *71, 130*
Le Breton, D., 66
Leeuw, G. van der, *73*
Lehmann, H., *6,* 21, *122,* 123, 137
Lessing, T., 53
Lethen, H., *4*
Lévi-Strauss, C., 2
Linck, G., *122*
Link-Heer, U., *78*
Lipps, H., 15, *53*, 59, 76
Lipps, T., 50, *134*
Long, R., 83
Lorenzer, A., 80, 92
Löw, M., *10*, 47
Luhmann, N., *5*
Lynch, K., *6,* 89

Mahayni, Z., 83
Marback, R., 88
Mark, D., 61 and n.
Marquard, O., *20, 98*
Massironi, M., *16, 18, 53, 54*
Mattenklott, G., 67
Matteucci, G., *148*
Mayr, A., *86*
Mazzeo, M., *115*

Mazzocut-Mis, M., *116*
Melai, R., *89*
Merleau-Ponty, M., 1, *5*, 7, 10, 15, 17, 21, 33, *36*, 37, 40, 50, 58, 98, 103, 106, 111, 114, 115, 118, 124 and n., 134, *139*
Mersch, D., *27*
Metzger, W., *5*, 19 and n., 131
Minkowski, E., 6, 11, 24, 37, 38, *57, 58,* 66, 69 and n., 107, *112,* 113, 116, *120,* 144
Minssen, M., 26, *56, 112,* 128
Mitscherlich, A., 88 and n., *89,* 91, 96 and n.
Monet, C., 83
Monke, S., *126*
Moore, P., *86*
Müller, R.W., *122*

Napoleon, 29
Niebuhr, G.B., 55.
Nietzsche, F., 1, *58*
Nitschke, A., *84*
Norberg-Schulz, C., 75 and n.
Norman, D.A., *27, 32,* 50, 81 and n.

Oetinger, F.C., *105*
Osborne, P.D., *22*
Otto, R., *59,* 73, *74*

Palágyi, M., *49*
Pallasmaa, J. *11*
Paul, *105*
Petzold, H., *44*
Piana, G., 11, *19, 32,* 36, 97, *114,* 139
Piattelli Palmarini, M., *4*
Pinotti, A., *37, 38, 49, 53*
Plato, 103
Plessner, H., 70 and n.
Porfyriou, H., *89*
Pratkanis, A.R., *146*
Pretor-Pinney, G., 56
Proust, M., 65, 118
Putnam, H., *53*

Quine, W. van Orman, 148

Raabe, W., *139*
Raff, T., 98 and n.

Rappe, G., *74, 103,* 105
Ratzel, F., *58*
Révész, G., 45
Rombach, H., 145
Rothacker, E., *12, 13,* 18, *26, 32, 35, 49,* 50, *129*
Rousseau, J.J., *127*
Rudert, J., *69*
Rumpf, H., *11,* 18
Rykwert, J., *84,* 88, *89, 90,* 91, 136

Sartre, J.P., 23 and n., 35, 140, 145
Sasaki, K.-I., *122*
Schafer, R.M., 85, *86*
Schapp, W., 4, *10,* 14, 115, *116*
Scheler, M., *20, 31,* 130, *132*
Schelling, F.W.J., *105*
Schmitz, H., *3, 4,* 5 and n., *12,* 15 and n., 16 and n., 17, 18 and n., *23,* 24, 26, *27, 28, 29, 33,* 34 and n., *35, 37, 40,* 44 and n., *45,* 46 and n., *47,* 48 and n., 49 and n., 56, *58, 68, 70,* 71, *72, 73,* 74, *75,* 85, *86,* 101, 102 and n., 103 and n., 104 and n., 105 and n., *106,* 108 and n., *110, 111,* 112 and n., *119, 120,* 121, *122, 125, 131, 134, 135, 138, 140,* 143 and n.
Scholtz, G., *12*
Schulze, G., *79*
Schürmann, E., 83
Scott, G., *95*
Searle, J., *147*
Seel, M., 2, 12, 82, *125,* 148
Sells, S.B., *4*
Simmel, G., *37,* 60, 65, 68, 91, 92
Simmen, J., *95*
Sitte, C. 89
Smith, B., 61 and n., *127*
Smuda, M., 61
Snell, B., *104*
Soentgen, J., *1, 3, 55,* 74, *102, 138*
Somaini, A., *84*
Sophocles, 103
Spinicci, P., *119*
Spitz, R.A., *17*
Spranger, E., *120*

Straus, E., 37, 38, 39 and n., 51, *85, 111,* 118
Strehle, H., 119
Ströker, E., *6, 53, 86, 124,* 130
Székely, L., *47*

Tacchi, J., 86
Tarpino, A., 22, 95
Tellenbach, H., *1, 3,* 5, 9, 10 and n., 26 and n., 33, *36, 45,* 64, 66, 67 and n., *68,* 69, 122, *123,* 124 and n., *126,* 130, *135*
Thibaud, J.-P., 35, *86,* 131, *136,* 144
Todorov, A., *30*
Turrell, J., 83

Uexküll, J. von, *20,* 32 and n.

Varzi, A., *148*
Vendrell Ferran, I., *108*
Venturi Ferriolo, M., *75, 89*
Verhoog, H., *16*
Vischer, R., *134*
Vitta, M., 96
Vizzardelli, S., 85
Volke, S., 83
Volkelt, J., 109
Volz, P., 56

Wagner, M., *98*
Waldenfels, B., *107*
Walther, G., *35*
Watsuji, T., *55*
Wellek, A., *115*
Welsch, W., 16, *20*
Wendorf, G., *94, 137*
Werner, H., *113, 115, 129*
Wertheimer, M., 54, 123
Whitehead, A.N., 14
Willis, J., *30*
Winkler, J., *86*
Wölfflin, H., 48, 94 and n., *95*
Woodsworth, R.S., *4*

Zola, E., 116
Zumthor, P., *79,* 93, 95 and n., 97, *148*
Zur Lippe, R., *7, 93,* 144